Copyright © 2019 Gary Palmer. All rights reserved.

The opinions and ideas in this book are those solely of the author, Gary Charles Palmer. Readers are advised that the author is not engaged in the practice of providing financial services, legal advice or other professional assistance. Should expert advice or legal opinions be required, it is suggested that the reader consult a qualified professional. Although every effort has been made to ensure the contents of this book are accurate and factual, the author makes no representations or warranties in this regard and specifically disclaims any responsibility for any liability or loss, personal or otherwise, that is incurred directly or indirectly as a result of applying the concepts presented herein.

About the author

A prolific author, a noteworthy historian, and a man of letters, whatever that is - these are but a few of the attainments he never achieved, although he did write a few letters, if that counts. Gary Palmer was born in Hartford, Connecticut in Dec. 1943, to Al and Sophie Palmer. His mom and dad were noted for...well they weren't really noted for anything, but they were nice people all the same.

At 7 he wrote, "I was born on a dark and stormy night" which wasn't true, but it showed his early proclivity for not having writing talent. His youth was mostly uneventful, except for the time he threw an unopened can of beans into a Boy Scout campfire at age 12. No one was injured in the explosion, but one kid got beaned.

His high school yearbook said, "Most likely not to achieve much", which he used as an excuse his whole life. Somehow, he managed to make it through college and grad school, and served in the US Army for two years, rising to the rank of first lieutenant, from second lieutenant. A HAWK missile battery officer, the Army gave him a commendation for not killing anybody, so he's got that going for him.

He had a 30-year career in commercial finance, where he learned that making huge loans to corporations having financial problems is fine as long as no recession ever occurs. He became interested in investing and learned all of the inherent mistakes by doing all of them, especially the one about having too much stock in the company you work for (Bank America).

He lives in San Diego, with his wife Pat. They had two boys together, both of whom say they remember their dad, sort of. Retired now, he does not play golf, does not have a dog (although some say he needs an emotional support one), knows three guitar chords, complains about his back all the time, and wishes he was Steve Martin. We tried to find a recent picture where he looked good, but couldn't find one, so we have attached one taken when he was somewhat younger.

About the author (an additional perspective)

When my father gave me a draft of his book on investing, I mentioned that perhaps the readers would be interested to know more tangible facts about his personal background and financial savvy. Initially he was reluctant because he is a modest man and he had intended the readers to be mainly close family and friends. When I convinced him to share his investing insights with a broader audience he relented and conceded to the addition of this brief summary:

- University of Connecticut, Bachelor of Science, Business 1966. Nominated for graduation with distinction.
- Michigan State University, Graduated with MBA, high honors, finished 7th in graduating class, 1967. Enrolled in PhD-business, cut short by US Army draft orders.
- 1st Lieutenant US Army, two years, HAWK missile battery officer Europe.
- Connecticut Bank & Trust, 4 years, Commercial credit, Loan Officer.
- Barclays American Business Credit, (Barclay's Bank Subsidiary) 12 years. Portfolio Review Manager - Reviewed, analyzed, and recommended action for a national portfolio of large, high risk, commercial secured corporate loans. Supervised team of 12.
- Bank America Business Credit, 14 years. Senior Vice President and Manager of Industrial loan division, Corporate Portfolio Manager of $3 Billion secured portfolio of US corporate, elevated risk loans. Final signature authority for new loans, $40 million. Presided over unprecedented milestone of zero loan losses for 5 years consecutively.
- Became passionate about in investing in the 1980's, successfully grew and managed a personal investment portfolio, and utilized corporate finance skills to develop an investing strategy for long term assets to enable robust retirement savings.

After retiring early at age 55 in 1999 and successfully navigating the extreme market pullbacks of 2000-2003 and 2008-2009, Gary's successful investment strategies have allowed him to live comfortably with an investment portfolio that still contains 84% of its original 1999 value - after 20 years of withdrawals.

On a personal note, I have found my father's acumens on investing more than impressive. His tactics and instinct on growing a financial portfolio have been incredibly successful, and as his son I have been privileged to have profited from his knowledge in my own personal finances. My hope is that you find the content of this book similarly beneficial.

— Jeff Palmer

TABLE OF CONTENTS

About the author	iii
About the author (an additional perspective)	iv
I. INTRODUCTION	**1**
PURPOSE & SCOPE	1
THIS BOOK	6
SOCIAL SECURITY	6
SAVING ENOUGH	8
SLEEPING AT NIGHT	11
STAYING INFORMED	13
WHERE'S YOUR SAVINGS?	13
CURRENT ECONOMIC ENVIRONMENT	18
A RISING RATE ENVIRONMENT ABRUPTLY ENDS	20
II. INVESTMENT CONCEPTS and TERMS	**24**
CORPORATE BASICS	24
CRYSTAL BALLS	24
STOCK PICKING	29
DID YOU FALL SHORT OF THE S&P 500?	41
DAY TRADING	41
HEDGE FUNDS and QUANTS	45
WHAT CAUSES STOCKS TO MOVE?	50
ETFs - EXCHANGE TRADED FUNDS - PASSIVE INVESTING	57
DYNAMIC ETFs	66
ACTIVE ETFs	67
MULTI FACTOR ETFs	69
FUNDAMENTAL vs. TECHNICAL ANALYSIS	69
PRICE EARNINGS RATIO – the P/E	73
High P/E's in 2018 - 2019	75
THE PEG RATIO	78
S&P STOCK SECTORS	79
GROWTH STOCKS	81
VALUE STOCKS	83
CYCLICAL and CONSUMER DISCRETIONARY STOCKS	87
DEFENSIVE STOCKS	89
INCOME and DIVIDEND STOCKS	90
MARKET CAPITALIZATION	94
MORNINGSTAR STYLE BOX	95
THE S&P 500 and the DOW JONES averages	96
FINANCIAL ADVISORS	97
ROBO ADVISORS	100
DIVERSIFICATION	103
FOREIGN EXCHANGE	106
BUYING ON MARGIN	109

STOCK OPTIONS	111
EMPLOYEE STOCK OPTIONS	113
MOMENTUM STRATEGY	114
REVERSION TO THE MEAN and CONTRARIANS	119
SHORT SELLING	123
CROWDED TRADES	127
TRADING ONLINE	130
LIMIT ORDERS	134
ROTATION	137
RE-BALANCING	140
BUYING AND SELLING CONSIDERATIONS	143
BUSINESS CYCLES	146
BETA	150
ALPHA	152
RELATIVE STRENGTH INDEX	152
MARKET PULLBACKS, CORRECTIONS and RECESSIONS	153
MARKET TIMING	158
REDUCING RISK	163
VOLATILITY	167
III. INVESTMENT CHOICES	**171**
CASH	171
GOLD (and precious metals)	174
ENERGY	178
INTERNATIONAL INVESTMENTS	183
EMERGING MARKETS	189
ANNUITIES	194
TARGET DATE OR RETIREMENT OR LIFE FUNDS	198
IPOs	201
COMMODITIES	201
BONDS	207
BOND TYPES	209
BOND RISK and INTEREST RATES	215
BONDS vs. BOND FUNDS and BOND ETFs	218
BONDS – My View	220
PREFERRED STOCK	223
HEALTHCARE	226
FINANCIALS	230
REAL ESTATE INVESTMENT TRUSTS	233
TELECOM	236
VANGUARD FUNDS	236
SECTORS I AVOID	238
CHOOSING ETFS	244
IV. YOUR RISK PROFILE	**249**
V. STRATEGY- ASSET ALLOCATION	**256**

VI. PORTFOLIO RECOMMENDATIONS	**259**
VII. ETF CHOICES	**262**
BONDS	263
COMMODITIES	266
COMMUNICATION SERVICES	266
CONSUMER DISCRETIONARY	268
CONSUMER STAPLES	269
DIVIDENDS	270
EMERGING MARKETS	270
ENERGY	271
FINANCIALS	272
GOLD	273
HEALTHCARE	273
INTERNATIONAL	275
LARGE CAP	276
LARGE CAP GROWTH	277
LARGE CAP VALUE	278
LOW VOLATILITY STOCKS	279
MATERIALS	280
MID CAP	280
MID CAP AND SMALL CAP GROWTH	280
MID CAP AND SMALL CAP VALUE	281
NEAR CASH	281
PREFERRED STOCK	284
REITs	284
SEMICONDUCTORS	285
SILVER	285
SMALL CAP	286
SOFTWARE	287
TECHNOLOGY	287
TOTAL US MARKET	290
TOTAL WORLD	290
TRANSPORTATIONS	290
UTILITIES	291
VIII. FINAL THOUGHTS (6/19)	**293**
OF GREATER CONCERN	295
ACKNOWLEDGEMENTS	298
ADDENDUM	298
APPENDIX 1	303
LIST OF ALL URLs	303

Note: The digital version of this book contains URLs to key concepts and information. For readers of the print copy, a list of these URLs is provided on page 303.

I. INTRODUCTION

All thoughts and opinions contained here are my own, based on my own experience. Many will disagree, which as Mark Twain said, makes horse races. Without opposing views, everyone would bet on the same horse, and markets would never reach equilibrium. Unfortunately, there's no way to get rich quick without taking excessive risk - it takes time. Hopefully this paper presents a common sense way to build wealth over time, striking a balance between risk taking and risk aversion, in a conversational style.

References to "investors" throughout this book refers to persons or other entities (such as an investment advisor or mutual fund) who commit capital with the expectation of receiving financial returns. Investors utilize investments in order to grow their money and/or provide an income during retirement. Non-professional investors, like us, are placing their own funds, those which they believe they will not be needed for everyday expenses in the near term, to some level of risk.

Hopefully this book will help you in determining where to place this money to get the best possible return, at a risk level you are comfortable with - and to have the knowledge of when changes to your investments are most advantageous.

PURPOSE & SCOPE

The main purpose of this book is to pass along some of the things I've learned about investing to my family and some friends for their use after I'm gone. Wives always outlive their husbands - I'm told women passed a law which requires it - and I recently realized my initial goal of living forever was probably wishful thinking. Prince Phillip and Keith Richards seem to have figured it out, but thus far I haven't. So, I decided to use my laptop for something other than watching cats on YouTube.

Most people I know don't know much about investing, whether that's by design I don't know, but the subject seems in some ways like a black box to many people. It's very confusing, nobody agrees on anything, especially the experts, and they have their own buzzwords for practically everything. Worse, it's really easy to make a serious mistake. Financial advisors have a way of making their past returns look great, but how do I know he or she won't cause me to lose my life savings, and buy a new Ferrari with my money? You read about people losing their life savings all the time. Can I trust these guys? (probably not).

What's needed is some basic knowledge and a simple to understand model so that you don't have to rely on anyone other than yourself.

I thought it would be worthwhile to provide some guidance in investing money for the long term, without paying exorbitant fees, appropriate for life savings or retirement money you might have in a pre-tax account like an IRA, 401(k), or company retirement plan, or savings on which you have already paid taxes (post tax account).

Other than savings plans, you may be lucky enough to inherit money that you have no immediate need for or realize proceeds from the sale of a large asset such as a house or piece of land. You will want to get these funds working for you as soon as possible by investing them as outlined in this book. (If you plan on using some of this money in the near future, say 1 year, it is suggested that you choose a safe, low volatility place to park those funds, such as a bank CD or US government bond ETF.)

My main motivation was seeing and hearing absolutely terrible and needlessly expensive investment advice on TV, newspapers, and articles on the internet, and wanting my family to preserve and invest their savings in the best way possible. Especially bothersome are the financial advice columns, where they answer purported letters from readers, and give answers knowing absolutely nothing about the person's life situation.

The worst of these "experts" are those who try to convince you that they know how to pick stocks and make you rich – just become a client. I suspect some of them are ex-day traders who failed at that venture but are trying to find an outlet for their market knowledge. They may mean well but suffer from the delusion that if you're smart you can "beat the market" by picking stocks. I also thought that it would be nice if those who come after me didn't have to start at absolute zero and make the same mistakes I did.

Not everyone will agree with my views on this stuff, but I'm an unbiased source with no axe to grind, which is a leg up on an investment advisor who has conflicts of interest all over the place.

The biggest problem with financial advisors is that in addition to helping you, they are looking to earn as much money as possible for themselves and their employers. Not necessarily in a dishonest or fraudulent way - it's only human that they want to do well financially themselves, but they also have an obligation to earn money for their employer. Every time an advisor recommends you buy a mutual fund, or suggests you buy an insurance policy, money is being paid to him or her. Do you think your advisor is going to recommend products or services which do not produce income for themselves or their employer?

As non-professional investors have become more aware of the significant impact of fund management expense ratios, or ER, they have moved toward lower fee products. Historical comparisons of similar financial products revealed that the compounding of expenses was the largest single factor in predicting fund performance. That is to say the fee structure was more important than any other factor for comparable asset funds.

This reduced fee movement has taken place across all forms of investing like ETFs and hedge funds, but especially in the case of mutual funds. With mutual funds losing billions of invested dollars annually to passive ETFs, they have had to drastically reduce their fees to reduce capital outflow, which hasn't worked very well, as their average fees still exceed ETF fees by more than 300% (2018).

One of the major factors which has stimulated the reduced fee movement has been the extremely low bond rates of the last ten years. If you are earning 2-2.5% on your bonds, and paying an expense fee of 1-1.5%, there's not much opportunity for growth in your nest egg.

The extremely low interest rates set by our Federal Reserve over the last 10 years have been a serious problem for those trying to save for retirement, however this problem has worsened considerably of late. In 2019 interest rates have declined to historic lows, with the US 10-year bond - the most often used benchmark for bond rates - yielding only 1.55% as of 8/19/2019. Interest rates are being driven lower because:

- The Fed has started to push rates down again - by .25% in June '19.

- Slowing economic growth in just about every developed country in the world, including China, and most European countries.

- Central banks are lowering interest rates in other countries to levels far below US levels (many of which are now negative) which is causing non-US governments and funds to buy US bonds.

- Trump's trade war with China and possibly other countries is causing the fear of a US recession, causing investors to buy bonds out of fear (which pushes the yields down).

What this all means is that those of us trying to save for retirement have an even more difficult job ahead of us. The probability of running out of money in retirement, a scary outcome, is now considerably higher. Savers, especially those in bonds, CD's and similar low risk options are getting hurt badly. The US ten year is now approximately .07% below the rate of inflation. In other words, the nest egg of cautious savers will decrease in purchasing power, every day.

Hence this book.

THIS BOOK

It's necessary to understand some of the fundamentals of investing first, so future decisions make sense in the economic environment which exists at that time. Therefore, first I cover general investing concepts and terms, and how the investment markets work, then I will describe the fundamentals of asset classes you can choose for your savings, and finally I recommend some specific choices you can make. If you have an understanding of the basic concepts explained here, you will be able to adapt your savings plan as needed, regardless of the economic changes taking place. You will only need common sense, and you will not need a paid advisor.

A lot of what is written about investing becomes obsolete rather quickly, especially in the technical age we live in. I have written this guide primarily in 2018-2019.

The focus of this book is on making the best <u>investment choices</u> and minimizing the fees and expenses of those choices. A financial advisor may be helpful with regard to advice pertaining to <u>other</u> life decisions, such as tax planning, estates, wills, health insurance, estate planning, college savings plans, etc., but you will not need one to invest your 401K or other life savings.

With regard to these other life decisions, I would recommend picking up the latest edition of Jonathan Clements' <u>Money Guide</u>. Clements is an ex-Wall Street Journal writer, also with no axe to grind, who dispenses common sense, and is not a Wall Street dinosaur with outdated preconceived ideas. He covers life decisions I have not addressed, such as, should I take out long term care insurance, make a living will, etc.

SOCIAL SECURITY

I have not included in this book a discussion of the alternatives and pros and cons regarding how and when to take Social Security for three reasons. First it is so complicated you actually need to devote another book on the subject, two, the enormous dependency on a person's life situation, and three the preponderance of articles already written on this subject.

By life situation include, among others: age and age of spouse, single or married, number of years worked and paid into SS, age of dependents, financial resources of spouse, still working or retired or partially retired, health of those eligible for benefits, tax situation and state of residency, school age children, disability eligibility of claimant and/ or spouse, health insurance or lack thereof, other income to live on while waiting to claim, and the list goes on. I read letters written to financial advisors on the subject and continue to learn about unknown complexities of the rules of Social Security - it must fill volumes.

Here's an example - If you are divorced, but were married 10 or more years and have not remarried, <u>you are eligible to receive half of your ex-spouse's full benefit</u>. This allows you to take your spouse's benefits earlier and postpone your own.

It's hard to try to generalize, but if your health is good and you have enough income to get by while you are waiting, it is a huge advantage to postpone taking benefits until the age at which benefits are maximized for you, typically age 70. However, because of the long list of issues affecting your decision, it's necessary to research the issue thoroughly. Once you start benefits it becomes difficult to "un-start" them. I took my benefit at my so called "full benefit age" and in hindsight I wish that I had waited. The added benefit of waiting until you maximize your benefit is huge, about 8% annually, and basically free money.

Because of the complications involved, there are a number of calculators available where you enter your own personal data - just google it. The SS system has one of its own. If you have a complicated situation consider spending $40 to run the calculator at maximizemysocialsecurity.com a highly acclaimed tool which was developed exclusively by Boston University economist Laurence Kotlikoff, with no involvement by the Social Security Administration.

SAVING ENOUGH

I have enjoyed investing for many years. It became somewhat of a hobby for me, not just because it was interesting and challenging, but also because it was very important since I retired at a young age, 55, as my employer was acquired, and our headquarters became redundant. With a long way to go without a paycheck, and years before Social Security was available, I had to learn how to live on investments.

Making enough and saving enough is a lot harder today than it was for me. Inflation has marched along, whereas most people's salaries have limped along. And staggering costs to buy (or rent) a house, especially in California, and the cost of sending your kids to college has risen so much, borrowing significantly is the only option for most people. Saving money with a growing family is nearly impossible, although a 401(k) or similar deferred tax plan is a huge help.

To me, the goal of investing is fourfold: 1. to have enough money to retire reasonably comfortably and be able to pay for expenses as they happen, 2. to be able to give back to your family while you are still alive, 3. to not be a financial burden on your children when huge healthcare bills come near the end of your life, and 4. to leave enough behind when you pass to help your children have enough money in retirement (I caved in and left out the 5th one about the Ferrari).

These are tough goals to achieve. Life is too unfair. Hard working people struggle, undeserving people come into money. Luck has way too much to do with it. But this should not stop us from doing the best we can with what we have, and not giving our money away because of excessive investment fees, or worse, bad advice.

The investing part is a lot easier than the saving part. Most people with families are quick to say that saving is impossible when you are barely, if at all, able to meet your existing expenses. I know because I used to say it. What makes it so difficult is the natural tendency for us to adjust our lifestyle right up to the level of our income. There are just too many things competing for our limited dollars.

The surest way of saving is having money subtracted from your pay before you receive it - through some sort of automatic plan. If you expect to save out of the dollars that are left over after paying your bills, you might find there isn't anything material left. A 401(k) or any similar plan which takes the money out in the form of a deduction, works best. Hopefully you'll adjust your lifestyle to whatever you receive. Then consider this money not available - no longer accessible for living.

In my case, I saved the majority of my retirement savings in the last 5 years I worked, largely because of an unqualified savings plan offered by my employer, which, looking back, provided me with the savings I needed in my retirement years.

Other than a critical medical expense, the only circumstance which I think you might consider using your deferred tax savings before retirement, is to buy your first house. This, not only because of the difficulty in coming up with the down payment, but also because houses are in themselves a savings vehicle, which also create tax savings. Given the choice however, between borrowing and using money you have saved in a tax deferred plan, I would recommend borrowing, if it allows you to leave your tax deferred plan untouched. When your financial situation improves, you can refinance that mortgage with something that fits your needs better.

When I was growing up it was assumed you would retire at 65, however life expectancy then was age 72 for men, 75 for women, which is hard to believe now. Your retirement savings only had to last 7-10 years on average. Today, many retire before age 65, or more accurately are pushed into retirement, often by downsizing, and we live longer - much longer.

One of the toughest problems retirees face is making sure their money lasts as long as they do. From the U.S. to Europe, Australia and Japan, retirement account balances aren't increasing fast enough to cover rising life expectancy, the World Economic Forum warned in a report published June 13, 2019. The result could be workers outliving their savings by as much as a decade or more. Life expectancy is now about age 85. It's simply not possible for most people to save enough money to live for perhaps 30 years comfortably, without significant investment income.

If you very cautiously, put your savings in a bank savings account, currently earning less than 1.5%, or a bank CD earning 1-2%, or bonds, earning 2-2.5%%, you will find that inflation, which compounds annually, will practically wipe out the buying power of your savings well before you pass. Government reported inflation is about 2.2% today, however labor costs have begun to increase again, and labor costs represent 71% of the cause of inflation. Also, many people, including me, find the government's inflation numbers do not reflect the level of price increases we see in our daily lives.

Think about medical care costs and health insurance premiums, college fees, the price of a movie ticket, a car repair, the price of a house. Every time you experience these, the price has increased. If you run out of money when you're older, the number one fear of retired people, there's not much you can do. Going back to work as a senior often means a low wage job. Social Security will offer a bare bones existence, and your healthcare decisions may end up being made by disinterested administrators - unless you have another source of income to remain independent.

The elephant in the room is healthcare. It can wipe out a lifetime of savings in 1-2 years. The number one cause of bankruptcy in the US is medical bills.

The median cost of a shared room in a nursing home is $86,000 a year, according to Genworth Financial. How do you plan for that? You can't. Will you get a disease which costs hundreds of thousands to treat, or end up needing nursing home care for several years? Will this happen before your eligibility for Medicare? Fidelity has recently published a study (4/18) on average healthcare costs. A 65 year old couple will need $280K for healthcare before inflation. Based upon my personal experience, the number is likely to be much higher, especially if cancer is involved.

(Long term healthcare insurance is a greatly debated and a complicated issue I do not tackle here. Many who bought it many years ago find that the reimbursement limits are far too low for today's costs, and insurers keep raising rates to keep up with rising costs. Many companies are no longer offering this insurance. If considering buying, research thoroughly and talk to others who have actually used the benefit).

All of this means it's more important than ever to save as much as you possibly can while working, invest those funds wisely, and not waste money on investment advisor's fees and expenses or bad advice.

Because of several factors, including the limitless amount of easily available information on the internet, online access to broker accounts, the simplicity of computer trading, help and research tools available free on brokerage websites, and the emergence of ETFs, you no longer need a financial advisor for making investment choices.

This is excellent because over a lifetime, their fees, which accrue even when you are experiencing losses, are enormous. These savings will add to your retirement balance. You can do this yourself, and it's not hard. You will also be happy that your investments are consistent with your personal beliefs and values, and that you have achieved some level of financial security for yourself and your family.

SLEEPING AT NIGHT

Investing is a highly individualized discipline, which requires tailoring, depending on the investor's life circumstances. Age, family circumstances, children's age and financial situation, health, and sometimes forced retirement, and many other factors make it difficult and potentially very harmful to publish financial advice to other people. Everybody's life is very different, more so than we usually recognize.

Does someone in your family have a serious illness or disability, do your parents have marketable job skills, is there an elderly grandparent needing care, is college coming for the kids, do you own a home, can you increase the mortgage, can you work past 65, is your job secure, can a spouse work if needed, can you work part time, and so on.

This issue is further complicated by the personal likes and dislikes which we all gain during our life, and other personal preferences and moral codes, which affect our ability to be "comfortable" with certain investments. Tobacco and gun companies continue to do well financially, but do you want to invest in them? How about fossil fuel companies? It's very important to be comfortable with your investments from all perspectives. Personal biases count, and companies or industries which run counter to your moral compass, can and should be avoided. My personal biases are revealed here. You will have your own.

This guide recommends the use of Exchange Traded Funds, ETFs, as your primary investment tool. ETFs may include individual companies you do not like, and this is unavoidable. You must take comfort that with ETFs, your investment is in a basket of companies, and that the amount invested in any one company is very small in dollar terms. Everyday new ETFs are created to fit investor preferences. If you want to exclude, for example, tobacco or gun stocks, keep an eye out for ETFs which specifically exclude those industries. (A new Blackstone group of ETFs was announced today which eliminate gun companies).

Investment funds using socially responsible investment criteria have come with a lesser return on average, although there are some reasonable options. As of 10/1/18, ETF.com lists 75 socially responsible ETFs already in existence, with 7.6B in assets under management (AUM). The largest of these ETFs is DSI, with $1.2B AUM. It has returned 9.5% YTD (10/1/18) vs. a 9.7% return for the juggernaut S&P 500.

STAYING INFORMED

I did not want this paper to be too lengthy. However, I did want the reader to have enough of an understanding of this subject matter so that you can make intelligent informed decisions on your own. I did not want to make recommendations without supplying the underlying reasons for them. It was hard for me to determine how much depth to include. I tried to strike a balance.

If you do want to read more on any of these subjects, it's pretty easy to just Google it. Good sources of information include books and articles written by Jonathan Clements, and Investopedia.com is also good for learning the basics. Bloomberg.com and Bloomberg TV is also trustworthy. CNBC TV is informative but ignore stock picking recommendations. (My investment club tried some of Jim Cramer's picks – a large mistake). I watch it daily, primarily to understand overall market and economic issues. The Wall Street Journal is very good, however ignore stock picks and especially the opinion pages, which are now another Fox news outlet since Robert Murdoch purchased the newspaper.

On the reverse side I would totally ignore Investor's Business Daily, (especially their relative strength index), and all stock picking recommendations from Barron's, Fortune magazine, and all stock market newsletters. Old school publications cling to the belief that you can beat the market picking stocks. I urge a lot of skepticism with regard to The Motley Fool (which used to be common sense but is now becoming a marketing tool to sell you something) and I would totally ignore website Seeking Alpha. When reading articles with investment advice, limit your scope to general economic and business news and investing information, but not stock picking recommendations.

WHERE'S YOUR SAVINGS?

If the funds you are concerned about investing in a 401(k), or a similar work-related tax deferred plan, then you are restricted by the rules of your employer's plan. Your employer may offer both a regular IRA or a Roth. Every company's plan is different. You should <u>contribute the maximum</u> amount the plan allows every year, (as long as the maximum allowed by the government is not exceeded) regardless of the rules concerning company matching contributions. The opportunity to save tax free is a huge advantage. If you think you cannot afford the maximum, consider contributing the maximum anyway and reducing some other expenses, or borrowing the difference (as long as it's not at a high rate of interest). You may, for example, borrow on a home equity line of credit, which you can pay down when your financial situation improves.

In calculating how much you can afford to save out of each paycheck, remember IRA deductions come out before your income taxes. These savings will reduce your taxes, and in effect, the government is subsidizing your savings by deferring taxes. If this is confusing, calculate your take home pay with and without the IRA deduction and compare. If you are contributing to a Roth, this does not apply because you pay the taxes on a Roth deduction today - the Roth deduction comes out of your pay <u>after</u> taxes are deducted.

With respect to your investment options, you will have to choose from whatever your employer's savings plan offers. Many company plans offer relatively few choices, and worse, carry above average fees. These higher fees, which come out of the employees' investment returns, allow the investment provider to charge the company less for the administration of the plan, or in some cases, may provide for payment kickbacks to the employer, and become profits to them (or reduce the cost of their contribution to your plan).

If you see expense ratios on the plan choices above 1%, or for index funds above say .5%, then the investment plan provider is charging more than you would be paying if you were investing the money in your own IRA. Despite this, these higher fees are still worth paying if your employer is also contributing some percent of your salary to your plan, which is free money.

After reading this guide, make investment choices in your company's plan that come as close to the parameters outlined here as possible, picking <u>passive index-based funds</u> wherever available, avoiding actively managed funds, and picking those choices with the <u>lowest expense ratios</u>. When you leave the company, you will want to roll over the plan to a self-directed IRA at a broker within 60 days, where you can invest in anything you want.

Don't place any funds in the plan in cash, or cash equivalents, such as a "stable value fund" which is similar to a money market fund. Invest your total balance. Cash for emergencies should be held outside a tax deferred plan in a low risk account such as a bank certificate of deposit, or US bond fund. Having to take money out of a tax deferred plan should be a last resort.

IRAs and all other tax deferred plans are usually referred to as self-directed plans, meaning that they are not company plans. You voluntarily set them up with a provider, such as a broker such as Fidelity or Schwab, and you are free to invest in anything you want.

In 2018, IRAs have annual contribution limits of $5500, $6500 over 50, whereas 401(k)'s allow up to $18500, $24500 over 50. Roth contributions are not allowed for high income filers. If you are rolling over a 401(k) which contains shares of stock, usually of your ex-employer, do not sell them, roll them over "in kind". Before, or shortly after you leave your employer, when you set up the rollover account with the provider, get a good set of instructions from them to make sure you do not create a "taxable event", where if improperly done, the government may tax this money as ordinary income.

With self-directed plans you will have to select either an IRA investment retirement account, or a Roth savings account. With an IRA you avoid paying any income taxes now, and you pay them only when you withdraw funds after age 59 and ½. With a Roth you pay the full income tax now, and when you withdraw those funds for retirement you pay no income tax, including all capital gains made during the period. With a standard IRA, capital gains are not treated differently, all withdrawals are taxed as ordinary income.

I decided not to include any discourse here on the advantages and disadvantages of an IRA vs. Roth, or of the many Federal rules which apply. Firstly, because the decision is involved, and has lots of variables depending on your personal situation. Secondly, there are many rules, and they sometimes are changed. Thirdly, because there is a preponderance of information available both on the web and from the IRA providers which outlines the advantages and disadvantages of each, and which to choose based on your personal circumstances. Google "IRA vs. Roth", and you will see lots of articles.

The most important difference between the two is that an IRA benefits people who are already in a high tax bracket, want to avoid taxes now, and expect to be in a lower bracket after retirement, which most people will be. With a Roth you pay your taxes now when you believe that your tax bracket will still be high in retirement (because of your income or higher tax brackets) and you will have many years of capital gains accumulated which won't be taxed. The absence of taxes on the gains benefits younger people, who will have many years of gains which accumulate. Older workers who are already in a high bracket usually want to defer taxes immediately.

With a Roth you will avoid paying income tax on your withdrawals in retirement, including capital gains, which is a great benefit, however sometimes overlooked, you may be able to save more initially with an IRA. This because you are not paying any taxes on these funds, whereas with a Roth, taxes will reduce the amount you are able to set aside. The higher your tax bracket, the more you will be able to contribute (from an affordability standpoint), and as a result your investment balance will grow faster in the IRA because of a higher principal investment. 401(k) deductions in your paycheck are subtracted before taxes are calculated, which will lower your current tax bracket.

One problem in making this decision is we have no idea what income taxes are going to be in 20 or 30 years. One perhaps oversimplified way of looking at the Roth vs. IRA issue, is deciding if you are better able to pay the taxes now, and enjoy tax free withdrawals in retirement, or you believe you will be better able to pay those taxes in retirement, as you make withdrawals. Age also plays a role since younger workers will see their capital gains accumulate over many years, and a Roth will reduce taxes on those gains to zero.

In my case, most of my deferred savings were accumulated late in life, when my children had finished college and my wife and I were both working, so our tax bracket was high. Part of this was caused by the fact that they hadn't invented IRA's when I started working (and cell phones were used as counterweights for elevators...see right.) When my income was higher, in my 40's, I was able to save more.

Image credit: Jamie McCarthy/Getty

The IRA saved me a lot of taxes. By spreading out my retirement withdrawals as much as possible, my tax bracket in retirement is now significantly lower than when I worked. A Roth wouldn't have worked as well for me. In most circumstances, it is wiser to push required payments, such as taxes, into the future, and avoid paying money upfront for a future benefit, like a timeshare property, health club membership, long term care insurance, etc.

The difference between the two alternatives can be significant. Before choosing I would run a free IRA vs. Roth calculator. One of these can be found at IRA vs. Roth Calculator. Your broker can also help you with this.

The Federal penalty for withdrawing funds from a tax deferred plan before age 59 & 1/2 is 10%. You can withdraw funds before that age with no penalty if the proceeds are used for a permitted purpose like buying your first home, medical expenses, and eight other purposes. You can also withdraw funds without a penalty from a Roth IRA (since you have already paid the taxes on your contributions) however there are rules there also, most notably that it has to be at least 5 years since the account was opened. Withdrawal rules can be found easily online.

The reality is you can probably find a way to qualify for a penalty free withdrawal, but you should consider it an absolute last resort. An IRA is a huge benefit to you, and if you reduce or withdraw the balance, you are hurting yourself. You benefit the most by contributing as much as possible to your IRA. Plan on never using these funds until you retire. Try to find other ways to manage cash needs. For example, when buying your first house put down as little as possible, and when your financial situation improves, refinance it.

Regardless of which type of self-directed plan you chose, you have the freedom to choose any investments you wish, hence this guide.

ECONOMIC ENVIRONMENT (June 2019)

At the halfway point of 2019, the market has been on a 10-year recovery since the devastating recession of '08-'09 which hit bottom in Mar '09. During that period the Fed, like most central banks around the world, reduced short term interest rates to zero (long term rates largely move on their own) which

has produced a remarkable recovery. The S&P 500 has tripled since Mar. 2009.

Extremely low interest rates (below zero in some countries) helps people borrow money to buy houses and cars and other things, which gets the economy going. However, the collateral damage of interest rates near zero is that people's savings can earn next to nothing, and this is primarily people approaching, and in retirement.

This has forced retired people out of low return vehicles such as bank CDs and government bonds, into higher risk assets such as stocks and high yield bonds, to find investments which have returns high enough that they don't run out of money in retirement. This has been affectionately called "chasing yield". It's not their fault that bank and bonds yields are as anemic as they are, and the fear of running out of money after your working years are over is a strong motivator.

As the economy recovered over this period (albeit somewhat slowly at about 2% per year) both stocks and bonds did extremely well. Stocks, because the economy expanded, and with it company earnings, went up – and bonds, because falling interest rates increased their value. In Dec. 2015 the Fed began raising interest rates gradually, and increased Fed fund rates by .25%, 3 times per year, in '17 and '18. They were doing this to bring interest rates to more normal levels, and to prevent the economy from overheating and causing harmful inflation. The Fed has determined that 2-2.5% inflation is the desired level, all things considered.

In 2018 the economy exhibited strong but not excessive growth, very low unemployment rates (a 50-year low of 3.7%), and a resumption of inflation at about 2% per annum. Wage growth has started to increase, after years of stagnation, albeit very gradually, and some signs of labor shortages are appearing. Meanwhile the Trump administration approved a very large corporate tax cut, and authorized huge spending increases, both domestic and defense related, which stimulated the economy even more - at a time when no stimulus was needed. The Federal government is moving into a period of very large deficits, which will require much greater borrowing through the issuance of more treasury bonds. This would normally signal an increase in yields, as the market is flooded with new bonds.

In October 2018 US interest rates started to fall at an unprecedented rate. The rapid decline of interest rates through 6/19 has been totally unexpected and has worried many that these low rates are signaling an economic slowdown and a possible recession. Many investors have sought safety in bonds, and defensive equity groups like utilities, and real estate. However, the stock market had one of the best first halves recorded since 1997, as bond yields produce minimal gains, perhaps as low as zero when measured after inflation.

Worldwide demand for extremely low risk US government bonds remains incredibly high. As of 6/19 the benchmark 10-year US Treasury bond stood at only 2.0%, after having increased above 3% twice in 2018.

Part of this drop in US rates is being caused by extraordinarily low bond rates in other countries, where central banks have been keeping rates low to stimulate economic growth. As of 6/19, approximately 13 trillion in sovereign bonds worldwide have interest rates of zero or below zero, including Germany and Japan.

Recession fears are being caused by: an economic slowdown in Europe and in China, the 10 year growth period we have experienced possibly coming to an end, the potential for Trump's trade war to reduce US company earnings, and possibly the very flat interest rate yield curve (explained further under "Market Pullbacks").

A RISING RATE ENVIRONMENT ABRUPTLY ENDS

The Fed, until 2019, had been increasing interest rates with the objective of returning rates to more normal levels, reducing the artificial stimulus of nearly free money, and hopefully preventing the economy from overheating.

In a rising rate environment it is not wise to increase or overweight investments in securities which lose principal value in periods of increasing interest rates - primarily bonds of all types, especially long maturities, and bond surrogates (asset classes that behave like bonds, described further below), such as utility stocks, REIT's, real estate, incl. homebuilders, and Telecom stocks. (see also Bond Risk and Interest Rates).

In late 2018 economic reports started to reveal a slowing world economy, especially in countries outside the US. Marked slowdowns in Europe, the Far East, and China were especially worrisome. However, in mid-2018 a worldwide trade war was launched by the Trump administration with China, Japan, Korea, Europe, Canada and Mexico (countries which sell more to us than we sell to them which causes a US trade deficit). Investor sentiment declined sharply, as did stock prices, and bond yields fell.

In the last quarter of 2018 stock prices fell significantly. This was caused by:

- Fear that the 10-year bull market was coming to an end
- A slowdown in the worldwide economy including the US
- Higher interest rates lure investors away from stocks
- Slowing in the key US housing and auto market
- Fear of corporate profit damage from the trade war
- Fear the Fed was pushing interest rates too high
- Corporate earnings slowing

Because of these factors, and also because of the continuance of tame inflation of only about 2%, the US Federal Reserve, through Fed chief Powell, testified to congress that their previous increasing interest rate program had been placed on hold, and that no further rate increases would be made unless the economy started to heat up too much, and/or inflation increased unexpectedly.

What a difference six months can make. That's how long it took for the Federal Reserve to go from hiking rates (with talk of more hikes to come) to suggesting it may cut rates imminently.

The turnaround in the 10-year Treasury yield wasn't any less abrupt. It went from a yield of 3.25% in November 2018 to a low of 1.50% on 8/30/19, propelling the iShares 7-10 Year Treasury Bond ETF (IEF) to its highest level since 2016. (Bond prices rise as yields go down.)

10 Year Treasury Bond Yield

Largely because of the Fed's actions, stocks recovered sharply in the first half of 2019 as investor's fears of a Fed created recession, dissipated, and investors were comforted that the Fed "had their backs" - meaning that the Fed was ready to stimulate the economy if the current slowdown continued or worsened.

Takeaway: As of June 2019, interest rates have declined substantially with the benchmark US 10-year bond falling from 3.25% to 2.0%. The lower rates are causing more investors to switch back to stocks, and lower mortgage rates are giving a boost to housing companies and REITs. Investments which are inversely correlated with interest rates, such as bonds, dividend stocks, REITs, preferred stocks, utilities, and telecom stocks, will do better as long as the Fed doesn't start raising rates again.

So, the rising rate environment has abated for now, and fears of an economic slowdown are pushing interest rates down instead of up. The principal fears of investors have reverted to the ill effects of a US trade war with both China and Europe, a negative fallout from the UK's inability to resolve Brexit, and whether the economic slowdown will worsen. With the US presidential elections coming in 11/20, most think Trump will declare an end to his self-inflicted trade "war" with China and other countries, to bolster his reelection chances, and this will boost company earnings, and the stock market.

Long term investors are not concerned with these headline grabbing risks. If you are investing money to be used in 20 or 30 years, the events of today will be a distant memory, but it is important to be aware of the direction of US and world economies, as these changes will eventually show up in the prices of investment assets.

II. INVESTMENT CONCEPTS and TERMS

CORPORATE BASICS

Depending on your familiarity with basic corporate financial reporting and terminology, I have included a <u>short</u> addendum at the end of this book to refresh your familiarity in that respect. Covered are a company's balance sheet, income statement, and cash flow statement, and the meaningfulness of each to investors. If you think you might need to revisit those topics, I would turn to that addendum now. It is only 4 pages. It will help you in understanding the concepts discussed in the remainder of this guide.

CRYSTAL BALLS

The first rule of investing is fully understanding that **<u>no one can predict the future</u>** - not the future price of stocks or bonds or oil or gold or anything. But we keep trying. Every day the "experts" tell us what is going up or down, and by how much, and they sound so convincing. Some people, especially financial advisors, cannot help themselves from telling others what is going to happen. I think it is a way for them to achieve an air of superior knowledge and intelligence. These experts will be wrong much more often than they are right - in the direction, amount, and duration of future events. There are so many variables and unforeseen events; it simply cannot be done – <u>at all</u>.

We do however, listen to those who prophesize, because we want to believe someone can tell us what's ahead - especially when it offers us the chance to make a bunch of money, or conversely, if we can avoid losing a large chunk of our life savings. It's reasonable to think that professional investors will have the ability to see which way things are going. Unfortunately, at any point in time, half of these "experts" predict things getter better, and the other half see a recession looming.

It's not a lot different from going to a fortune teller (I'm going on a trip far away), especially when the future is described in glowing terms (I'm going to be coming into a lot of money). Its human nature - someone you know says, "I have certain inside knowledge...buy IBM". You want to believe it could happen, you envision yourself making a boatload of money, and you buy. You reason; if the price drops, I'll just sell, how bad could it be? This is how day traders are born.

Consider predicting the price of oil, for example. Say the oil producing countries of OPEC agree to limit their oil production. The price of oil immediately increases in anticipation of lower future supplies of oil. Will all of these countries actually comply with the agreement? Later it's revealed some countries do not. Oil supply is still too high, so prices fall. Without warning, a huge new supply of oil is discovered somewhere, and prices drop further. These kinds of supply demand shifts will make scrap paper out of historical chart analysis.

Between 10/1/18 and 12/24/18 the price of WTI (West Texas Intermediate crude oil) dropped 43.5% - <u>no one</u> saw or predicted that decline. Everyone who held energy related stocks got trashed. Human actions and world events are not predictable. Many oil traders and experts who have guessed wrong for several years, are finally admitting to the impossibility of this effort. There are just too many variables and new ones are continually created (like Trump selling oil from the US strategic oil reserve - or not). Computers do not help. Computers can predict the <u>probability</u> of future events, especially in rational environments, however as we all know, humans are only *sometimes* rational. Hillary Clinton learned this the hard way. Computers predicted she would win the 2016 presidential election with an 84% probability, based on poll results, only days before the final vote. She lost. Could all those polls have been inaccurate, or was it the rare occurrence of a low probability event?

In polling, the wording of the question prejudices our answer without our knowing it, and worse, people answering surveys often don't answer honestly (or answer what they think is expected). They don't want to look foolish, or uninformed, and they might not even understand the question. Half of a couple dozen of those questioned by Jay Leno on the street in LA didn't even know who the vice president was. The utter failure of the 2016 presidential polls proved that <u>applying computers to predict human behavior is not reliable.</u>

No one has been able to develop a computer model for investing which consistently outperforms its market benchmark average, over an extended period of time.

Stock prices have been repeatedly shown to be <u>virtually random</u> in the short run, especially in periods under 3 months. <u>A Random Walk down Wall Street</u> by Malkiel, which many consider the authority on the subject, is considered conclusive. However, in the longer term, stocks will **always** follow the earnings of the underlying company(s), 100% of the time. If a company's earnings per share are increasing, their stock price will go up and vice versa, as long as the time period considered is long enough, like a year or more.

In the short run, a company's stock will go up or down based upon current sentiment but will confuse a rational observer. There is a lot of noise, irrelevant news, however we have no way of knowing which is relevant and which is noise. Daily stock prices are also moved by day traders, essentially gamblers, and chartists, who mistakenly believe they are able to predict future prices based on previous price and market history.

No one has found a way to predict the future, so you must abandon the effort, and ignore those who prognosticate. It is sometimes difficult to not get sucked into the fallacious belief that financial experts and analysts can predict the future price of something. Pundits can be quite convincing, pulling out loads of graphs and charts of correlation.

When you see or hear about guaranteed methods of making money in the stock market, **roll your eyes**. It is an old but true cliché that anyone who could predict stock prices would be rich beyond imagination and not tell anyone how they did it (because then it wouldn't work anymore). If someone says they have a method of beating the market, they are probably about to ask you for money.

When you are listening to market pundits, listen for words like," We don't know for sure, but the probabilities favor…", or, "We can't predict near term direction, however in the longer term its likely…, and words to that effect.

Quoting Josh Brown of Ritholtz Wealth management, "There were many years during which stocks have rallied as the economy had performed worse than expectations. There are also years during which economic data was strong but stock prices were weak. And then we've seen literally everything in between. No one can reliably predict which of these scenarios is more likely to occur in advance. Understanding the economy is a helpful exercise. Placing market bets as a result of this understanding is a carnival game on the midway".

Takeaway: The vast majority of experts predicting future stock prices are not worth much more than fortune tellers. If you think about it, people who forecast something will go up or down will always be right if you wait long enough, because everything does go up and down, at some point. Predict a recession and you will always be right - eventually. Unfortunately, this information is totally worthless. Fortunately, there is a way to invest successfully without having to listen to these predictions.

In the next section you will read about the abject failure of active fund managers in "beating" the stock market averages.

STOCK PICKING

Stock picking is dying a slow death among most investors who are only interested in the long-term growth of their savings, without spending every day wondering which way the market is going. Investment advisors claim they can pick stocks and do better than the market averages, which is what they have to say, or they will be seen as having no value. Statistics show, over time, they will not only fail to beat the averages, but that they will fall significantly short of them.

According to recent (7/2018) data from S&P Dow Jones Indices, over the 15 years ending June 2018, 92% of US large cap funds fell below the S&P 500 index, 95% of US mid-cap funds trailed the S&P Mid-cap 400, and 98% of US small cap funds fell below the S&P small cap 600 index. Shortening the period to 3 years, overall 86% of funds failed to beat their benchmark index.

The report concludes, **"For many investors, the ability to invest in low-cost, passive, unmanaged index funds and outperform 92% of high-fee, highly paid, professional active fund managers seems like a no-brainer, especially considering it requires no research or time trying to find the active managers who beat the market in the past and might do so in the future"**

This finding holds for every category of fund, including large-capitalization stocks, mid-caps, and small-caps, as well as for the primary investment styles of core, value, and growth. There are even some categories and time horizons where fully 100% of active funds fail to beat their benchmark. More than 58 percent of U.S. equity funds either folded or merged during the 15-year time frame, as investors moved into index based passive investments.

According to Wells Fargo, through 2018, there hasn't been a year when more than 50% of managers outperformed their fund's benchmark since 2009. According to Kiplinger, about 2/3rds of actively managed funds do not meet or exceed their benchmark, interestingly by about the amount they charge for their services, a little over 1%.

2018 was the 4th worst year since 2001 for active managers failing to exceed their benchmark index (In other words, if they manage a small cap fund, their benchmark index might be the Russell 2000, or similar small cap index). 69% of large cap active managers fell short of the large cap S&P 1500 in 2018. An even worse result occurred in 2015, 2011, and 2014.

From an asset-weighted perspective, active funds lagged by 47 basis points in 2018, and 58 basis points on a three-year annualized basis. (CFRA research). In other words, if you had self-invested in the index, you would have done .58% better than the average active manager and paid an ETF expense fee of say .05-.15%, instead of 1% or more.

The results are even worse if you consider persistence - the ability of top performing funds to continue their outperformance over successive quarters. S&P Dow Jones Indices released their "Persistence Scorecard", data covering the two years ending March 2018, which showed a vanishingly small percentage of funds remain in the top quartile of performers over a two-year period.

Of the 557 domestic stock-based funds that were in the top quartile in March 2016, "only 2.33% managed to stay in the top quartile at the end of March 2018," the report read." Fewer than 1% of large-capitalization stock funds stayed in the top quartile, while 3.85% of small-cap funds did. Zero midcap funds stayed in the top group over the period.

The results weren't much better over longer time horizons. Fewer than 22% of large-cap funds stayed in the top half of performers over three consecutive 12-month periods. That represented the best percentage of the asset-class sizes: just 13.46% of small-cap funds stayed in the top half of performers, while 7.59% maintained a top-half ranking.

This data reveals the fruitlessness of trying to identify outperforming funds to invest in. Funds that beat their benchmark in a particular quarter are unable to repeat those results in subsequent quarters.

This study concluded by saying, "Beyond the performance data, active funds tend to charge significantly more than their passive equivalents", and that, "These fees are the principal reason for their underperformance".

I have included all this detail because financial advisors and professionals speaking on TV and writing articles for the major financial journals, are telling people just the opposite - that they are able to choose winning stocks on a consistent basis. In truth they rarely ever beat their benchmark, and if they do, they will not duplicate the result over periods longer than a one or two quarters. If you review the prospectus of a fund which outperformed its benchmark, you will find that the result was usually not because of a majority of good picks, but rather that the fund held one or two stocks during the period which had an extremely large price increase, offsetting the marginal picks or underperformers. A one-off event.

A number of studies have been performed to attempt to determine why actively managed funds do so poorly. Among the findings:

- First and foremost, the cost of management (these are not inexpensive people),
- A tendency for active managers to be continually buying and selling, chasing quarterly performance results, which results in excessive asset turnover, or churn rate, which is costly and results in higher taxes,
- The propensity to chase momentum stocks selling at high prices, often to "dress" their quarter end report *(see sidebar)*.

Quarter End Reports
For marketing purposes, funds want to show on quarter end reports that they have invested in whatever the best performing stocks were for the quarter, so they buy them as the quarter comes to a close. Similarly, they don't want to be seen as investing in the notable losers in the quarter, so they sell them, even if a loss is realized. None of this gerrymandering can or will occur with index investing.

- The need to keep 5% or more of assets in idle cash for customer withdrawals,

- Large funds find that their size can become an impediment to performance, and it can reduce or limit their acceptable investment choices (they cannot buy low dollar stocks, or stocks which trade thinly).

- As funds get larger their performance starts to mimic the averages purely for arithmetic reasons, so after their overhead costs are added in, they fall short of the average.

- As more and more money flows into passive index funds which buy all of the companies in an index, good or bad, managers have an increasingly difficult task to find outperformers. In other words, passive investing is creating its own success, by making an asset manager's job even more difficult.

The Wall Street Journal proved over decades that darts thrown at a newspaper page of stock listings usually beat expert's choices. It's extremely counter intuitive. It seems logical and rational that smart educated financial experts could choose investments which would do better than totally random picks. This was probably the beginning of the end of the stock picking, because it revealed how poorly the experts did. Doing research and applying years of investing experience was not able to overcome the randomness of market and world events. The newspaper finally discontinued the exercise, probably because it was an embarrassment to the investing community (especially to the "experts" who picked big losers).

Many if not most people who are financially educated believe they can pick stocks and beat the averages. It's seems easy. The markets include lots of terrible stocks: companies losing market share, losing money, negative cash flow, in a dying industry, drowning in unstoppable pension obligations, unable to service huge debt, and perhaps on the verge of bankruptcy. These undoubtedly drag the average market return down. If you avoid these, and only pick healthy companies, for example, those increasing market share, profitable, well managed, unburdened by excessive debt or pension obligations, strong balance sheets, in growing industries, etc., its seems logical to assume that you can't help but beat the averages. It doesn't work, why?

Primarily because the market, on a worldwide platform, is extremely close to being perfect in pricing stocks. Companies doing poorly or struggling have already had their share price beaten down to a point where enough buyers have emerged to stop the slide and establish equilibrium between buyers and sellers. These buyers believe the stock is a buy, because they believe the company is taking steps to remedy their problems, and they see it as a buy low opportunity. The same is true on the upside. Companies doing extremely well have had their prices go up so high sellers have emerged, believing the stock has become overpriced and an opportunity to take profits. Price equilibrium is reached.

If you accept that all stock prices are at the equilibrium, due to a free and rigorous stock market exchange, then you start to see how stock picking becomes much more difficult. You have to be able to find stocks whose price is an anomaly, and for some factual reason, will move toward the equilibrium price you believe is more correct. In other words, you have to outsmart a market which has already properly priced all listed stocks.

Since all market participants theoretically have the same public information available, this is quite an undertaking. In fact, it's very highly likely that professional researchers whose job it is to follow that particular stock have more knowledge about the company than you do. They visit the companies; attend all public meetings, interview executives and competitors, and spend much more time than we do in making their evaluation of what the company's "fair value" is. What we think about the company is based upon an incomplete knowledge of the facts.

I attended a presentation by UBS, United Bank Switzerland, which has a significant investment operation in the US, where they noted that as a starting assumption for all portfolios, that all stock prices are already priced properly and at market equilibrium. They recognized the futility in believing they could find underpriced or overpriced stocks. This approach means, in effect, that there are no bargains. That every weak company has already been appropriately discounted in price, and every strong company has already had its price elevated to reflect its fair value, based upon all publicly known information. If you recognize this, you can start to realize the difficulty in picking winning stocks - especially year after year.

One of the most popular sources of stock picks is financial newsletters. People subscribe to them for their investing advice. The letters claim an amazing track record of continuously beating their benchmark average, which is not true. Without going into details, there are many ways for them to lie with numbers. No one ever asks to see proof of their superior results anyway, so they make all sorts of false claims. In truth they produce terrible advice, and after losing subscribers because they did poorly, eventually close. Their track record is terrible. Of 28 newsletters in 1980, 2 are left. Since 2001 more than half of all newsletters have folded. In the past 15 years only 7% of all newsletters beat their benchmark.

Anyone can start a newsletter, there are no requirements. All you have to do is run ads which assert amazing returns, and show their happy subscribers having drinks on a huge yacht. People buy the letters hoping for the stock picks which will make them rich. The only people making money are the publishers, not the investors. Do not waste your money with financial newsletters. They have reinforced the studies which show that stock picking by "experts" does not work.

One reason stock pickers fail is that companies will always present to the public the most favorable condition possible. Insiders, (the company establishes who they are) who are aware of the company's true financial situation, are not allowed to speak publicly about the company's financial condition, except in a window of days at the end of each quarter. In public releases, companies will exaggerate their strengths, and often neglect to address their difficulties. Wells Fargo did not disclose their fraudulent sales practices program until they were sued. They had known about it at the board level, for <u>10 years.</u>

If a company has a significant problem they consult with their legal staff and their public accountants to determine if they are legally required to divulge the issue under SEC rules. The test is materiality. Companies will not tell you if a competitor has or is releasing a better product than theirs. They will not mention the loss of customers unless it is so large it's in the news. They will not mention senior management conflicts or evidence of malfeasance, until they're forced to. They will euphemistically refer to damage control changes as "restructuring to modernize and improve customer satisfaction". They employ communication consultants to 'spin' news releases positively.

Wells Fargo deceived investors for 20 years with a steady stream of very favorable public information which inflated their stock price. They convinced many investors of their superiority, including Warren Buffett. Now they are referred to as a company which has "lost its way". The list of companies not telling investors about serious problems is endless – the financial rewards for not revealing weaknesses are too compelling.

The result is that analysts develop a positive view of the company, place a higher valuation on the stock, and label it a "buy".

As an example of just one of the fallacies of trying to pick stock winners, experts always say chose companies with "strong management". This is just not possible. How can any outsider possibly know this? Companies have public relations departments to convince investors that their company's management is first class. So, the only way of determining this is to look at past performance. So how well does that work out? Here are a few examples.

<u>GE</u> increased earnings steadily for years which investors thought indicated management's superiority. The CEO was

Time magazine's "man of the year", he was thought to be unequaled. Now we have learned profits were "managed" for decades, using creative and improper accounting, inadequate reserves, horrible acquisition and subsidiary disposal experience (buy high, sell low), poor strategic decisions, and now the company is struggling. The dividend was reduced to 1 cent, and the stock dropped from $55 to $7. Now considered a falling knife.

<u>Wells Fargo</u> a Wall Street darling, loved by Buffett, with a great PR department that convinced everyone that the company was best in class. They were found to be cheating every class of customer they had including checking, credit cards, overdraft fees, mortgages, car loans, insurance, investment advisory, and more. Senior management and the board were fired, and the bank is under prohibition by the Fed. An absolute failure of management. Described now as a textbook case of management incompetence.

<u>Valeant Pharmaceutical (now Bausch Health)</u> The stock climbed continuously, up 3000%, they could do no wrong. Articles about the "gifted" management team were everywhere. Hedge funds piled in. They were found to be manipulating accounting, creating bogus subsidiaries, recognizing sales to themselves, and overcharging customers egregiously. They fired senior management and were so humiliated they had to change their name. The stock fell from $250 to $11.

<u>Bernard L. Madoff Investment</u> Undoubtedly the epitome of investor's misjudgment of management. Before he was found to be a fraudulent con artist running a Ponzi scheme, he was known as a super smart investment manager with impeccable credentials, revered by his peers, trusted implicitly by his investors, a charitable pillar of New York, Chairmen of the NASDAQ stock exchange. He created $16 billion of fake money and lived lavishly off other people's life savings – and kept the fraud running for 18 years.

A blogger on Fidelity recently wrote, "Why is it that after I buy something, the price goes down?" When prices are accepted as being fairly valued and at price equilibrium, the odds of the price going up or down, in the short run, is exactly 50%.

When you look backward at stock picking mistakes, more often than not it was because of unforeseen events. In business, as in life, things happen which surprise everybody. World events like wars and catastrophic weather, consumer preference changes (like buying online), technological change (like phones with cameras built in), continuously change the playing field.

You buy Intel and phones start wiping out computers. You buy stock in an ocean shipping company and oil prices plunge, resulting in lower revenues. I call these the "whims" of business. No one saw it coming, it just happens. Often, it's because of issues you were not aware of – you can never have complete knowledge.

In 2007 Warren Buffett made a 1 million dollar bet with Protege Partners that the S&P 500 index would beat a group of any 5 hedge funds, picked by them, over 10 years. The hedge funds had complete freedom to change all portfolio positions, vs. a fixed index. The results were announced with the 2/2018 Berkshire Hathaway letter to shareholders. The index beat all 5 funds easily. The hedge funds returned between .3% and 6.5% - the S&P 500 returned 8.5%. Buffett's conclusion: **"Americans pay staggering sums to investment advisors every year and get worthless results - gambling on stocks is a losing investment bet**".

In March 2019 Warren Buffett disclosed that not only he, but his two senior asset managers, all failed to beat the S&P 500 index in the previous 10 years. That's a powerful admission. It comes from a man so wealthy and successful he has no difficulty being humble - he's not trying to sell you anything.

When the major stock averages drop collectively on a particular day, or week, or month, the experts and financial advisors are quick to say that it has become a "stock pickers" market. As evidence they point to a handful of stocks which went up in price, during a period when most stocks, and the market averages, were down. They say, in effect, "These particular stocks have done well, while the market averages have fallen – this proves that someone who chose those stocks will have beaten the market averages", which is true.

What they fail to mention is that there is **absolutely no way to predict which stocks are going to be in the group of price gainers - <u>especially</u> year after year.** Stock pickers talk about their successes, like gamblers, and avoid discussion of total long-term returns. When producing past results, they selectively choose favorable time periods, and make inaccurate comparisons. San Diego financial guru Ray Luchia was banned from the industry for making false claims about his past returns. (I attended his seminar and I don't believe he had false intentions; it was just that financial advisors often get caught up in overselling their historical track record).

The steady rise in the stock market from 2009 to 2018 has been used as an excuse by fund managers for failing to beat the averages. They claim they are at a disadvantage in rising markets where all investors benefit, but that in falling markets they would excel. A test of this contention was performed by Bloomberg in Oct. 2018 when the market fell by approximately 7% in one month, the worst drop in 7 years. Only 42% of actively managed funds that invest in large cap stocks, did better than the S&P 500 index. In other words, if you had purchased a passive fund indexed to the S&P 500, your results would have exceeded 58% of actively managed funds. The best and brightest can't even equal the return of a brainless index.

Fund prospectuses enumerate the investments which turned against them in the quarter, and how those investments were sold or reduced. They might say for example, "losses were experienced on Kroger Foods, due to the unexpected entrance of Amazon into Whole Foods. This stock is no longer held." The implication is that this problem won't reoccur. It won't. However, in the next quarter there will be other mistakes resulting in the sub-par results.

I noticed in reading my mutual fund prospectuses in past years that they almost always fell short of that index. <u>None</u> of my investments beat their benchmark, which at the time were mostly Fidelity mutual funds with expense ratios of around 1.5%. It finally occurred to me that, duh, **buying the whole index guaranteed my results would not fall short – ever.**

The movement away from using asset managers, and the corresponding declines in their fees as a means of retaining customers, has not gone unnoticed by investors. A 10/18 article by CNBC noted that a selection of 10 large publicly traded asset-manager stocks — including Invesco, BlackRock, Franklin Resources, T. Rowe Price and Legg Mason — were off an average of more than 25 percent from their 52-week highs.

This article goes on to say, "low-cost index funds are dominating the collection of new cash from investors over the active strategies these managers specialize in."

Investors are gradually waking up to the fact that the fees they have been getting charged by these firms have been excessive and are largely avoidable by using ETFs with extremely low expense ratios. More than 50% of the S&P 500 index is now owned by passive index funds, and the number continues to increase. As of 9/30/18 43% of all US assets are invested passively, and 80% of all new dollars invested goes into passive investments (Bloomberg).

Dow Jones Indices LLC reported as of 12/31/18, that statistically, an active manager charging a 1% fee has a <u>7% chance</u> of beating a comparable passive index fund which charges .03%, over a period of ten years. This holds true for all fund categories including international stocks.

As I was finalizing this book, Morningstar, an authoritative and unbiased source for investing well known to investors, released the results of an ongoing study which I thought wrapped up this section nicely. In an article posted on Sept. 13, 2019, Marketwatch.com said the following:

> *"The drumbeat of bad news for actively-managed asset management keeps getting stronger. On Thursday, Morningstar released its semiannual analysis of active funds compared to passively-managed peers. The picture is not pretty for anyone*

trying to beat the market, especially when combined with the additional challenges of picking the right active manager and paying their fees.

Only 23% of all active funds topped the average of their passive rivals over the 10-year period ended June 2019. What's more, the cheapest funds succeeded more than twice as often as the priciest ones (33% success rate versus 14% success rate) over those 10 years.

Morningstar found that over the past 10 years, only 8% of active U.S. large blend funds outperformed their average passive equivalent."

This is just more evidence that active managers are not able to achieve results which are able to surpass the fees they charge. This is quite startling when you consider that their fees are commonly between 1 and 2%.

> ***Takeaway***: I hope I didn't beat this horse excessively, however the single biggest reason to invest passively - the basic principle behind this guide - is that neither you nor a professional can pick stocks and do better than the indices over time. It's a hard thing to accept, especially for those with financial experience. Buying a single company stock like Apple or Netflix, as opposed to buying a basket of stocks in an index, is in many ways like playing a single number on the roulette wheel. A high risk of losing, a large payoff if your number comes up. This might be fun and exciting to try with a few extra bucks - but not a great idea with your retirement savings. Without a *real* crystal ball you are just rolling the dice - not much different than Vegas, except no free drinks.
>
> It has turned out that the *cost* of super smart investors, backed by loads of super smart researchers, and banks of computers, *is greater than* the extra return they (sometimes and temporarily) are able to achieve, relative to overall market returns.

DID YOU FALL SHORT OF THE S&P 500?

When the stock market is up you may see that your increase was less than that of the S&P 500 in percentage terms, even though you are invested solely in index funds. One reason this occurs is because most people hold some cash, and that cash has a very low yield, so it reduces your total return. The S&P 500 has no cash component. There is nothing wrong here, it simply means you have chosen not to invest all of your money. If the overall market is down, your uninvested cash will mitigate this decline.

This is one of the principal reasons why financial advisors also fall below the S&P 500 index. They are rarely 100% invested. They hold cash as "dry powder" to make future investments when stock prices fall, using a "buy on the dip" strategy for increasing returns, or when they believe a certain stock is temporarily underpriced. They also may hold cash to fund client withdrawals, and also have cash from previous sales or dividend returns which they haven't invested as yet. They do not let their cash increase too high however, as it will affect their return negatively.

DAY TRADING

There is an abundance of articles written about how day trading is a losing enterprise. An endless number of studies have shown you are likely to lose between 90 and 100% of your capital doing it. Recommendations of financial advisors are always the same - don't do it.

Day-traders stare at price charts, and statistics referred to as market "internals", and try to divine the future based on perceived patterns in the market that have occurred before. An example might be that 90% of the time, the stock of oil companies goes up during the 10 days after the price of oil increases by 5% in a 1-week span. You set your computer to follow this statistic and act accordingly.

There have been hundreds of studies which show the futility of stock trading. A 2010 Berkeley study on day traders in

Taiwan found that the average trader lost 0.25% of their portfolio daily, and 93% quit day trading within five years. I don't want to make that case again here, if you are interested further, Google it. So why do so many people do it?

The lure of making a lot of money in a short amount of time, from the comfort of your recliner is just too great. Stock prices are so volatile, if you were somehow able to buy at the lows and sell at the highs caused by daily price movements, your return would be enormous by the end of the year. The idea is you needn't get bogged down worrying about how well or how poorly a company is doing, what their balance sheet looks like, or whether profits are up or down. Since stocks are moving up and down every day, just take advantage of that movement.

It's similar to a carnival game. The essence of a carnival game is that it has to look easy but be very difficult. The carnival basketball hoop looks so *close*; how hard can it be? I can shoot free throws and that hoop is a lot closer. If it doesn't look easy, no one will play *(see sidebar)*.

Carnival Basketball
The carnival basket hoop is close, but it is considerably smaller than regulation size, with little margin for error, and the ball bounces more than a regulation ball. You basically need to get it in without touching the rim, or it bounces out. It may cost you $50 for a $15 Panda Bear.

So how do day traders pick stocks? By using any of a thousand different stock trading tools which use charts, chart patterns and shapes, arithmetical models, algorithms, and forecasting tools which are available just about everywhere. The major brokerages all have some sort of proprietary computer based analytical tool to help you.

All of these tools and methods rely primarily on previous price and volume activity. In essence, they presume that what the stock has done before can somehow predict its near term price movement. There are countless different inputs that can be used when building trading systems. Technical indicators are the most common, but some trading systems incorporate fundamental data, such as revenue, cash flow, debt-to-equity, or other financial ratios. Others even incorporate options activity, news, tweets, and other data from around the web that could provide a signal.

The only requirement is that the data must be represented in a way that a computer can analyze. These systems all seek to identify the immediate term supply/demand characteristics of a security, which will indicate the direction of price in the next hour or day or week. In other words, they ignore all the research that shows stock prices are random (events with no pattern, where all possible outcomes have an equal probability of occurrence) in the short term and predict the future.

If any of these systems actually worked the demand for it would be incomprehensible. Whoever invented it would keep it a secret because if everyone adopted it, the market as we know it would stop working. Everyone would bet on the same horse to use Mark Twain's analogy. The market only functions if for every buyer, a seller can be found, and vice versa. If this Holy Grail of investing was ever found the market would cease to exist.

If you're still not convinced, think about hedge funds. They have thrown literally billions of dollars and the smartest people they could find at developing algorithm-based computer models. Their collective results in recent years has been worse than awful, as noted under the hedge fund discussion which follows below. 1,057 hedge funds shut down in 2017 - the most in any year since the financial crisis. It looks at this juncture (10/18) like more hedge funds will liquidate this year than any other, measured either by numbers or dollars under management. The computer models failed, investor returns have been abysmal, and fund managers then decide to return (what's left of) their investor's money, before being humiliated by massive, or total, withdrawals.

To make money investing takes time and patience, which can be frustrating when you are anxious for a substantial gain relatively quickly. The problem is exacerbated when you see a stock go up by 4 or 5% in one day and you think, I just have to find more of those. Share prices may or may not respond to what is currently happening with the company from a business perspective, until the period chosen is long enough to follow the earnings trajectory and outlook for the company. Amazon, from a business perspective is doing great, everyone agrees. The stock as of 10/9/18 was selling for $1,870/share, up $641 or 42% from Jan. 1. However, if you had bought it on Oct. 1, nine days prior, you would have lost $56/share. Why? Because short term sentiment, and not company results, moves stocks in the short term.

Market timers and traders jumping in and out of stocks are continually trying to predict not what everyone else will do, but what everyone else *thinks* other people will do. For example, say Greece announces they will have difficulty servicing their national debt. We know that this has a negligible or non-existent effect on the earnings of American companies. However, there will be some selling, because traders are worried that **others** will sell, simply because **they** perceive everyone else may sell, purely out of fear. They might reason - I know this event does not affect US businesses, however since it may result in some selling, I will sell before the prices go down. This is what is described as a "trading event", where stocks move in reaction to an event which has no bearing on business fundamentals. It is also called "noise" and is of no concern to a long-term investor.

> *Takeaway*: Trying to take advantage of short-term stock price movements is gambling not investing. The risk is not suitable for your life savings. Getting rich from your easy chair is a pipe dream.

HEDGE FUNDS and QUANTS

Hedge funds have provided another example of how experts have not been able to pick investments which consistently "beat" the averages, no matter how many whiz kids they employed, or computer algorithms they develop. Hedge funds were originally created for very wealthy investors who paid very hefty fees to have their money invested by very smart and experienced Wall Street icons, backed up by often complicated and complex investing tools, outside the understanding of most investors. The original concept was that they would employ hedging techniques to maximize profit and protect from downside losses by both buying and shorting securities at the same time.

This approach had some success in previous generations, but for the last decade hedge funds have done extremely poorly. In recent years, many hedge funds have resorted to very large investments in a small number of companies, percentage wise, hoping they could score big gains via a lack of diversification. This has resulted in some colossal disasters, like Bill Ackman buying Valeant Pharmaceutical (now Bausch Health) ($250/share down to $15).

A number of hedge funds today are attempting to achieve above market returns using large computers and so-called quant algorithm technology. This is nothing more than the very old theory that somehow a formula-based method of securities picking can outperform humans. The computer is fed thousands of variables, and it then buys and sells as dictated by its algorithms, automatically, removing the biases held by humans.

Many quants use a model where securities or asset classes are classified based on risk. Risk is usually measured by volatility – more volatility equals more risk. The system attempts to exploit inefficiency in the market, where risk/reward ratios are not in alignment. It buys anything where it deduces that expected return exceeds risk, and vice versa. Early returns at these funds were quite good, but no longer. Quant funds actually had losses in 2016 and 2017.

There are a number of reasons why hedge funds have done very poorly:

- No one has been able to develop a set of algorithms which work consistently.
- The models often assume future behavior will replicate past behavior, which is only sometimes true.
- Today's markets are very liquid and efficient, eliminating risk imbalance opportunities.
- Steep management fees.
- Computers cannot predict things which have never happened before – key people die, wars erupt, dictators emerge, people invent new things, etc.

Many if not most computer models have a propensity to favor investments moving up in price, also known as momentum strategy. It is common sense to assume something doing well has a reason for doing so. Momentum based quants buy whatever is going up, and sell whatever is going down, perhaps not bothering to determine a reason.

Momentum theorists argue that you do not need to understand why something is doing well, you just buy it. However, as the price of an investment rises, human subjectivity kicks in. Some investors start selling to "take profits" – as fear the stock is overvalued. No one can predict at what price level that will happen. If more investors fear the beginning of a downturn, they sell, and an actual downturn is triggered. In past years, high transaction fees prevented some of this hyperactivity, however computers have resulted in very low transaction fees and greater trade volumes.

Psychological reactions of investors, like the fear of a dollar loss, can be irrational, and often is. Stock markets are well known for overdoing buying and selling, pushing prices unreasonably too high or too low. An old saw is that the stock market is fueled by greed and fear, and fear (often irrational) trumps greed. Traders often mimic what everybody else is doing, which we now refer to as momentum investing. Since the computer assumes rationality, the computer's choices are often wrong, in contrast to a chess computer, which is programmed to assume the opponent makes his best possible play.

Hedge funds keep trying to find the holy grail of investing and failing. As of 2018, hedge funds as a whole have been a failure, trailing the results of passive index investments every single year from 2008 through 2017 – 9 years, despite these funds being manned by the best and brightest on Wall Street, and algorithmic based computer modeling.

Since 2008, hedge funds produced a net gain of just 5.5%, vs. the S&P 500 return of 12%. YTD through Sept. 2018, equity hedge funds have earned 3.5%% vs. the S&P 500 which has gained 9.9%. For the same period, a straight 60/40 stock/bond portfolio returned 8.9%.

Quant funds have done even worse – they were up 1.7% through 9/18 vs. 9.9% for the S&P 500. Hedge fund closings are being announced nearly daily. 1,057 hedge funds shut down last year and 125 hedge funds closed in the second quarter of 2018. These results underscore the reality that smart people cannot "beat" the market. Fortunately, being rich doesn't mean you can buy high returns.

As of today, there is no accurate way of measuring how much of stock trading volume is performed by machines acting on predetermined criteria. Highly regarded investment professional Lee Cooperman estimates that 80% of shares are machine generated, without regard to investment fundamentals - such as corporate revenues, profits, P/E, etc. Instead these machines are reacting to headlines coming across the news wire, stock price momentum, daily share patterns, etc.

Flash traders program computers to act in less than 1 second to trading patterns, generally buying on strength and selling on weakness.

The effect on the market of computer algorithmic trading is arguable, but one effect is clear - Increased volatility. Computers act instantaneously to news reports and buy and sell aggressively. This is a digital version of act now, ask questions later. When you come home from work you may be surprised to see a huge drop or gain in one of your holdings. It's likely the "algos" have been busy. This is another reason to own diversified ETFs.

When you own individual company stocks you are vulnerable to large drops in a single day simply because of a news headline. Today Amazon stated it is going ahead with an online site focused on selling furniture, and the stock of competing Wayfair dropped over 5%. Who needs that kind of risk?

Thus far computer driven trading has not succeeded as a long-term investment tool. The computer cannot see future events, like North Korea shooting down a US airplane, or Amazon deciding to sell groceries in stores, any better than humans can. They also cannot judge which of several market moving factors will have the most influence, and which will be acted on and which will be largely disregarded by investors.

The Wall Street fund managers who operate these funds have done quite well because of substantial fees, which are paid annually, regardless of the fund's performance. Hedge fund fees have dropped to help reduce the continued outflow of invested assets but are still extraordinarily high. As of 9/18 average hedge fund fees are 1.4% of assets plus 17% of gains. Why people are still giving them money is beyond me.

There have, however, been some side benefits to the onset of computer trading. Liquidity in the stock market has improved, allowing investors to buy and sell in seconds, while reducing the buy/sell price spreads. Also, computers have been programmed to "buy on the dips" (buying whenever prices have moved lower) which causes prices to recover to the upside quickly, reducing market pullbacks both in frequency and duration. In a market which continues to move upward, buying on the dips can be the only opportunity to buy "bargains".

Wealthy investors have begun to realize that hedge funds do not have a sustainable investment methodology, do not have superior investment picking skills, and worse, cannot even do as well as a simple S&P 500 index fund. Their terrible performance continues. According to Hedge Funds Research, hedge funds are down 1.7% for the YTD through 10/31/18, compared to the S&P 500 benchmark index which is up 1.4%. Hedge funds are realizing record withdrawals this year.

> *Takeaway*: It's unnerving that the majority of stock trades are done today by computers which are not following the basic fundamentals of corporate investing, however that is the world we're in, so you have to live with it. The way I look at it, the machines can have the daily micro gains, and fundamental investors will prevail over the long term - which is all we care about anyway.
>
> So far, the serendipity of future events, and the irrationality of investors, have prevented the successful predicting of stock prices by computer driven quantum analysis, except in intra-day, high frequency trading.

WHAT CAUSES STOCKS TO MOVE?

Somebody said stock markets always move in the direction that makes a fool out of the most numbers of people. Anyone who has been involved in investing feels the same way. You analyze something to death, run backward and forward charts, read everything written about it, calculate probabilities, analyze all the factors influencing the target, and come to a conclusion. You wait for a low entry price, and then buy.

You may make the huge mistake of telling others about your decision and encouraging them to buy it too. If you're really unlucky, you do this for a living, and you drag all your clients into the same investment. Two days later Amazon says they are going to start selling drug prescriptions, and your stock drops 10%. This is why Wall Street offices are on the upper floors of huge buildings.

Prices of company stocks move <u>in the short term</u> based upon <u>SENTIMENT</u> – which is a human behavioral characteristic. It may or may not be based on underlying facts, it changes, sometimes quickly, it's not predictable, and it leads to random prices in the short run. Sentiment is affected by almost everything from unrest in Italy to an analyst's unfavorable evaluation. Humans have an inborn tendency to believe that things are going to continue in the same way as they have in the recent past, (the recency effect) and this leads to momentum buying and selling. Day traders use computer models to identify technical trading patterns and try to capitalize on price movements using a very short time frame.

Sentiment may be with respect to a certain stock, a business sector, or consumers taken as a whole. With regard to the latter, investors pay close attention to The Michigan Consumer Sentiment Index, a monthly survey of U.S. consumer confidence levels conducted by the University of Michigan. It is based on telephone surveys that gather information on consumer expectations regarding the overall economy.

This index is designed to capture the mood of American consumers with regard to their economic well-being and outlook. Whether the sentiment is optimistic, pessimistic or neutral, it signals general information about near-term consumer spending plans. Because consumer spending accounts for roughly 70% of U.S. <u>gross domestic product</u> (GDP), the survey is regarded as one of the many important economic indicators followed by businesses, and participants in the investment community. It asks questions which are forward looking, and as such, is believed to be predictive of the near-term strength of the US economy. Monthly movements are not meaningful - look at quarterly results.

Prices of company <u>stocks in the long term</u> (one year or longer) will however, <u>always, 100% of the time</u> follow the <u>EARNINGS</u> of the underlying company(s), up and down. When a company has net profits after taxes, its equity, total assets less total liabilities, will generally increase. Each fractional shareholder will then theoretically "own" a greater dollar value than before the profit was earned, or in another way, each share has a greater value. As a long-term investor, you are trying to identify the factors which will determine whether those earnings are going to go up, level off, or start declining.

The most significant factor in moving stock prices as a whole, is the economy - but not the only factor by far. A strong growing economy will lift most boats, whereas a stalled or shrinking economy will make it much harder for corporations to increase profits. This relationship only works over longer periods.

Each day, investors are treated to news about the economy and information about how the stock market has done recently. It can be very difficult to process what's going on because at any given moment in time, there may be very little correlation between how things are going in the real world and how prices are acting on Wall Street.

The noted fund manager and author Ralph Wagner once described the relationship between the economy and the stock market thusly:

> "There's an excitable dog on a very long leash in New York City, darting randomly in every direction. The dog's owner is walking from Columbus Circle, through Central Park, to the Metropolitan Museum. At any one moment, there is no predicting which way the pooch will lurch. But in the long run, you know he's heading northeast at an average speed of three miles per hour. What is astonishing is that almost all of the dog watchers, big and small, seem to have their eye on the dog, and not the owner."

The man is the economy, moving steadily ahead, and his destination is quite easy to predict, similar to an economic trend. The dog is the stock market, going this way and that, without a discernible reason, but alas, he ends up in the same place as his owner. Different paths, but they both end up in the same place.

Sometimes a company will report good earnings however the share price will go down. This is because in the short term, market sentiment moves the share price, and there may have been elements in the report which disappointed investors.

Sometimes the share price moves down because it had gone up significantly before the report, and investors are following the old adage to "buy on the rumor and sell on the news". This adage suggests that when news is reported, it only confirms a trend which has already been "baked into" the stock price by investors. Over time however, the share price will reach an equilibrium which is based upon a multiple of its earnings per share.

When analysts publish estimates of company earnings, they are likely to be quite accurate for the next quarter or two. For the following two quarters their estimates are likely to be close. After that it becomes an educated guess. Being able to forecast earnings for a year is of little help to an investor hoping to build up their savings over 20 or 30 years.

Think of how ludicrous it is to invest in something with great upward price momentum, when you do not plan to use these funds for decades into the future, when that momentum will be a distant memory. Today I read a recommendation to buy Starbucks because of good quarterly earnings growth.

Ask yourself, when I retire in 20 years will Starbucks still even exist? What if Amazon decides to open its own coffee chain and sells coffee for $2.00 a cup, and delivers it to your home or office for free? (maybe they'll even hold the cup for you).

There is an infinite number of variables affecting the stock market, because stock markets act like a barometer of constantly changing worldwide investor assessments of business and economic conditions. The variables include not only economic and market factors (historical and current), but political and world events: Is a lack of rain in Columbia reducing the coffee crop; has conflict in the Middle East worsened; is a hawkish Federal reserve governor going to retire; will the senate pass a healthcare bill? The list is endless.

Even if you could catalog them all you somehow have to figure out how their simultaneous behavior affects your target variable. Add to this the numerous events happening within companies that the public never sees: Is market share falling? Is management misbehaving? Are they cooking the books?

Have they lost key personnel? Are class action lawsuits brewing?

Now add the introduction of new things: inventions, cultural change, human behavioral change, and you can see why everyone fails at predicting short term price movements. What happens to Levi Strauss if kids stop wearing jeans? (maybe that's a good thing).

Can we all agree this is ridiculous?

The best approach to cautious long-term investing is to view everything from 20,000 feet. Ignore individual companies and daily movements. If you're trying to plan a traffic intersection, you don't drive around in it, you view it from above, completely ignoring what each car is doing. To be successful in investing is to identify major economic influences such as how our economy and others are doing, and how particular business segments are likely to fare going forward.

ETFs allow you to ignore individual companies and **focus on the business sectors which are most likely to succeed** in future years. As you move forward and facts change, you modify and update your portfolio, ignoring daily market activity as so much noise. Diversification protects you from the incorrect choices you make. It's impossible not to make some mistakes. ETFs also allow you to invest in the entire market, not bothering to try and figure out who is going to do well. Stocks go up 80% of the time.

Statistics conclusively show that over time, corporate earnings are the single greatest factor in determining the direction of stock prices at the company, or total market level. The second most influential factor is interest rates. This is why analysts watch the Federal Reserve closely to determine the direction of interest rates over the next few months and next year.

Increasing interest rates puts the brakes on the economy in myriad ways. Just to name a few, consumers face higher interest costs on their existing loans, and higher mortgage rates and auto loan rates affect purchases negatively. Corporations also pay more in interest on their loans, negatively impacting their earnings, reducing their availability of cash to buy capital equipment and expand, reducing their growth expectations, and possibly reducing their hiring plans. The government sector will pay more in interest on the national debt, have less funds available for economic stimulus programs, possibly curtail expenditures on existing social programs and military spending, and possibly cause a need for higher taxes which will reduce consumers' ability to make purchases.

There are very few beneficiaries of higher interest rates, most notably banks (and other lenders), insurance companies and financial companies, and retired folks who receive higher returns on their savings (however these higher rates will reduce the return on bond funds that they own, a concept explained further under Bond Risk and Interest Rates).

When Fed officials or the Fed chairman make public statements concerning the future direction of interest rates they are often described as either "hawkish", meaning they are leaning toward higher rates going forward, or "dovish" meaning they think rates are already at a proper level, or think they might need to move lower, so as not to stifle economic growth. The Fed has only two mandates - increase employment in the economy (via economic growth) and prevent excessive inflation - a difficult balance.

Patience is a key to investing. It takes time for your investments to grow, especially when you are diversified. Diversification reduces your ability to make large gains quickly, but more importantly reduces your risk of a large loss.

Takeaway: Since stocks move in a random manner in the short run, you may experience a drop in value soon after making your investments. This does not mean you made a mistake. If you made sound ETF choices as outlined in this paper, you will do well. There are millions of investors who are younger than you, depositing money in their 401(k)s every month, and looking for a place to grow their savings, which will push equities higher - just as all the generations which have preceded us.

It's hard to focus on a future 20 or 30 years from now, how can we, it doesn't exist. We may however be able to see some changes slowly taking place, like the obsolescence of coal for power, or large department stores with marble floors. Placing bets on individual companies, and how they'll do 25 years from now, is one of the most foolish ideas I can imagine.

Hopefully by choosing index funds in a commonsense way, you result will reflect growing economies, and will not be affected significantly by companies who fail to adapt and grow, and/or fail altogether. Sears wasn't successful (ironically initially based on a catalog sale format), and those who invested paid the price. It's impossible to predict who won't be around 20 years from now, so don't try.

ETFs - EXCHANGE TRADED FUNDS - PASSIVE INVESTING

The typical mutual fund, now referred to as an <u>actively managed fund</u>, has highly paid (human) managers backed up with many specialized analysts who buy and sell investments based on their own judgment. Expenses and the related expense ratio for these funds are high, to cover the related salaries and employee expenses, often including very large bonuses. Typically, these funds hold weekly meetings where analysts make presentations to management on which investments they believe should be bought or sold. The fund is bound only by its relatively loosely worded defining characteristic, such as US bonds, or high grade equities. However, the fund's parameters allow management a great deal of discretion in these decisions (so as not to limit their choices).

Investors are rapidly abandoning these funds because, as outlined above, they perform worse than the market averages. The minority who do outperform their benchmark will do so only temporarily. Their temporary investing success is usually the result of a small number of very "right" decisions, and over time, those funds will fall back below the averages with everyone else. In a down market, as occurred in late 2018, actively managed funds do even worse. Their stock picking ability does not improve; however their fees continue to reduce your principal, exacerbating the decline in the overall market.

The high cost of salaries for the experts, research, and marketing people (direct selling) is the most significant reason for their subpar performance. Managed funds like mutual funds and hedge funds have to charge expense fees of 1.0-2.5% or higher to cover costs, and also charge a boatload of other fees. Expense fees have a very large impact on long term investment performance. The compounding effect over many years causes a huge drain on long term results.

If you invest $10,000 for 30 years and the investment earns 7% per year, you would have about <u>$45,000</u> if you are paying fees of 2%. However, if your fees are .5%, as many ETFs charge, you would have about $70,000.

Kevin O'Leary gives us his example. If you save, say, $5,000 for one year, a typical stock market returns in a diversified, low-cost index fund means that a year later you will have $5,365.

Let's say the next year you save nothing additional. But you leave that $365 gain invested. In 10 years at a typical stock market return your money will more than double, hitting $10,115. That's because every year your gains are reinvested and growing as well. Wait another 10 years and you have $20,462. Ten more years and you have $41,396. The money just keeps on doubling with no extra effort at all.

If you add $5,000 every year to your savings, your balance at the end of 40 years is $1.2 million. Five thousand dollars multiplied by 40 years is $200,000. The extra $1 million is all from compounding gains.

Because fees appear to be small, investors often overlook them – 1-1.5% just doesn't seem like much. However, that fee is charged annually, whether your investment balance goes up or down. If you buy a mutual fund, one that costs you around 1% of your balance per year in fees, that's 1% of your entire retirement savings being subtracted each and every year. It's not 1% of your savings in that year or 1% of your gain. It's 1% of everything you've ever saved and all the money that you've earned from compounding your gains, taken from you.

Thus, the effect of a 1% fee in a stock mutual fund is that you lose one-third and up to one-half of your potential gains to the fund's managers. You've effectively sandbagged your own retirement.

If you are invested in bonds, which have much smaller returns than stocks, the effect of expense fees is even more injurious. If you compare a fee of 1.5% to an average bond yield of 2-2.5%, you can see how much of your return you are losing -

and in the years when your return is below zero, the 1.5% in fees continues unabated.

Charging high fees is a great deal for the fund managers. They take no risk and receive a significant portion of your gain. All for doing what? The implicit promise is that they will get you a better return than the stock market alone. Ironically, those fees mean that the vast majority of active stock fund managers can't give you a better return, especially after decades of charging fees on your gains - negative compounding.

With regard to fees, Morningstar's Ben Johnson says, "Every dollar is worth fighting for".

As the late John Bogle, founder of Vanguard, often said, the "humble arithmetic" of low-cost investing is indisputable. He saw this phenomenon early and using index funds with low expense ratios, developed a way for investors to experience excellent investment performance over long periods, without having to be monitored daily. Instead of trying to beat the benchmark, you buy the benchmark, and its return becomes your return.

The fund follows a predetermined index exactly. A computer makes all transactions, and no management personnel are required to make investment decisions. Index based funds are also called "rules based" investing, meaning the fund follows a set of predetermined rules without variance, and also called "passive" investing, meaning all fund purchases and sales happen automatically, without need for management input. As a result of the markedly improved performance of passive funds with low expense ratios, investors have moved sharply in that direction.

A January 2019 Federal Reserve Bank of Boston study, "The Shift from Active to Passive Investing: Potential Risks to Financial Stability?", found that "Passive funds made up 45% of the assets under management (AUM) in equity funds and 26% in bond funds, whereas both shares were less than five percent in 2005."

Investors have been moving approximately 40 billion dollars out of actively managed funds into passively managed funds every month. The balance invested in ETFs now exceeds 4 trillion dollars, increasing over the last year by a stunning 34%. Of the close to $500 billion in funds added to index funds over the last year (2018), 70% has gone into funds charging 1/10th of a percent or less. ($100/year for $100,000 invested). This has forced investment companies to lower expense ratios to try to be competitive, and as a result, some managed funds now have more reasonable expense ratios, albeit still higher than ETFs.

ETFs are funds which follow a particular benchmark like the S&P 500, or energy stocks, or Australian stocks, or whatever. The fund ties itself to an index or basket of investments which match predetermined criteria, like healthcare companies. Investors pick ETFs with pre-determined rules which match their own expectations for those market segments most likely to do well going forward.

New ETF funds are being established frequently, to tailor investments to every customer's preferences. Fund providers are anxious to capture every possible corner of the market, sometimes in new and creative ways.

As of mid-year 2019 there are approximately 2300 ETFs, so the variance of choices is vast. ETFs can follow common stocks, bonds, commodities, debt of foreign countries, or just about any imaginable investment there is. The difference is you buy the category, or sector, not the ingredients. Computers do the investing, as funds are received by the fund. You purchase and sell ETFs just like stock, during the open hours of the New York stock exchange. Small investors can diversify their portfolios to a much greater extent than ever before, as there are no minimum investment requirements. Diversity is the single greatest factor in long term investment return.

ETFs are called passive because once the parameters or rules are established; a computer takes over, buying and selling to match as accurately as possible the defining index or basket of investments. The rules for that ETF are never changed (see also dynamic and actively managed ETFs below), and the index being followed is never changed. If investors don't like the performance, or believe their basis for choosing it has changed, they sell it, just like a stock, paying only a transaction fee the same as a stock sale, around $5 for most brokers. If an ETF does not attract a sufficient amount of investors to operate profitably, it may close and liquidate, dispersing funds back to the owners.

You can buy large sectors, like all US stocks, or European bonds, or drill down to micro categories, like investment grade US corporate bonds. These sectors break-down further into subcategories, where you can pick and choose to avoid categories of companies you don't want. For example: healthcare ETFs breakdown into 6 basic types: (1) Pharmaceutical companies, (2) Healthcare Providers—hospitals, nursing homes etc., (3) Healthcare insurers (Aetna, Cigna) etc., (4) Healthcare Equipment and Supplies, (5) Biotechnical companies, and (6) All of the above, in an all-inclusive healthcare ETF. Some of these segments are better choices than others, and with an ETF you can focus your investment, and not buy the entire sector.

Similarly, real estate investment trusts, REITs, breakdown as follows. (1) Office buildings, (2) Apartment and condo buildings, (3) Malls/shopping centers, (4) Hotels and lodging, (5) Storage and warehouses, and all of the above.

ETFs offer several important <u>advantages over mutual funds</u>. These include:

1. Lower account management fees – the expense ratio (ER) is the easiest and quickest way to measure the annual cost to you, and is computed in the same way by investment funds. This is the only fee charged by the ETF manager. The only other fee you will pay are those assessed by your personal broker, for the transaction, usually about $5/trade. (brokers may have fees for special situations).

2. Greater diversification - a collection of stocks or bonds, not a single entity. More diversification results in less volatility and reduced risk.

3. ETFs trade in real time while the market is open, usually within seconds of entering your order. Mutual funds do not trade until the NAV (net asset value) is calculated after the market closes. You benefit from ownership immediately, and know the exact execution price, not the next day. Your brokerage account will show your share ownership in real time.

4. Taxes - Unlike mutual funds, ETFs do not record or pay out capital gains, and the related federal and/or state taxes. You will owe taxes only when <u>you sell them</u>. Mutual funds are required to report and pay out capital gains to you every year, which you will owe taxes on in the current year.

    Note: *There is no capital gains tax on any trade within your IRA or Deferred Tax Plan (401(k). You are taxed at the ordinary tax rate for your bracket only when funds are taken out of the IRA Plan - regardless of their source. You will owe capital gains taxes on any gain on any sale from investments which are not in a deferred tax plan (your post or after tax accounts). If you hold on to an ETF you in effect postpone any capital gains tax until you decide to sell, the same as an individual stock transaction.*

5. ETFs have no sales load, which is an upfront commission to the sales agent.

6. ETFs have no minimum investment. You can buy as few shares as you want.

7. ETFs trade like stock so you can place stop or limit orders, sell short, buy on margin (a loan from your broker – not recommended), exercise put and call options, etc.

8. ETFs are more transparent. With an ETF you will always know what you are invested in, it does not vary. This feature is called transparency. Holdings are reported

daily. With an actively managed fund you will find out quarterly what the manager has bought and sold during the previous 3 months.

9. Dividend reinvestment can be done manually by purchasing additional shares with the cash received from dividend payments, or automatically if the ETF allows.

10. With ETFs there is no difference between the daily price and the NAV (net asset value)/share. Mutual funds will have differences which complicates understanding of price vs. value.

11. ETFs have no 12b-1 fees for marketing and distribution, no redemption fees, and no account service fees. (Mutual funds are starting to drop these fees out of necessity).

12. ETFs do not need to carry idle cash balances to cover potential redemptions, which are a drag on performance.

13. Actively managed funds often have very high asset turnover, or churn rates, which is costly and wasteful, as managers change their holdings. Short term holdings result in higher capital gains taxes. ETFs do not change its investments from one security to another. It only buys or sells the index components to match incoming sales and distributions.

14. ETFs have "Authorized Participants" (APs) which create and redeem shares to keep ETFs priced at fair value. For example, if demand for an ETF increases and a premium develops, APs step in to create more shares and push the ETF's price back in line with its actual value. If there's a rush to sell and a discount develops, APs buy ETF shares on the open market to reduce supply. This helps to lower fund expenses and reduce ETFs' tax burden.

There also are **inverse ETFs**, which go up if the securities in its index go down, also called a "short" or "bear" ETF. There are also **leveraged ETFs**, which move 2 times or 3 times the movement of the securities in the index. Both of these products have elevated risk, and potentially much more volatility, which requires close monitoring in the event you start experiencing losses and need to take action. They are therefore more suited to traders than long term investors and are not recommended for the average investor.

One thing to keep in mind is that with an ETF, the fund will buy everything in the index according to its rules for inclusion. It does not have the freedom to exclude securities from companies doing poorly. Therefore, you must make sure you understand what is in the index and choose highly diversified ETFs which will mitigate the effect of badly performing or failing companies. Note however that these failing companies, like Sears for example in a retail ETF, will be bought at the market price, which already reflects its questionable future.

There have recently been articles trying to evaluate what the possible effects are of the huge movement toward passive investing. With investors buying the market averages instead of individual stocks, the entire market tends to move up and down together. Stock charts of the averages are mirror images.

This is not a bad thing (unless you are a stock picker), however buying the market average indices will cause highly priced stocks to go up even higher, and even weak stocks will go up with the rising tide. Some say this has pushed stock market prices too high (relative to earnings), and this is creating weak companies to be overpriced. However, the opposite is also true. When ETFs are sold, everything in the index is sold, pushing major averages lower, taking down both the good and bad, as they did in Oct. 2018.

Much has been written about the overall effect of ETFs on the market, however, thus far there is nothing conclusive. However passive investing is a huge benefit to the individual investor, and this has come as a dis-benefit to highly paid wealth managers, as investors realize they are unable to financially justify their fees.

In the mid 90's the amount of total US invested dollars which was tied to an index was close to zero - today 43% are passively invested (10/2018), as are 80% of new dollars invested. Stock picking experts often disparage ETFs. They have to because as their assets under management decline, their fee income also declines.

Takeaway: **In 2018, $506 billion went into index-based investment products - $153 billion of that amount came out of actively managed funds. There are strong reasons for this. With index based products you will reduce risk through diversification, while reducing fees to an absolute minimum.**

Don't give a significant chunk of your return to somebody else. A recent study by Morningstar found that in 2018, despite significant fee reductions by mutual funds, **the average actively managed fund charged almost twice as much in fees as the average index fund (1.9X).**

Fees aren't all that matters, you still need to pick investments that make sense, however when comparing similar ETFs, the lowest fee offering will probably return more, over the long term.

DYNAMIC ETFs

It should be noted that because of the popularity of passively managed funds, investment firms have rolled out some hybrid funds which follow an index but also allow for management the discretion to change investments – adding some investments and removing others regardless of whether they are in the index. These are often called dynamic ETFs.

The euphemistic term "dynamic" meaning we follow an index, but when we decide we're smarter than the index, we don't follow it. This in an attempt to get the advantages of a rule based passive fund but allow for the manager(s) to adjust the investment choices, and or underlying rules, whenever they deem it prudent. By establishing these funds, managers are trying to capture some of the money flowing into rules-based funds, without letting go of their belief that smart people can do better.

In general, the results of these funds have been poor, fees are higher, and they under achieve their passive counterpart. When researching an ETF, read under the "profile" and beware if it says management may make changes to the investments or to the index, or rules used in buying investments, without obtaining permission or approval from the fund's participants.

Takeaway: Avoid actively managed funds posing as index-based funds.

ACTIVE ETFs

An actively managed ETF is another hybrid product which uses an ETF format but does not follow an index. It has a manager or team making decisions on the underlying portfolio allocation, not adhering to a passive investment strategy. An actively managed ETF will have a benchmark index, but managers may change sector allocations, market-time trades or deviate from the index as they see fit. This produces investment returns that do not perfectly mirror the underlying index.

An actively managed ETF has some of the same benefits of a traditional exchange-traded fund such as liquidity and tax efficiency, making them better than traditional mutual funds. They tend to have lower expense ratios than mutual funds, but higher expenses than index-based ETFs, in order to pay for management expenses. Unlike an index-based fund, whether management will do better or worse than their benchmark index, is not known, as with any mutual fund.

Traditional ETFs can be counted on to follow an index faithfully, which allows investors to know the holdings and risk profile of the fund. This helps keep a diversified portfolio in line with expectations. Fund managers of an active ETF, however, have the freedom to trade outside of a benchmark index, which makes it more difficult for investors to know the future makeup of the portfolio.

As with a mutual fund, the potential to outperform comes down to the underlying manager. Some will periodically beat their benchmark, but research finds that active management will underperform a passive strategy over the long term, for reasons outlined in this paper. It comes back to managers falsely believing they can beat the market averages by enough of a margin to pay for their higher expenses.

There is some evidence however, that ETFs have drawbacks when it comes to fixed income portfolios. Sometimes there are not enough bonds or the type and maturity needed available intraday; cap weighted indexes mean you will hold a much greater amount of large company frequent issuers; the less liquid aspect of bonds, which are issued in irregular batches, make it hard for the ETFs to accurately match their benchmark; indices will buy more of upgraded bonds (buying high); and lastly a number of bond market technical problems can be sidestepped by active managers.

There are a number of articles on this subject which you may wish to read if you intend to have a large exposure to bond ETFs. (Google active management of bond funds). Is having an active bond ETF manager worth the higher expense ratio they charge? So far the answer appears to be no. Passive bond funds have generally done better than active managed funds primarily because of lower fees. (see more under Bonds).

In certain bond categories, such as ultra-short bond funds for example, all or most of the ETFs use active management, as indexing is difficult in some asset classes. All that matters to you is the return, so compare the results over more than 2 years and pick the best performer. If you decide on an actively managed bond fund, pick one with a low ER.

Takeaway: Avoid actively managed ETFs, except for certain categories of bonds, where active management may be a necessary evil, such as ultra-short bond funds. When choosing, look for a low expense ratio, as total return differences between similar bond funds are minimal.

MULTI FACTOR ETFs

Most ETFs are single factor, meaning they include stocks in their index which are all of one particular descriptive factor, such as growth, value, large cap, small cap, low volatility, high beta, consumer cyclical, Australian, etc. In the past few years we are seeing more multi factor ETFs, meaning the index being used has screened companies such that they meet two or more descriptive factors, such as value/cash flow, or large cap/ dividend growth, etc.

The concept is simple, the ETF is capturing all or each of the factors which investors deem to be the most important in future price growth. Investors have used computers to screen companies which meet their chosen criteria for selecting the best stocks to invest in. Primary examples of important factors include; value, momentum, size, quality, low volatility and dividends.

These new ETFs run these screens for you and put all of the stocks which meet the criteria into the index.

The concept of these ETFs seems quite logical. I have looked at the return of some of these ETFs, and the results have been disappointing. Their performance has been mediocre, and the expense fees tend to be higher than for most ETFs.

The jury is still out here. Logic would tell you that if the right selection of factors is chosen, their performance should exceed market averages, but as of this writing, multi factor ETFs have performed no better, and in many cases worse, than have the broader market ETFs. There is no clear reason for this unsatisfactory result. It seems that to some extent these funds are trying and failing to find the holy grail of investing, a well-worn path indeed.

FUNDAMENTAL vs. TECHNICAL ANALYSIS - ANALYZING COMPANIES

There are two basic ways investors use to analyze a company's stock value, fundamental and technical.

Fundamentalists believe correctly that the underlying economic and financial fundamentals of a company are the only meaningful measure to use in analysis, over the long term. These include the trend in sales, trend in profits, trend in profit margins, cash flow vs. debt service, strength or weakness of the balance sheet, the level of debt, the level of net worth (equity), strength of management (as measured by past results), strength or weaknesses of the company's industry, strengths or weaknesses of their competition, etc.

Also important is the company's business plan (how they make money), and its sustainability, changes taking place in their industry, their susceptibility to technological or legal changes, barriers to entry facing competitors, (Buffett calls this the moat) and a host of other economic and financial factors.

Technical analysts, on the other hand, analyze market price statistics. They use charts of historical stock prices and other ratios and statistics in an attempt to predict future price changes based upon previous results. They use terms like, resistance level, support level, double top, triple bottom, head and shoulders, double cross, and crossing the moving average, to describe stock price chart patterns, which they believe portend future price direction. They believe historical price and volume statistics repeat themselves, and analysis of them will forecast future changes. They also analyze technical movements of the market as a whole, also referred to as market "internals".

History is the best way to show that this method of analysis is fundamentally flawed, except in the very short run, where charts and statistics may indicate the relative supply and demand of a stock.

You may read that, say, when a stock crosses its 50-day moving average, historically it has continued in that direction 75% of the time over the next 30 days. However, the fact that because something happened 75% of the time after some other things happened in the past, does not mean that the probability of it happening is 75% the next time. It's merely an observation. All of the millions of variables at work are never exactly the same, and more importantly, business and economic variables have much more to do with stock price direction than comparison to historical events. The probability of getting heads on the next coin flip, after 10 heads in a row have come up, is still 50/50.

A 2008 study by researchers from New Zealand and Australia tested more than 5000 technical trading strategies in 49 different country indexes, finding that none added value "beyond what may be expected by chance."

Technical analysis, in my opinion, is a dinosaur left over from decades of traders on Wall Street trying to find the holy grail of investing - the elusive crystal ball.

Technical analysis should be avoided unless you are a trader. A trader jumps in and exits frequently based upon daily market trends, including up and down volume, percentage of stocks crossing moving averages, number of new highs vs. new lows, relative strength indicators, put/call volumes, and other technical patterns with goofy names like the stochastic oscillator.

If I hear someone going on about the technicals I use fast forward. Do oil prices really go up and down based upon whether two lines on a chart cross? Or does it have to do with real world supply and demand changes?

Ironically, many computer-based trading models, which focus on the super short run of stock prices, program the computer to buy and sell based on technical patterns, and as a result can create a self-fulfilling prophecy in the very short run, seemingly verifying the legitimacy of technical analysis.

Technical analysis is often used in markets where there is no reliable way of accurately determining the current supply vs. demand fundamentals - such as the future price of oil or gold. Russia is selling gold to build reserves, however India is adding to reserves. Professionals working the numbers every day can't predict the price, so how can the rest of us?

Takeaway: As a long-term investor you can ignore all technical analysis which is more suited to traders trying to determine if a stock or commodity is temporarily over or under sold. **Over time, fundamental factors will always prevail in determining stock prices.** A common expression is that when investment markets act irrationally for reasons sometimes known and sometimes not, they will always return to fundamentals. If the price of Facebook stock keeps going up, despite the fundamental fact that many users are deleting their accounts, or using it less, you can be sure the price will eventually correct for that fact, and go down.

You just have to be patient sometimes for the fundamental factors to play out in a company's stock price. I recommend decaf.

At the expense of oversimplification, fundamental analysis applies to things that are real - technical analysis suggests patterns which are imagined.

PRICE EARNINGS RATIO – the P/E

A company's stock price is a function of: how many shares were originally issued by the company, subsequent issues, purchases of its own shares, shares distributed to executives, the number of shares presently outstanding, what the initial price at the IPO was, stock splits and reverse splits if any, and the movement of the stock price since it was first issued. In other words, it's complicated. A stock with a high dollar price per share doesn't mean it's expensive. In fact, it might be the opposite. Alternately, a low dollar priced stock may actually be expensive. <u>The absolute dollar price of a stock is meaningless</u>. You need something to compare it to so you can determine if the current price is high or low relative to other investments.

Since stock prices, at their core, reflect the earnings power of a company, the best way of evaluating and comparing those prices is the price earnings ratio, or P/E. This is simply the current price per share divided by the company's earnings, or profits, per share. If a company's stock price is $30/share and the company earns a profit of $2/share, the P/E is 15. This is also called the "multiple", as in, what multiple of earnings is the price? The P/E tells the investor how the company's current earnings compare with the market price per share.

This same concept holds true for companies acquiring other companies. In making an acquisition you must be sure your payback takes place in a reasonable period of time, for it to be a good investment. Historically, for a company growing moderately, other companies have been willing to pay about 15-20 times earnings, the same as the individual investor described above. This is a complicated calculation, taking into account growth rates, tax rates, and a whole host of other factors, but as a rule of thumb, about 15-20 times earnings is often at least a starting point in determining a company's selling price. This analogy is not perfect however, because buying a whole company gives the buyer absolute control, which has a considerable value beyond what a minority share purchaser receives.

So the "multiple" is a shorthand way of comparing stock prices of various companies, which puts them on an apples to apples basis. Historically speaking, and I am oversimplifying here, companies with stock P/E's of under 15 are generally considered value, or cheap, or low priced. P/E's of 15-20 are considered to have an average price, and P/E's of 20 and above are considered expensive.

The multiple of earnings investors are willing to pay depends on a number of factors: Are earnings growing and by how much? How much is the dividend and is it likely to continue? Is the company in a slow growing industry like banking or utilities, or a fast growing industry like computer software or online retailing?

Generally, banks and utilities have low multiples under 15X, and high tech companies have high multiples of 30X or higher. If the P/E of a stock seems illogically high or low, it's sometimes the result of a onetime charge to earnings or a onetime gain, for example when a large asset is sold.

There are two different types of P/E's. One is based on last year's earnings, and one based on the current year's _expected_ earnings. These are the "TTM P/E" – for trailing twelve month P/E - and the "forward P/E", respectively. The TTM P/E is the price divided by the profits for the last twelve month fiscal period. The forward P/E is the price divided by the average consensus earnings _estimate_ for the current fiscal year. Since this is an estimate, the forward is less reliable; however, it's important to know because investors want to determine where the P/E is likely to be within the next 12 months.

The stock market is said to be forward looking. When you buy a stock, the historical earnings of the company are certainly important and relevant, but you are primarily interested in how well the company is expected to do when you own the stock, and therefore the forward P/E is a key number. If a company is healthy and earnings are growing, the forward P/E will be lower than the TTM P/E.

When P/E is being discussed or written about, and it is not designated which P/E they are using, generally speaking today they are usually speaking about the forward P/E. The forward P/E will have adjustments incorporated in it which are not reflected in the TTM P/E such as acquisitions, tax changes, new or discontinued operations, and other changes in the company's business.

The stock price per share is easily determined by looking at the market listing. The earnings per share is less definite because it is usually determined after so called non-recurring expenses are eliminated. Investors want to "normalize" earnings, by eliminating expenses which are not expected to re-occur. Common examples of non-recurring expenses include lawsuit losses, money paid to acquire another company, large casualty losses, write offs of bad debts or worthless assets, and employee severance expenses.

You do not need to calculate the P/E. The company's earnings per share and P/E are publicly reported and appear on all finance web pages like Fidelity or Yahoo. If you see differences from one site to another, usually it's because of a onetime event. (Johnson and Johnson's TTM P/E is either 266(Yahoo) or 24 (CNBC) due to a tax charge).

High P/E's in 2018 - 2019

As of May 2019, US stock prices are considered to be relatively fully valued, or at the high end of historical P/E values, by most investors. This is because the market has been going up quite steadily since March '09 after the financial collapse of 2008 – over 9 years. Since 1936 the S&P 500 trailing P/E has averaged 17. As of May 2019 it sits at 21. At 21 times earnings are considered expensive, or fully valued.

The average S&P forward P/E is 17, also at a historically high level, but not considered excessive by most, primarily because of very low current interest rates, by historical standards.

Most professional investors believe that the current very low unemployment rate, historically low interest rates, solid economic growth around 2%, a reduced corporate income tax rate, very heavy corporate stock buyback programs, and a low inflation rate, (about 2%), creates justification for these elevated P/E averages.

With bond yields at very low levels, many investors have reduced their bond holdings and bought stocks, looking to get a return greater than 2%, which also pushes up P/E levels, also referred to as the multiple.

On the other hand, some investors believe P/Es are too high to be putting new money to work and believe that a return to traditional levels is likely.

A possible influence on the above average level of P/Es is that the demand for stocks has increased, for the reasons mentioned above, whereas the supply of stocks is actually shrinking. The number of NYSE stocks has decreased from approximately 5000 to about 3500 today. This is because the pace of corporate mergers and acquisitions is far outpacing the number of new IPOs. This paints a picture of a lot of dollars chasing a shrinking number of stocks.

If US companies' earnings continue rising as they have recently, and stock prices stall for a period, also as they have recently, we will "earn our way" out of this issue, as P/E's will decrease.

Some investors believe that high P/E levels are a reason to increase stock selling and reduce buying, unless and until P/Es return to historical levels. History has shown attempts to move in and out of the market based on current conditions, which is called market timing, is a very unwise strategy.

If a market downturn occurs, ignore the financial news for a while to avoid getting nervous and upset. If anything, consider the downturn as an opportunity to buy something at a cheap price if you have uninvested cash. If investors increase selling, and/or reduce buying, their uninvested cash will increase, and their returns will suffer. At some point they will have to resume buying to put their idle cash to work. This will cause prices to strengthen again.

> ***Takeaway***: As a long-term investor, primarily investing money in an IRA or 401(k), short term market cycles are not a serious concern, other than to review your holdings and make portfolio modifications from time to time, while increasing antacids and cutting back on caffeine. If stock prices are high based upon historical P/E levels, it may be wise to increase portfolio diversification, or take other defensive measures which are discussed below, but without resorting to aggressive selling.

THE PEG RATIO

Investors found that comparing companies based on their P/E ratio alone, left out an important factor – the company's earnings growth rate. If a company is growing rapidly, an investor will gladly buy a stock with a higher P/E because the company's earnings growth has the effect of reducing the P/E going forward. On the other hand, a slow growing company's share price will justify a lower P/E because the E is the denominator. I don't mind paying 25X earnings if those earnings will grow rapidly in future years, and vice versa.

The PEG ratio (price/earnings to growth ratio) is a valuation metric for determining the relative trade-off between the price of a stock, the earnings generated per share (EPS), and the company's expected growth.

In general, the P/E ratio is higher for a company with a higher growth rate. Thus using just the P/E ratio would make high-growth companies appear overvalued relative to others. By dividing the P/E ratio by the earnings growth rate, the resulting ratio is better for comparing companies with different growth rates.

The PEG ratio is considered to be a convenient approximation.

The growth rate is expressed as a percentage value, and should use real growth only, to correct for inflation. For example, if a company is growing at 20% a year, in real terms, and has a P/E of 20, it would have a PEG of 1.

A lower ratio is "better" (cheaper) and a higher ratio is "worse" (expensive).

The P/E ratio used in the calculation may be projected or trailing, and the annual growth rate may be the expected growth rate for the next year or the next five years. It's only important that in such an analysis, an apples to apples basis is used.

S&P STOCK SECTORS

Standard and Poor's currently divides the stock market into 11 sectors. They presently are:

Financials: The financial sector consists of banks, investment funds, insurance companies and real estate firms, among others. In general, the majority of the revenue generated by the sector comes from mortgages and loans, which gain value as interest rates rise.

Utilities: The utilities sector consists of electric, gas and water companies as well as integrated providers. In general, the sector generates consistent recurring income by charging consumers and businesses that provide higher-than-average dividend yields.

Communication Services: On September 24th, 2018 a Communication Services sector was added to replace the Telecom sector. This new sector is comprised of stocks which may have been previously classified in the telecom, technology, and consumer-discretionary groups. It will include Disney, Netflix, Comcast, Facebook, and Google (Alphabet). It will increase the Communication sector as a percent of the S&P 500 from approximately 2% to 11%. Tech will decline from 26% to 20%, and Consumer Discretionary will decline from 13% to 11%.

Consumer Discretionary: The consumer discretionary sector consists of retailers, media companies, consumer service providers, apparel companies and consumer durables. In general, these companies benefit from an improving economy when consumer spending accelerates.

Consumer Staples: The consumer staples sector consists of food and beverage companies as well as companies that create products consumers are unwilling to cut from their budgets. In general, these companies are defensive plays capable of withstanding an economic downturn.

Energy: The energy sector consists of oil and gas exploration and production companies, as well as integrated power firms, refineries and other operations. In general, these companies generate revenue that's tied to the price of crude oil, natural gas and other commodities.

Healthcare: The healthcare sector consists of biotechnology companies, hospital management firms, medical device manufacturers, pharmaceutical companies and health insurers. In general, the sector is considered to be both a growth opportunity and defensive play since people will always require medical aid.

Industrials: The industrial sector consists of aerospace, defense, machinery, construction, fabrication and manufacturing companies. In general, the industry's growth is driven by demand for building construction and manufactured products like agricultural equipment.

Technology: The technology sector consists of electronics manufacturers, software developers and information technology firms. In general, these businesses are driven by upgrade cycles and the general health of the economy, although growth has been robust over the years.

Materials: The materials sector consists of mining, refining, chemical, forestry and related companies that are focused on discovering and developing raw materials. Since these companies are at the beginning of the supply chain, they are vulnerable to changes in the business cycle.

Real Estate: The real estate sector consists of companies invested in residential, industrial, and retail real estate. The main source of revenue for these companies comes from rent income and real estate capital appreciation. As a result, this sector is sensitive to interest rate changes.

Which of these sectors to underweight and overweight, and when, is discussed further below.

GROWTH STOCKS

Growth stocks are stocks which are growing earnings at an above average rate. They are highly favored by investors, and as a result are expensive – they have price earnings ratios which are above average. Whereas the average trailing price earnings multiple of the S&P 500 is approximately 24X as of this writing, growth companies have multiples of 30X or higher. They are expensive, in Wall Street vernacular. The above average P/E results because investors are willing to pay a higher multiple for the rapidly rising earnings, which will cause the stock price to appreciate at an above average rate. So high growth companies, like tech oriented companies, seem like an obvious choice to buy. There are many growth stock ETFs.

So why doesn't everyone buy only these growth companies? The answer is that many investors don't believe that buying stocks at high prices (relative to earnings) is wise, and that if and when their earnings begin to slow down or actually decrease, their stock price will drop precipitously and quickly. If they show a few quarters or more of weak results, their stock price will decrease until the P/E comes down to a more average range. A multiple contraction, as this is called, results in a very large percentage drop in the share price.

If a growth company earns $3/share and trades at a P/E of 30 its selling price is $90/share. If a weak earnings report results in a drop in the multiple to an average market multiple, say 20, times $3 = $60, a decrease of $30/share or 33% - a brutal decrease for the investor. Sometimes a growth company's multiple will drop even when reporting favorable earnings, when investors find some element of weakness in the report - perhaps management's caution of possible slower growth ahead (their "guidance".)

A growth company must continue a high earnings growth rate to sustain their high valuation. The problem is that everyone knows that companies cannot sustain a very high growth rate forever. For every Apple which continues to defy gravity, there are 10 other companies which have lost their mojo.

Eventually, almost all companies will begin to level off and stabilize as they mature. Will Apple continue to sell iPhones or some other new product at a breathtaking rate forever? No, but when will the trend end? (The trend is your friend, until it's about to end).

As a long-term investor, you may not want to be obligated to follow these trends closely. Also, if you want to buy low and sell high, it's very difficult when your purchase price is high to begin with.

Apple's earnings growth has been nothing short of astounding, yet their trailing P/E is only 20. Long term investors are cautious that when Apple's earnings begin to level out, the price will fall quickly (which it did in 2018).

Because growth stocks are considered a higher risk/higher return investment, buying them used to be considered best suited to younger investors who will be living through many up and down cycles, and less well suited for people in their 50's and 60's or retired. This rule of thumb was based on the historical investor who owned perhaps 15 or 20 stocks, where one disaster could reduce your overall return to zero.

Most investors today disagree with this, and believe that these fast-growing companies are the future, and don't we want to be part of the future? No one wants to own the next buggy whip company, but will Campbell soup end up that way? The millennials do not favor very salty food packed in a tin can.
Would you prefer to invest long term in a semiconductor company, or a laundry detergent company? Everyone needs laundry detergent, but will these companies be able to grow profitability when their product is a commodity?

Financial managers tend to recommend large well-known companies as people feel more comfortable investing in companies they are familiar with. Also, foreign investors buying US names tend to pick companies that they recognize and are familiar with. As a result, the P/E's of a relatively small number of high growth companies has risen to where many consider their prices too high. Examples include the FAANG stocks: Facebook, Amazon, Apple, Netflix, and Google. These trades are said to be "crowded", as many investors are buying a very short list of companies.

With the advent of ETFs, all investors, including older investors, have a way of participating in the growth sector with the risk that some of these companies will start to slow down and mature, mitigated through diversification. If any of the companies in the ETF start to slow down, it won't affect the performance of the group significantly. Growth stocks have outperformed all other sectors for the last ten years. For a middle-aged person, a sizable portion of their portfolio should be in the growth category - say 15-25%.

You may do better by buying lesser well-known growth companies, with lower P/E's. To do this consider ETF's categorized as mid-cap growth or small-cap growth.

As you would expect, growth stocks do better than the market averages or value stocks, during periods of strong economic growth, as we have had for the last 10 years. If the economy slows or contracts, value stocks will likely perform better.

VALUE STOCKS

A value stock is one that trades at a lower price relative to its fundamentals such as earnings, sales, and dividends, than market averages. The P/E ratio is the most often used measure to define a value stock. As of 8/28/18 growth stocks had an average P/E of 20 times current year (2018) earnings, whereas value stocks had a P/E of 15 times. They may be said to be "undervalued", sometimes called cheap, because their price is lower than the price indicated by their basic financial fundamentals. This group is the exact opposite of growth stocks. They appeal to risk averse investors, and those seeking "bargains" that they believe have an above average opportunity for price increases.

There are a few reasons why a company's stock might be in this category. Most notably, companies in slow growth industries like utilities and banks. Older companies like Ford and Exxon are in mature markets and growth for them is difficult and often slow. Also mature companies like Procter and Gamble or Kellogg, where new products are infrequent and innovation is slow or non-existent. Also in this category are companies whose stock has been beaten down in price because of potential issues the company faces. These issues could be short term in nature, soon to be forgotten, or they might include a more serious problem, such as too much debt, lawsuits, adverse legislation, reduced demand for their products, and many others. Retailers who have not embraced e-commerce currently find themselves being sold off by investors.

Value investors try to separate the wheat from the chaff. Starting with a list of low P/E stocks, they try to determine the cause. Why are investors paying less for this stock? If they believe the cause is something that management is addressing or has plausible plans to remedy, they might consider buying. If the company's problems are systemic, or caused by a continuing loss of customers, perhaps it's a "falling knife" – a company which continues to have fundamental problems.

The stock market is notorious for over buying today's winners, and over selling today's losers. The market has already discounted the company's weaknesses by pushing the price down, perhaps excessively. Value stock buyers look for an opportunity to buy low and sell high. Since the price is already low because of slow growth or financial stress, the probability of further decline is also lower. These companies will offer investors a turnaround plan which may or may not be successful, but if it is, the potential price appreciation is significant.

On the other hand, some investors are more comfortable with steady eddy type stocks and are willing to accept lower returns from owning them. Food and beverage, and consumer staples, are examples where sharp declines are not likely because regardless of world events or economic problems, consumers will continue to buy these products. Another desirable factor with value stocks may be a relatively high annual dividend. Companies in this group usually pay a higher dividend to attract buyers, as an offset to their slower earnings growth potential.

While waiting for a recovery, a value stock buyer earns a favorable dividend, usually higher than a bond coupon interest rate. The stock in General Motors spiked upward recently when they announced a major shift to electric cars. Just changing the company's future direction uplifted the stock. Management in slow growth industries must continue to make changes in their business plan to not find themselves becoming obsolete. As an example, Ford recently announced they would eliminate all but two sedan models being sold in the US.

ETFs can again be the answer here, where a value ETF is focused on certain quality characteristics, rather than just buying low P/E stocks. They define what kinds of companies are in the index, so investors can focus on a group of good companies that currently happen to have a low P/E and not companies facing insurmountable problems. The diversification of the index reduces the risk that some companies might fail.

Funds with both growth and value components is said to be "blended". A balanced portfolio will have both growth and value stocks.

Throughout the economic recovery in the US which has continued since 2008, growth investors have done much better than value investors. Value investors believe that buying low is the key to long term investing, however in the last ten years this has not been true. As was noted earlier in this paper, the market has already priced stocks appropriately to their fundamentals

Periods of strong economic growth will benefit companies categorized as growth. Value stocks are more likely to fare better in market contractions. Investors watch this relationship closely, looking for a shift to better performance among value investors, which may happen if the US economy starts to slow down. If businesses start to see a leveling off of sales growth, or an actual decrease in sales and/or earnings, you will see many investors switching to a value approach. Value stocks are expected to decrease less than growth stocks if we enter a downward economic cycle and are therefore deemed a more defensive choice.

If you are buying value stocks as a steady business with a strong dividend, this is an accepted investing style. However, if you are buying value stocks which have fallen in value, and you are making the assumption that the market has undervalued them, this may be a faulty assumption. In some sense you're making a financial bet that you are a better judge of the company's future than the market believes. Taking a position against the collective wisdom of millions of investors may be presumptuous.

Before leaving the discussion of what a value stock is, it should be pointed out that using only the P/E as the definition has a serious shortcoming. Some very large companies are growing so rapidly they have very small or nonexistent profits by ordinary accounting standards. They may be investing heavily to gain market share and are not trying to maximize profits at this point in time - Amazon and Uber are examples, which may have very high P/Es, or no P/E (no profits).

> ***Takeaway***: If you decide to favor value stocks in your portfolio, start by going to ETF.com and look at a list of value oriented ETFs. Of those you chose to look at further, make sure to view the top 10 holdings. You may not like what you find. The ETF may be packed with financials which have a below market P/E, and may also include companies which are performing poorly. Safe choices are VTV, MGV, VOOV, and VONV(Russell 1000).

CYCLICAL and CONSUMER DISCRETIONARY STOCKS

"Cyclicals" are stocks which do well when the economy is growing strongly. These include car manufacturers, airlines, appliances, furniture retailers, clothing stores, and hotels, travel, and restaurants – things people spend on when they have discretionary income available. When the economy is growing, unemployment is low and the GDP is rising, investment managers will overweight this portion of their portfolio.

Conversely, these are the products which people often cut back on during a recession. Cyclical stocks are the flip side of consumer staples, which people continue to demand even during an economic downturn. Cyclical stocks rise and fall with the business cycle.

Nine of the eleven S&P categories are considered cyclical, in other words, most stocks. This makes sense because when the economy is growing, most companies will do better. The two non-cyclical sectors are Consumer Staples, and Utilities.

This seeming predictability in the movement of cyclical stock prices leads some investors to buy cyclical stocks at what is perceived as the low point in the business cycle and sell them at the perceived high point. When the economy is doing well, people can afford to buy new cars, upgrade their homes, shop and travel.

Conversely, if a recession is bad enough, cyclical stocks can become completely worthless as companies go out of business. Companies that manufacture boats are a good example of a business that prospers in good times and struggle just to stay in business during economic downturns. When times are bad, boats are the last thing one thinks about.

Consumer cyclical stocks can be further divided into durables and nondurables. Durable goods companies are involved in the manufacture or distribution of physical goods that have an expected lifespan of more than three years. Companies that operate in this segment include automakers, aircraft manufacturers, appliance manufacturers, and furniture makers.

People pay attention to the government's durable goods orders index, as it is an indicator of future economic performance. When durable goods orders are up in a particular month, it may be an indication of stronger business activity in the ensuing months, and vice versa.

Non-durable goods companies produce or distribute soft goods that have an expected lifespan of fewer than three years. Examples in this segment are sports apparel manufacturers and retail stores.

> *Takeaway*: It is advantageous to overweight cyclicals in periods of good economic growth and underweight non-cyclicals, and then reverse when the economy is slowing down measurably.
>
> It's anyone's guess whether our economy is likely to have a recession in the near term or continue growing satisfactorily. Therefore, the best strategy is to under and overweight based on your personal assessment rather than going to extremes and over-adjusting a market sector of your portfolio to 100% or to zero.

DEFENSIVE STOCKS

Defensive stocks are those which are expected to continue to do well, even in weak economic conditions. These include consumer staples (necessities), like food and beverage stocks, and food retailers. Also considered defensive are healthcare, telecom, and utilities for obvious reasons – you need them even when funds are tight. Some people, including myself, believe healthcare should be categorized as a growth industry as well, which will do well in any economic environment.

When economic reports start showing signs of a slowdown or recession (see Pullbacks, Corrections and Recessions) you will see the defensive stock categories increase and the cyclicals decrease. Since we are often wrong about when these economic slowdowns will actually occur, it is wise to not eliminate one group over the other, but underweight and overweight these groups according to your best guess as to which way the economy seems to be heading. Also be skeptical of one-month reports which may not indicate a trend. If you see, however, the unemployment rate increase for say three or more months in a row, you may wish to start making some gradual portfolio adjustments.

Many of these defensive stock categories are in slow growth industries like food and beverage and utilities. To attract buyers, companies in these segments have relatively high dividend payouts, which is a major reason why investors buy them. When bond yields increased to around 3% in 2018, many investors sold this group and prices fell significantly. Investors moved from defensive names with strong dividends to bonds, where coupon rates had improved, but have less price volatility. Rising bond yields represents a significant risk to high dividend stocks.

Consumer staples had fallen precipitously in 2017 and 2018. It is not known if this has happened because the economy of the US was growing strongly, or because investors now see this group as having systemic issues (or both). The group has done better in 2019.

These companies are seen as vulnerable to significant increases in materials prices, which will happen if inflation pushes prices higher. However, they have a limited ability to raise their prices due to strong competition. This squeezes their profit margins, in an already slow growth industry. Adding to the group's downturn has been traditional grocery retailers in this segment losing sales to Walmart, Target and Costco, new e-commerce grocery retailers, and the entrance of Amazon into brick and mortar grocery sales (purchase of Whole foods). These changes are reducing the number of investors turning to this group as a defensive measure.

Value stocks have trailed growth strategy stocks for the last 10 years. Whether this is a permanent change, or only because we have been in a recovery from a very serious recession, is not known.

INCOME and DIVIDEND STOCKS

Income stocks are those paying a high dividend steadily and increasing the dividend periodically. Investors have begun to pay more attention to dividends, as studies have shown dividends play a major role in long term returns. They seem small, but they add up. Standard & Poor's has reported that **more than one third** of the long-term total return of the S&P 500 can be attributed to dividends.

Fast growing companies, especially tech companies and young companies need to plow back their free cash flow (profits after making debt payments) in building the company. They need to make heavy capital expenditures and build their labor force. They often need to borrow heavily. Therefore, they will usually pay a very small dividend or none at all. They can't afford to pay shareholders more, as their available cash flow is limited by growth needs. Conversely, older companies that have matured and are growing slowly, if at all, have a diminished need for cash, and therefore can afford to pay higher dividends.

Investors invest in tech companies and younger growing companies, not for the dividends, but because they expect the share price to grow as the earnings of the company grows. Think Google, Amazon, Facebook, etc. Since mature companies like Procter and Gamble and Kellogg will have small growth numbers, they pay higher dividends to offset the slower appreciation in their stock price. If they didn't, investors would choose other stocks.

Other business segments with relatively high dividends are REIT's, telecom, and utilities. They, along with other slower growing industry groups which have high dividend rates, are often called "bond surrogates". Bond surrogates are stocks which have steady dependable cash flows and pay good and reliable dividends. Investors buy them as a lower risk investment choice similar to bonds, but with a higher yield than bonds, and having some appreciative value potential, and a lower volatility than stock market averages.

As the Fed has been increasing interest rates, bonds have fallen in principal value, offset only by their approximate 2.5% coupon rate (10-year government 5/2019). Investors, concerned about this principal risk, as well as their very low return, have turned to bond surrogates. There has been an explosion in new dividend favored ETFs, which have been created to appeal to different investor preferences, and also to avoid undesirable companies, like high risk companies, and companies which have had to suspend dividends in the past.

The only problem is that bond surrogates, like bonds, will also respond <u>negatively to rising interest rates</u>. The idea is that you trade off any chance of a big gain in stock price in order to have a reliable source of dividends, as a way of avoiding low yielding bonds. This strategy works fine unless and until interest rates are on a steady move upward.

A caveat for dividend stocks is bond yields. When the 10-year US Treasury bond went over 3% in 2018, some investors began to sell dividend stocks and move these funds into bonds. A low risk 3% bond is a strong competitor to a dividend stock paying 3-4% but having equity risk attached to it.

Shifts in investor sentiment like this argue for maximum diversification. You never know when something unfavorable will affect your portfolio, so it's never wise to be extremely overweight in any one market segment.

Dividend stocks are often favored by older investors, those near, or in retirement, who seek regular interest payments to supplement their Social Security and/or pension payments, while providing the potential for some capital appreciation with less volatility. They may use their dividend checks for living expenses, as opposed to re-investing them. Many of the ETF's categorized as income or dividend will pay their dividend monthly instead of quarterly to appeal to those investors. This cautious approach reduces risk but also lowers returns.

For reasons which escape me, most of the articles I read about investing for retired people concentrates on buying income stocks such as strong dividend payers, utilities, REITs, and bonds, so as to provide income for living expenses. Completely absent is a discussion of buying equities for capital appreciation, which during most periods will exceed the income from bonds and bond surrogates, and then selling small quantities of those securities as needs require. If you are investing funds in a deferred savings account, there are no capital gains tax to consider. Taxes on IRA withdrawals do not differentiate between principal, income earned, or capital gains.

If you consider that you may be retired for a period of 20 or 30 years, you can see how important capital appreciation will be to you. Comparing the <u>Barclays U.S. Aggregate Bond Index</u> with the S&P 500 index between 1980 and 2017, stocks averaged an annual return of 12.2% while bonds returned 7.9%. A 50/50 portfolio (stocks/bonds) would have earned 10.0%. If you go back further the difference widens. Between 1928 and 2013, stocks earned 11.5% while T-bills and T-bonds averaged 3.6% and 5.2%, respectively.

As of 5/2019, the S&P 500 had an average dividend of 1.9%. The long term average is 2.1%. Popular large cap dividend ETF SDY ($16B) has an average dividend of 2.4%.

> ***Takeaway***: Generalizations are generally ill advised, however generally, the more bonds you hold the lower your return will be, and the lower your volatility will be, because stocks and bonds move in opposite directions, most of the time. With bonds, your portfolio balance will not increase as much in strong economic periods and will not decrease as much in slow or declining periods. This tradeoff gets to the heart of your own appetite for risk and volatility (see also the section Your Risk Profile discussed below).
>
> Buying income or dividend stocks instead of bonds gives the investor an opportunity to realize capital appreciation with somewhat lower volatility than average equities entail (but also the risk of a reduction in value).

MARKET CAPITALIZATION

A company's total market capitalization is merely the total number of shares outstanding times the current price per share. This is the most common standard used in comparing company size. This standard has more or less replaced ranking companies by total revenues, or total profits.

Investors generally divide company stocks into three size categories. Large Cap refers to large companies, over 10 billion. In the US this usually translates to the S&P 500 - the largest 500 companies in the US. Mid Cap stocks are midsize companies which typically are defined as a $2-10 billion cap, as included in the S&P 400 index (there are other indexes). Small cap stocks run between 300 million and 2 billion. There are a number of small cap indexes; the Russell 2000 is probably the most popular. Less popular categories are the mega cap (biggest of the large cap) and the micro-cap (smallest of the small stocks).

Most funds are market capitalization weighted, meaning larger sized companies will have a much greater weight in the fund than smaller companies. You will read for example that Apple or Amazon is the largest company in the world, or the US. They are using market cap as the determinate measure. I am not a fan of the concept of total market capitalization, or market cap, because it is largely a meaningless number. The price investors are putting on a stock and/or the number of shares outstanding doesn't translate into our normal concept of size such as total sales, total profits, or total employees for example.

The problem with this weighting is that increases or decreases in the stock price of a single, or perhaps two or three companies, can dominate the results of a fund, in effect eliminating the diversification provided by the index investing concept, which was intended by the investor. That is, a large price movement in the largest component(s) will have a dramatic effect on the value of the entire index.

This happens to a great extent with high tech or growth indexes because of Apple, and energy indexes because of Exxon. In choosing ETFs, it is important to see how concentrated the fund is by looking at the top ten holdings.

There is a total of approximately 3,500 US stocks listed on exchanges in the US. If you owned a large cap 500, midcap 400, and the Russell 2000, you would own approximately 2,900 of that total. There are also ETFs which include the entire US stock market, such as Vanguards VTI, which seeks to match the return of the entire US market.

MORNINGSTAR STYLE BOX

Morningstar, a company specializing in investment research, invented the style box to help investors better understand the makeup of a stock fund or index. The box has 3 columns and 3 rows – a 9 square matrix. The 3 rows are labeled large cap, mid cap, and small cap. The 3 columns are labeled value, blend, and growth, corresponding to the stock categories described above. By blackening or coloring one or more of the 9 squares, it tells you what kind and size of stocks the fund primarily holds. You will generally see these boxes wherever there is a general description of the fund or index. It will give you a basic understanding of the types of companies the fund is primarily invested in.

	Value	Blend	Growth	Size
				Large
				Mid
				Small

THE S&P 500 and the DOW JONES averages

The S&P 500 index is an index based on the 500 largest U.S. companies. It is a durable, diversified index, and its return since 1928 has averaged 10%.

This index has become the standard against which many funds measure themselves. If you only invested in one index, this would be it. To justify their existence, stock pickers believe they must "beat" this index, and they usually fail, and when they succeed it will be temporary. This index should be your largest holding—perhaps as much as 15-20%. There are many S&P 500 index funds. The best performers have the lowest annual expense ratio. The vanguard VOO is presently the best with an expense ratio of .04%--only $4 per year for each $1,000 invested. (The total stock market ETF ITOT has an ER of .03).

This index is highly diversified, contains only very large companies in a relatively stable U.S. economy, and up until Trump, a stable, democratic, political climate. The companies in this group have 40% of their sales from overseas markets (creating worldwide exposure by buying US companies), and for all of these reasons, it is a favorite of investors worldwide.

The index is a market capitalization weighted (see below) which means large companies will affect the index more than smaller companies.

The Dow Jones Industrial average has historically been the average most people look at to see how the market is doing. This bellwether status however is slowly disappearing, especially among professionals and active investors. The average is flawed as an indicator of the overall market movements for a number of reasons. The "Dow" only contains 30 very large company stocks; therefore, it is poorly diversified and large gains or losses in one or two of these 30 will affect the results excessively, like Boeing.

Also, the Dow is share <u>price</u> weighted, which means the companies whose stock price is high in <u>dollar</u> terms will affect the average disproportionately. This makes no sense at all, however, to change the rules would eliminate its comparability with historical numbers. Because of this arcane rule, companies like Amazon and Google will not be added to the Dow because their share price is too high and would unduly influence the "average". Most indices are market cap weighted.

(In past years companies would "split" their shares, lowering the share price and compensating by granting more shares, however this practice is not presently popular, and in fact quite rare.)

Recently large swings in high dollar stocks in the Dow have caused the average to swing wildly in both directions, causing many investors to become frightened of the excessive volatility. News outlets continue to focus on the Dow average because this old standard is all that many know about the stock market. The S&P 500 is much more representative of the US market.

A common mistake is to pay attention to the point gain or loss in market averages, when the only truly significant measure is the percentage change. As the market moves higher, point changes become less significant in absolute terms. The most significant measure to you personally, and the only one that matters, will always be your percentage gain or loss.

FINANCIAL ADVISORS

A financial advisor may make as much money from your retirement portfolio as you do. If the market moves downward, the advisor will continue to make money, as you experience losses. The advisor will take fees, some of which are not visible or known to you, including fees they receive from the fund providers, for acting as a sales agent. The IBM Institute estimates that globally, $1.3 trillion is destroyed annually by excess management and advisory fees. The Council of Economic advisors estimated that in 2015 US investors lost $17 billion in their retirement accounts due to advisors with conflicts of interest.

A friend of mine asked me to review her portfolio, which had been constructed by a financial advisor who earned 1% of the portfolio's assets – a common arrangement. There are two apparent sets of expenses here – the advisors fee, and the underlying fund's expense management fees. Not apparent are fee kickbacks, paid to the advisor, paid for by the client. The portfolio contained mostly actively managed funds, which had high fees, 1-2%, meaning total "apparent" fees of 2-3%, also a common situation.

There were some index funds in the portfolio, however they were the "B" shares, or "C" shares. These "share classes" have been created to provide income to pay advisors who put their clients into these funds. These share classes receive the same underlying funds' performance; however they have much higher fees – not only nearly double management fees, but sometimes upfront fees as high as 3.5%, and sometimes back–end fees, which are charged if you sell before 12 months.

Several class action lawsuits against financial advisors for placing clients in expensive funds are working their way through the courts. Today, March 12, 2019, the Wall Street Journal reported, "<u>Almost 80 investment advisory firms agreed to pay back more than $125 million to clients who were steered into higher-cost mutual funds without being clearly told about cheaper versions, the result of a government effort to persuade financial firms to self-report misconduct</u>. (largest fine - Wells Fargo)

The advisor is only required to put you in "suitable" investments – no matter the costs. The higher fees allow the fund provider to pay the advisor for acting as their agent, in addition to the fees you are paying them directly.

If you end up paying a total of 3% in fees, from all sources, that represents about 43% of the long-term average increase in the US stock market. In other words, almost half of <u>your</u> returns will go to somebody else.

Paid financial advisors are biased because their compensation is in part determined by the advice they are giving you. If you ask about whether to buy life insurance for example, they say yes, they recommend a certain insurance company or broker, you buy insurance, and your advisor gets a check from the insurer because he acted as their agent.

It is naive to think that a wealth advisor is going to give you advice which results in reduced income for themselves, or their employer. Because of their knowledge of the investing business, it is easy for them to take advantage of less knowledgeable clients. Their recommendations just happen to be fee rich, no surprise there. Follow the recommendations herein and you will avoid these guys and your savings will grow faster.

It's impossible to know if your advisor is acting in your interest. As Warren Buffett said, "Don't ask the barber whether you need a haircut".

You no longer have to pay for a financial advisor for investment management. The advent of computerized brokerage accounts and low fee ETFs which do not require active management, are eliminating their need.

You may however, need answers to life's broader financial issues, such as do I need life insurance, should I borrow from my 401(k) for a house, do I need long term health insurance, will I owe capital gains taxes on this sale, etc. Answers to these questions can be researched on-line, and I would also recommend Money Guide by Jonathan Clements. Use the index for particular questions.

Takeaway: Seeking advice on a particular life issue makes sense, hiring a fee-based advisor, not so much.

ROBO ADVISORS

Robo-advisors are a financial investment service that provide automated financial planning services with little to no human supervision, using a web-based platform. A typical robo-advisor collects information from clients about their financial situation, future goals, and risk appetite through an online survey, and then uses the data to construct an investment plan. You can have the program automatically invest your assets if you choose, or you can do it yourself. This is a relatively new concept. Betterment, the first such advisor was launched in 2008, and the level of sophistication has improved dramatically since then.

It's important to understand that these services are primarily focused on what assets you invest in, and less so on personal life planning with regard to things like life and other types of insurance, wills and estates, divorces and taxes.

Its sounds like a dangerous concept, and it has a bad sounding name, reminiscent of robo phone calls, but I believe it is a satisfactory choice for people who do not wish to do their own investing, and are willing to pay a modest fee for help - usually about .25%. It uses index funds to simplify the choices, and steers investors to low expense ratio funds which are key to good returns. The fees of using the service are very low, because of the elimination of salaried employees, ranging from zero to .5% of assets. This compares with 1-2% for human advisors. These fees will add to the expense fees of the underlying funds.

The advent of modern robo-advisors has completely changed that narrative by delivering the service online to consumers. After a decade of development, robo-advisors are now capable of handling much more sophisticated tasks, such as tax-loss harvesting, investment selection, and retirement planning. The industry has experienced explosive growth as a result; client assets managed by robo-advisors hit $60 billion at year-end 2015 and is projected to reach $2 trillion by 2020.

Other common designations for robo-advisors include "automated investment advisor," "automated investment management" and "digital advice platforms." They are all referring to the same consumer shift towards using computer-based applications for investment management. They are also more accessible than humans, available 24/7 online. Furthermore, no minimum dollar investment is required. In contrast, human advisors do not normally take on clients with less than $100,000 in investable assets, in order to produce sufficient fees.

Web based Robo advisors are also convenient, as you can use them to check your holdings or make trades immediately from your home or office.

Over 200 robo advisors are operating, including standalone companies such as Betterment and Wealthfront, and now the major brokers including Fidelity, Vanguard, and Schwab have also rolled out programs. Shortcomings include the lack of human help and understanding, the handling of complex issues, and the degree the program "understands" your risk appetite and personal biases. If you say your risk appetite is "medium", what does that really mean?

If you want to read more about this subject, Investorjunkie.com has an informative section on Robo advisors where they summarize the programs, list pricing, compare features, and rate them. As of 10/18, Wealthfront is rated highest.

The biggest problem I have with robo-advisor programs is the adherence to traditional rules of thumb with regard to the proportion of bonds owned.

I ran a test in mid-2017 for a 50 year-old retired male with a moderate risk profile against four different programs. (Betterment, Wealthfront, Schwab, Future Advisor). The proportion of bonds recommended averaged 40%. These numbers are way too high in my view for three reasons. A retired 50 year-old has to make his money last for perhaps 35 years. Today bonds only return 2-3% so unless you have say,

3-5 million invested, you will not generate much income. Secondly, since the Fed began raising rates in 2016, bonds have lost principal value, causing the total return to fall below 2%. Lastly inflation is currently running at 2.5%, which means if you have bonds earning 2.5% you have a zero real return. I own no bonds today for both of these reasons but will add them when interest rates normalize.

Although I believe robo-advisors are a good idea to help people lacking investment knowledge at a very low cost, I cannot agree with the proportion of bonds typically recommended, especially in today's environment. If you decide to use a robo advisor, I would see if it's easy to change the asset allocations they are recommending, and if so, reduce the bond component and substitute equities by the same amount, depending on your age.

Some robo plans offer financial planning advice as well as investment guidance. I would be careful here, as everyone's personal situation is different, and not suited to generalizations. I would stick with the asset choice program.

Robo advisors are now being offered by most large banks and brokerage firms, as it is seen as a major growth business, as investors move to passive investing, and high cost personal advisors are used less often. Each offering is slightly different, and you need to understand the details before you pick one. Here are the issues to address if you are contemplating using one:

- What are the fees and how are they calculated? Are the fees clearly shown to you? Estimate what your annual fees will be starting out.

- Do the fees include access to a human advisor? Never? Sometimes? For an extra fee?

- Do they put you, or recommend you use, ETFs **they operate and manage?** This is a conflict of interest. You want them to recommend ETFs managed by <u>unaffiliated</u> companies, as Betterment does.

- Do they use actively managed funds? These are more expensive and not recommended.

- Is there a trial period?

- Enroll and **get their recommendations before actually making the investments**. Actually, make the investments after you have reviewed them and are comfortable with them.

- Pay particular attention to the amount of bonds recommend. Consider modifying their asset allocations by reducing the bond component, if it looks high after reading this guide.

- Do not use an advisor recommending the "B" or "C" shares in a fund, which entails much higher fees.

- If you believe you are going to want to talk to someone about your finances often, these plans are probably not for you.

TIP:

Wells Fargo has been abusive to its customers in every business service they offer including checking, credit cards, insurance, loans, mortgages, and wealth advisory. The way they have treated their customers is deplorable. I would not use them, ever.

DIVERSIFICATION

The most important factor in successful investing over time is diversification. Everyone knows that you can't put all of your eggs in one basket. Studies show that the more diversified you are the better you will do over the long haul. By giving up the big gains, you also don't have the big losses.

In previous days, experts said to be well diversified in a stock portfolio you needed to own 20-25 stocks. This results in excessive risk. If you own 20 stocks equally, you have 5% of your money in each. If just 1 or 2 of these companies does very poorly, it will drag down your overall result so much that your overall return will be poor. Who can pick 20 winners? Nobody! An ETF allows you to invest any sum, large or small, and you will immediately own every stock (or bond, or commodity) in that index. With an S&P 500 ETF, you will own minority shares in the largest 500 companies in the US. Spreading the risk this broadly results in long term stability and superior long-term returns.

A well-known stock pundit from CNBC recently wrote (9/18) that holding 20 or 30 individual companies was actually too many for most people, and that they should hold only about ten! I can't imagine worse advice. Put your life savings in ten picks - insanity squared!

At one time the most widely held stock in the US, GE, fell from $55 to $7! Maximizing risk does not work. This would require you to guess properly on every choice you make. All investors, except this one apparently, knows this is not possible. This is like going to a roulette wheel with 3500 numbers and picking only ten. Good luck with that.

Diversification requires investing in a broad range of asset types - you could include equities, bonds, commodities, real estate, foreign assets, emerging markets and high yield bonds. More aggressive investors add artwork, sculptures, and rare objects like antiques, and classic cars. (Forget baseball cards, comics, coins, stamps, and other "collectables" which may not appreciate). The theory is that not all of these categories will do poorly at the same time, and your resultant return will be better. Inflation, which is a permanent way of life, will cause dollar growth in most of these categories, even when other factors remain unchanged. Remember, inflation is not the increase in the prices of things, it's the decrease in the value of the dollar.

As a passive investor seeking high diversification, I do not want my returns in equity funds to be whipsawed up and down by the results of one or two companies. Therefore, the best way to eliminate this effect is to choose highly diversified ETFs. However, most ETFs and funds are capitalization weighted – large companies have a greater influence on the index. This causes the index to be unfairly influenced by the performance of mega companies, such as Exxon is to the oil ETF XLE.

More preferable are <u>equal weighted funds</u>. These funds include all holdings equally. If there are 50 companies in it, it holds 2% of its total funds, in each. If one company does terribly, the index won't be affected materially. The problem is there are not very many equally weighted funds out there, and because of this special feature, the fees can be a bit higher (like .35-.65% for example). This may be worth it in some cases, such as biotech funds where prices are extremely volatile at the company level.

Equal weighted funds mitigate the risk created by a small number of high momentum stocks with super high P/Es, like FAANG. If those stocks start to turn lower, it will have an outsize effect on the ETFs performance. You can mitigate the FAANG risk in the S&P 500 for example, by owning RSP, which I own. Its ER is only .2%.

To see if the fund has high concentrations in a few companies, go to the funds main page on Yahoo or Fidelity and click "holdings". They will show the top 10 investments held. If the top 10 represents more than say 35% of the total, or the top one or two is more than 15%, look for a better choice. If most of the investments represent about the same percentage, for example about 2-3%, it is probably equal weighted.

Hopefully in the future more equal weighted ETFs are offered.

Being diversified means not only using diversified ETFs, but also including some investments, even in your least favorite asset classes.

FOREIGN EXCHANGE

Foreign exchange, or forex, or FX, refers to the currency exchange rates between various countries. A great deal of time is spent on the financial channels on TV, such as Bloomberg and CNBC, devoted to lengthy discussion and analysis of which countries' currencies were up or down, and the reasons why. I suggest you pretty much ignore most of it.

Exchange rates are most important to currency traders. These are professionals, usually working for large banks, who make huge currency trades on a daily basis. These people were originally for making sure the bank had appropriate currency balances, but now it has grown into a profit center. This is a highly specialized market suited only for professionals.

Currency changes will have some effect on your domestic stock holdings, primarily large companies with a significant proportion of overseas sales. An increasing dollar will have a downward impact on sales and earnings overseas, and vice versa. A lot of attention to the value of the dollar by US investors is because approximately 40% of the sales of the S&P 500 companies are in overseas markets.

The most important concept to remember is that if the dollar falls, domestic companies benefit, because they will be able to lower prices in foreign countries without reducing their profit. This, over time, will boost sales. Also, if and when they repatriate their foreign sales into dollars, it will translate into more dollars therefore higher earnings. This is why countries who are trying to increase their GDP try to push their currency down. China has been accused for years of keeping its currency artificially undervalued so as to help their exporters, and overall economy, to grow. Conversely, if the dollar goes up it will hurt domestic company's sales abroad.

Throughout 2017 and the first 4 months of 2018 the dollar has declined, and this has helped US corporate profits. Recent increases in interest rates by the Fed have lifted the dollar 5.8% between April and late July 2018, which will dampen the profits of businesses who sell significantly overseas. This trend has not reached a worrisome stage, however if the dollar continues to increase some companies will start to disclose if profits are impaired by a rising dollar in their financial reports.

Currency moves will have its most significant impact on your international stocks. When you buy international stocks, particularly companies with significant US sales, those companies will have their reported profit affected by how their currency changes with respect to the US dollar. If you own stock in Toyota, and the yen gains vs. the dollar, their sales will be negatively affected.

Currency changes actually have a much greater effect on the cost of commodities. Commodity prices generally move inversely with the US dollar. This includes oil and gold. Dollar weakness since Jan 2017 has moved commodity prices higher. The broadest measure of the dollar vs. a basket of other currencies, known as the dollar index, is DXY:CUR. This index is the most often referenced in watching dollar movements. <u>No one has been able to predict accurately how this index will move, so it is of little value in portfolio planning.</u>

Currency risk is not avoidable for the average investor, but fortunately this is not problematic. Changes in FX rates are typically very small, changing by 2-4 digits to the right of the decimal point. Also, if you own multiple country ETFs, like Europe for example, overall FX changes will be mitigated by the averaging effect of several different countries. Further, without going into detail, when a country's currency moves in one direction for an extended period, counterbalancing forces build up in the opposite direction, which ultimately stops and reverses the trend. Currencies will normally cycle up and down multiple times over the long term.

The S&P 500 exhibits an extremely low correlation to the US dollar. If you look at a chart of the two, it is difficult to draw any meaningful conclusions. The concern among investors over the value of the dollar is overly exaggerated. All of the above means average **long term investors can basically ignore FX.** Since no one can predict future dollar movements, it's of no use in formulating investment strategy.

Takeaway: Long term investors do not need to be overly concerned with world currency fluctuations. However If the currency of a particular country is moving significantly lower over an extended period of time, 6 months to a year or more, it may mean something seriously negative is happening, and you may want to check your investments to see how much exposure you have there, if any.

If a country is having difficulty paying its national debt, as has Greece in recent years, has runaway inflation, or political crises, you should eliminate any investments there, regardless of the fact that their low price looks like a bargain. If a country's currency keeps dropping, whatever they import will continue to go up in price, possibly causing runaway inflation, and also making debt payments owed in a foreign currency more expensive to pay. Lastly, do not invest in any currency per se that is, owning the actual unit of exchange in a foreign country. It is pure gambling.

BUYING ON MARGIN

Buying on margin means you have taken a loan from your broker in order to buy securities. The securities you buy are collateral for the broker and must be held by them to cover your loan. You have done this because you believe strongly in a particular investment, do not have enough cash to buy it (or don't want to use your cash), and are willing to pay interest on a secured loan to be able to make a purchase.

The margin requirement is set by the Federal Reserve. Today the margin requirement is 50%. To buy on margin you must put in at least 50% of the purchase price, with the remaining 50% (you can borrow up to 50%) coming from your broker loan. **Interest rates are steep, between 7 – 8%** as of this writing, which is determined by your broker. To do this, you believe that your return will be greater by borrowing money and paying the interest, than it would be if you sold some other investments, giving up the return you were earning on them.

Buying on margin is very risky. If the stock falls in price you may receive a margin call, meaning your collateral has fallen below the 50% requirement. You will have to either: make a loan payment to bring down the loan; pledge additional shares as collateral; or sell the shares, take your loss, and fully repay the loan. If you do not have either the funds to reduce the loan, or additional shares to pledge, the broker will start selling your stock, and does not need your approval to do this, until the loan is below 50% or repaid in full.

All of this can be triggered by a short-term market pullback, where you are required to sell at a loss, plus pay the loan interest. In a steep market pullback, thousands of investors will get margin calls, forcing them to sell, which pushes the market down further (causing more margin calls).

Takeaway: Buying on margin is best suited to professional traders, with a short time horizon for the trade, who have sufficient cash balances to cover a downturn should it occur. Day traders with limited available cash trying to borrow their way to investment gains are paddling their boat near the falls. Regardless of the temptation to make money using other people's money, <u>do not buy securities on margin</u>. The downside is large losses.

STOCK OPTIONS

Stock options' trading is an investing strategy suited only to professionals, and stock traders, who make short term bets on the near-term price movements of stocks. Traders are not interested in the long-term fundamentals of the company, relying on very short term price movements, sometimes as short as one week, to make a profit and then get out.

Options are not suited to long term investors, and especially to those who only wish to check their investments occasionally. Not done properly, options trading can result in serious losses, and require a fair amount of study to understand fully.

Not being appropriate for long term investors, I have included only a short description here so you will have a rudimentary understanding of what they are, and if you choose to skip this section, it will not be of consequence.

A stock option is a contractual right, sold by one party to another that gives the buyer the right, but not the obligation, to buy or sell a stock at an agreed-upon price within a certain period of time. A stock option is considered a call when a buyer enters into a contract to purchase a stock at a specific price by a specific date. An option is considered a put when the option buyer takes out a contract to sell a stock at an agreed-on price on or before a specific date. If you do not exercise the option you purchased, by the maturity, the option expires, and you lose whatever you paid for them.

The idea is that the purchaser of a call option believes that the underlying stock will increase, while the seller of the option thinks otherwise. The option holder has the benefit of purchasing the stock at a discount from its current market value if he believes the stock price will increase prior to expiration. If, however, the purchaser believes a stock will decline in value, he enters into a put option contract that gives him the right to sell the stock at a future date. If the underlying stock loses value prior to expiration, the option holder is able to sell it for a premium from current market value. You do not have to actually exercise a call or put, you can just sell the option. You might do that if you have a profit in it you wish to realize, or you no longer think holding the option has profit potential.

These contracts are nothing more than bets that the underlying stock will go up or down. So why not just buy or sell the stock? The primary answer is leverage. With options you can invest a small amount of money relative to the potential gain, which can be very large, in relative terms. Also, if your option purchase become valueless, your loss is limited to what you paid for them.

Options are suited to traders interested in very short-term price movements who want to bet on that movement, but not actually become an owner of the shares. Also, options players build 'strategies" where they execute more than one option at the same time, in order to reduce risk by limiting losses if they are wrong. The idea is to build a strategy where the potential profit exceeds the potential loss. Using options is also a favorite tool for traders with a limited amount of dollars available, who are trying to score outsized profits.

If and only if you have enough of an interest in investing to become well studied in stock options, you may wish to consider the strategy of buying puts to reduce losses if the stock drops. For example, before the 2008 crash, your puts would have gone up in value as your stocks went down. Put options grant their owners the right to sell 100 shares of stock at the strike price. Although puts don't provide 100 percent protection, they can reduce your loss. It's similar to buying an insurance policy with a deductible. Unlike shorting stocks, where losses can be unlimited. With puts, the most you can lose is what you paid for the put option - if the price turns against you, you let the option expire unused.

By picking a strike price that matches your risk tolerance, you guarantee a minimum selling price -- and thus the value of your investment cannot fall below a known level. This is the ultimate in portfolio protection. The reason the vast majority of conservative investors don't adopt this strategy is that puts have an expense, yet they may never be used, and they must be monitored closely as the contract has an expiration date.

I would not use options without a commitment to understand them fully and be willing to monitor them often. The Najarian brothers have educational materials available for no charge, if you decide to become educated in options.

EMPLOYEE STOCK OPTIONS

Employee stock options are given by employers to compensate employees by giving them the right to buy shares of the company at a discount or at a favorable fixed price. The employee has the option of exercising the option, within a given time frame, or not participating. If the company's stock goes up the employee will make a profit, theoretically incentivizing him or her to work hard to make the company's profits increase. The terms of the option are determined by the company, and terms vary widely.

As an employee you must be aware that in addition to your job, buying your employer's stock increases your concentration of risk in this single company, and you do not want to increase this risk so much that if your employer does poorly or fails, your financial condition is injured materially.

Employees in a large company may believe they can adequately access the company's earnings potential and financial stability, but also may not - as I learned the hard way. To avoid concentrating your risk (as an employee and as a stock owner), exercise the option when it becomes available, and then immediately sell the stock, taking the profit now, and forgoing any future gains the stock might realize if you held it. Some companies will simply remit the gain to you if you so designate on your purchase option. This gives you a guaranteed gain, a rare occurrence in investing. Take advantage of the gain and forego any possible future profits, and use the funds to invest elsewhere, or perhaps reduce some of your debt.

I received employee options late in my career, and I used the proceeds, over time, to reduce my home mortgage to zero, which I was very glad I did when I reached retirement, and my monthly expenses were lowered significantly. This meant I needed to withdraw less funds from my IRA, and it continued to have positive returns. It is much easier to borrow than to reduce debt, and employee options can give you a golden opportunity to do so.

The mistake often made is thinking that since this monetary gain was given to me with no cost, I can be greedy and hold the stock hoping for further gains, because I'm playing with "house" money. In fact, it's your money, and investing it is no different than investing your "other' money. Money is fungible, there aren't different kinds of money. If you chose to invest it that's OK, but why should it be in your employer's company?

(My biggest financial mistake was holding too much stock of my employer, Bank of America. As the largest US bank, the thought of it failing was inconceivable. The stock went from $55/share to $3.75 in Dec. 2008, the dividend was reduced to 1 cent/share, and the bank required a government loan to continue.)

An even worse scenario is a stock option exercised, and the stock held, followed by a significant drop in the price of the stock. The discounted price of a non-qualified stock option is considered "compensation" by the government, and is taxed at ordinary income tax rates, regardless of what happened to the stock value after it was purchased. You may end up selling the stock at a loss just to pay taxes on a gain you never realized – a double edged sword. When the tech stock crater hit in 2000, a number of employees of high tech companies were required to file bankruptcy, because they did not have the funds to pay income taxes on their employee options.

MOMENTUM STRATEGY

There are an endless number of stock buying strategies, however momentum is one that is often discussed and worth knowing about.

Momentum in nature refers to the tendency of things to keep going in the same direction as they have in the past (until a disruptive event occurs). Stock prices often reflect this characteristic.

When a company's stock exhibits an upward trend, it attracts more buyers seeking profits, and less sellers, who want to continue profiting from the gains. The stock shows up on lists of top performing companies and even more buyers jump in. The trend is self-generating.

If a stock keeps going up, the RSI or relative strength index (see page 152), goes up. The stock will then show up on buy lists in Investors Business Daily, and on computer generated measures of stock strength shown on stock analysis web pages. This creates more buying, however, these results are being generated from just one variable - that the recent price movement has been trending up, and not from any fundamental reason, such as strong sales or profit growth.

Buyers might not know why the stock is climbing and may not care. They want to ride the wave. This is momentum investing, where investors overlook or ignore the fundamentals of the company and invest solely on the price trend. Quite obviously this strategy is best suited to traders, who follow the market closely. They will watch for signs the trend has, or is about to, reverse, or they will pre-program their computer to unwind the trade if momentum shows signs of weakening (like reduced daily volumes).

The reverse also happens. When a stock is falling, fewer new buyers will be interested, and many existing owners will decide to take their losses and sell, pushing the price down. There may be a fundamental reason for the decline, like the company is reporting losses, or it may be simply momentum investors selling because of recent price movement downward. Their thinking might be, "I don't know why the stock is going down but I'm getting out before I lose any more money". There's increased risk in buying a falling stock, and there's no reward for being a hero. The Wall Street adage is, "don't try to catch a falling knife".

The defining characteristic of the momentum investor is not becoming overly concerned about why the price is going the way it's going – you buy things that are going up, and vice versa. It's not totally illogical. You argue, "I'm not exactly sure why the stock is going up (or down) but there must be an underlying reason since so many investors are buying (or selling), so I'll act in the same way.

A second type of momentum investor, perhaps more common, is one who observes stocks steadily moving up or down, and decides it is a momentum candidate. He then, and when I say *he* remember this may be a computer we're talking about, decides to investigate the possible fundamental business reason(s) for the stock's steady movement in one direction. If the fundamentals support the movement, he decides to buy, or sell.

By fundamental meaning real world business issues such as increasing sales, increasing profit margins, increasing net profits, increasing market share, reduced borrowings, announced stock buybacks, increased industry expansion, etc. The same sort of analysis on the downside, where negative trends in the company's business is causing investors to bail out of the stock (or short sellers to sell short).

Momentum players use stock screeners to identify momentum stocks, where you set your computer to list stocks exhibiting a pre-set qualifier. For example, you have the computer list all stocks where the price has gone up (or down) three or four or five days in a row, or four days out of the last five, or three consecutive weeks, or months. Whatever you believe is the best measure of momentum. When you, or the computer, identifies a stock meeting your momentum criteria you buy it (or sell it). You may also have the computer execute the trade automatically, as a quantum investing firm does. Computers around the world are busy executing buy and sell orders even when the lights are out, and all the employees are tucked under the covers.

You can see how momentum players are in a sense feeding off one another, mimicking the buy/sell actions of others and riding the wave until it ends. The adage is, the trend is your friend, until it's about to end. The massive increase in the price of Bitcoin is a perfect example. People were buying not because of a fundamental reason, but because everyone else was buying. These frenzies usually end ugly. Momentum is obviously not a safe strategy for long term investors.

Pure momentum strategy is dangerous because it can be mindless. Many people have been burned by this strategy, and it is generally considered ill advised. However, that being said, most investors are aware that it is very dangerous to ignore a trend. Algorithmic trading can be a powerful force which you do not want to stand in front of.

If a stock is going up (or down) consistently, it may be because momentum players have latched on to it. A telltale sign of this is an extraordinarily high P/E, where buyers have pushed the price beyond normal investing parameters (e.g. Chipotle). If so, when it does eventually reverse, it may go the other way quickly and by a large amount. If you are not a trader watching the market every day, or have your computer programmed to notify you of a reversal or have pre-set sell (limit) orders with your broker, you can sustain a large loss.

Investors who classify themselves as value investors look for stocks which they believe have been beaten down in price unjustifiably, giving them an opportunity to buy at a "bargain" price. What may happen however is that the price may continue going downward after they bought because momentum players are selling or shorting the stock.

This has happened to GE in the last few years, whose stock keeps going lower even after many have bought the stock after deciding the stock represented a value purchase. Buying a stock which has gone down in value significantly, because it looked to be a "bargain" price, only to see the price continue downward is often called a value trap.

The anti-hero for momentum investors is the reversion to the mean principal discussed further below. Many investors, and computer algorithms, follow an investment strategy which is to sell the stocks, or stock sectors, which have been going up in previous weeks and/or months, and buy those they have been going down, or lagged the overall market - expecting the prices to eventually revert to the mean, or average.

Takeaway: Momentum and reversion to the mean are both investment strategies which are based on previous stock price movement rather than fundamental factors as a basis for making investment decisions. As such they are not suitable for a long-term investor.

Strategies such as these are of primary concern to traders and technicians invested in individual companies, looking for short term profit opportunities. ETFs mitigate the risk of unforeseen stock price movement. If you are holding a growth ETF and one of the components has a bad earnings report, for example, the effect of that one company will be insignificant. With ETFs there is no need for you to be concerned with daily or weekly market movement.

REVERSION TO THE MEAN and CONTRARIANS

In nature we notice a tendency of measurable things to revert to the mean, or average. Things which have exhibited much greater than average or below average behavior for a prolonged period, have an increasingly probability of reverting back to average behavior. Several years of very dry weather are followed by above average rain years. Roll snake eyes three out of ten rolls, and then they stop showing up, with the expected average (one out of thirty-six) eventually returning. The number of examples is endless. The postulate is, if you look at long enough periods, the measured results of a variable will approach the average.

Casinos are continuously profitable because of it. Mega trends like climate change and cultural change will move the average slowly, but the reversion still occurs. The longer the period of your measurement of what is average, the more likely a return to the average will occur.

Stock prices also exhibit a tendency to return to the average, although this is not anywhere near an exact science. Stock market prices are determined by humans, and human behavior is obviously very difficult to predict. With stock markets, above or below average activity, be it in prices, or volume, or volatility, or any other metric, will often revert back to average. This can be explained in part by the behavior of business cycles. When things move in one direction for an extended period, forces build up in the opposite direction which pushes the metric back toward the average.

For example, say milk prices keep going up for some reason involving supply and demand. Farmers see this and take steps to increase their revenue by producing more milk. They may buy more cattle, increase cow fertilization steps, increase feeding, reduce cow slaughters, buy more milkers or storage, or transportation equipment, hire additional workers, etc. When enough farmers do this, more milk is produced, and the price will fall back toward average levels.

With stocks, when the price of a stock, or group of stocks, goes up by more than all other stocks on average, some owners may decide to sell and realize their profit. If energy or healthcare stocks do well above average for a period, it is common for selling, or possibly a reduction of new buyers, to materialize, because the price is seen as too high. Stocks or stock sectors are often described as leaders or laggards. Many investors and computer programs expect leaders to slow, and laggards to catch up. Seems simple, however one never knows when those reversals will occur.

To oversimplify a bit, if a stock, or stock sector (like an ETF), or an industry, experiences above average movement up or down, the probability of a return to average becomes greater as time passes. Trends moving in one direction will not go on indefinitely. They usually, but not always, return to average, if you wait long enough. 2017 may be described as the FAANG year because of the huge gains made by Facebook, Apple, Amazon, Netflix, and Google. The reversal happened in early 2019, when investors abandoned the FAANG stocks in droves, and as a group they underperformed the overall market by a large margin.

For some investors, and also some computer driven funds, this phenomenon has become a strategy. They buy any stock, or group of stocks, which have gone down significantly for an extended period, and vice versa, selling anything which has outperformed. This is sometimes referred to as a contrarian strategy. There are enough investors employing this strategy that it has become somewhat self-fulfilling. The contrarians actually contribute to the likelihood that a reversion to the mean will occur.

There are two significant caveats here. First before buying anything which has gone down significantly, it's important to make sure that there is not a lasting fundamental reason for the decline, as with a failing company like Sears, Radio Shack, or Toys R Us. Similarly, that there is not a lasting fundamental reason for a category of stocks to decline, like coal mining, cigarettes, or perhaps big box, high overhead retailers, like JCPenney or Macy's.

A contrarian is going against the trend. The risk is that you cannot accurately identify the point at which the reversion will begin, and while you're waiting, you may sustain losses. GE has been going down since Jan 2016 - will it bottom, or continue further?

The cyclical nature of oil prices has a similar effect on companies in the energy sector. When the price of oil goes to an extraordinarily low, or high price, you will hear many pundits recommending buying or selling this sector, anticipating a reversion to the mean and a return to "average" prices.

Oil price swings caused by supply and demand changes are met by counter movements taken by both suppliers and users. For example, if oil inventories are falling and prices increasing, drillers will increase exploratory drilling, increase pumping, and activate previously shuttered wells. Likewise, if prices are increasing, users may seek to use alternative fuels, like electric production plants switching to natural gas, and new plants being designed for natural gas use.

Therefore, it is logical to assume a reversion will occur.

It's possible that at some point no reversion will occur. Fossil fuels are at the beginning of a very long-term secular decline, due to the pollution of the atmosphere. Despite moves to decrease our usage of fossil fuels, the need for them will continue to exist for many decades, especially in less developed countries, and therefore sector profits will continue for many years.

My personal preference is to pass on the energy segment altogether, not only for the secular issue, but also because the extreme volatility in the price of oil, drags all the energy related companies in its wake. A risk I prefer to leave to others.

Observation of market activity is very convincing that a large number of investment funds, to include computer driven funds, are using reversion to the mean strategy. At times you will see market leaders lagging, and market laggards gaining, for no fundamental reason. Healthcare stocks will do poorly one day, and then recover completely the next day, with no underlying reason for doing so.

For example, because of increasing interest rates, utilities and REITs were driven down from 2016 to 2018, yet you will often see those segments go up even on days when interest rates were moving higher.

Buying the laggards and selling the leaders is a popular strategy which pushes overall returns toward market averages and reinforces the argument for a passive approach to investing.

Computer trading has exaggerated stock price movement because similar computer models are being used by many firms, and also because of a greater number of transactions occurring. For example, stocks will increase dramatically on a good economic report, as thousands of computers are buying on that news.

When a particular market segment rises substantially on a given day, computers will often start responding to their reversion to the mean instructions and sell the same group theoretically after realizing a gain, later that day. You may notice that stock prices often exhibit a "U" or upside down "U" pattern during the day. Down in the morning, recover in the afternoon, or up in the morning, fall off in the afternoon.

Thank computers for this.

Takeaway: If you are a long-term investor, reversion to the mean activity is irrelevant because you will hold your investment through years of market prices adjusting to unsustainable price movement in one direction. Also remember not to let your babies grow up to be either cowboys or stock traders - both occupations are hazardous.

SHORT SELLING

Short selling, which is selling stocks which you do not own, is a strategy used to make a profit by selling shares of a company which you expect to go down. You borrow the shares from your broker. Short selling is not appropriate for long term investors, which requires close monitoring, a potential large dollar risk, and a "bet" which may come closer to being described as gambling. I have including a basic description here, for general knowledge purposes, as you will hear investors talk about shorting quite often.

Shorting stock has long been a trading technique for speculators, day traders, hedge funds, and individual investors willing to take on a potentially substantial risk of capital loss. Shorting stock, also known as short selling, involves the sale of stock that the seller does not own, or shares that the seller has taken on loan from a broker, in the expectation of a lower price in the future. Traders may also sell other securities short, for simplicity I'll discuss stock shorts only.

Short sellers take on these transactions because they believe a stock's price is headed downward, and that if they sell the stock today, they'll be able to buy it back at a lower price at some point in the future - which is called "covering". If they accomplish this, they'll make a profit consisting of the difference between their sell and buy prices. Some traders use short selling purely for speculation, while others want to hedge, or protect, their downside risk if they have a long position—in other words, if they already own shares of the same or a related stock outright, often referred to as a long/short strategy.

Some investors believe it is easier to determine when a company is facing serious negative issues which will result in stock price drops, than predicting tomorrow's winners. Examples would include companies whose product is being replaced by technological changes, cultural changes like customers switching to online purchasing, companies with negative cash flows, or inadequate ability to repay loans, companies using questionable accounting or business practices, etc. It wasn't hard to see how cell phone cameras would nearly wipe out the mass market camera manufacturers, for example.

Most investors buy shares of various companies and depending on their trading mentality, either sock them away for the long term in their investment portfolios (buy-and-hold investors) or trade them on a short-term basis (day traders and swing traders). Buying shares is referred to as "going long", while "long only" means investors who only buy stocks and do not short them. For example, many mutual funds can only go long, and are prohibited from shorting stocks.

Stock purchases can either be made in a cash account, where the investor puts up the full amount of the stock purchase; or in a margin account, where the investor puts up part of the buy transaction amount for the stock purchase and borrows the rest from the broker using the stock as collateral. Short selling, on the other hand, is usually conducted only in a margin account.

While investors go long in expectation that the stock will appreciate in price, traders go short in anticipation that the stock will tumble. As noted earlier, short selling makes it possible to sell what one does not own. The short seller achieves this by borrowing the stock from a broker, and immediately selling the stock at its current market price, with the sale proceeds credited to the short seller's margin account. At a future point in time, the short seller will cover the short position by buying it in the market and repaying the loaned stock to the broker.

The difference between the sale price and the purchase price represents the short seller's profit or loss. Let's assume you short 100 shares of hypothetical stock ABC at $10 per share; after a period of time, the stock has declined to $5, at which point you buy it back. Your gross profit on this short sale is thus $500 ([$10 - $5] x 100 shares). Your net profit will be somewhat lower, owing to the costs involved with short selling.

In addition to the normal cost of the trade transaction, the investor pays margin interest, which is the interest paid on the margin debt incurred for the short sale, plus the actual cost to borrow the stock, which can be quite high for stocks that are heavily shorted or difficult to borrow. Plus, the <u>short seller also has to pay the lender of the stock any dividends</u> or rights declared during the course of the stock loan.

Continuing with the above example, assume that the stock you shorted at $10 spikes up to $22, at which point you decide to cut your losses rather than run the risk of it moving even higher. In this case, your loss would be $1200 ([$10 - $22] x 100 shares). In percentage terms, your loss is 120%, since you lost $1200 on your initial investment capital of $1000. Obviously, losses of greater than 100% of your invested capital are mathematically impossible on the long side, since you cannot lose any more than the total amount of your investment.

Therein lies the major risk of short selling, the fear of infinite losses. While the maximum loss for a long investor is the amount invested in a security, the maximum loss for a short seller is theoretically infinite, since there is no upper limit to a stock's price appreciation.

If the price of a stock you have shorted keeps rising, increasing your losses, you will at some time have to buy the stock back at a loss to close out your position. Sometimes when a stock increases significantly and the short sellers are in a "short squeeze" they will buy the stock and cover their short which pushes the price up even further. During a short squeeze the short seller may be forced to cover their short position at an artificially high price that may only be temporary in nature.

The percentage of short sellers in a stock is a publicly reported number. A stock with a large percentage of shorts means a lot of investors are expecting the price to decline, which is a negative. However, by the same token, these short sellers must at some point buy the stock to cover their short position, and therefore, as a group, represent positive future demand for the stock - a positive.

> ***Takeaway***: Intuitively, it seems, it would be easy to just short companies experiencing significant business problems, however, remember the market is already discounting those stocks. Unless you are the type of person who spends time reviewing their portfolio daily, and is comfortable with the substantial risks of shorting, avoid this strategy, as most typical investors do.

CROWDED TRADES

You may hear stock market commentators referring to crowded trades. They are referring to stocks which are extremely popular, and because they are held by so many investors, the price has been pushed upward, perhaps to an "overbought" condition. Further, they may be an element of above average risk inherent in the stock, because with so many holders of the stock, any negative news or unfavorable information released about the company could trigger a large number of investors to sell. Today you could put Apple, Facebook, Netflix, and Google (Alphabet) in this category, and many others like Microsoft, Boeing, and Visa.

There can be several reasons why a stock is widely held. For the most part these are very large companies, perhaps in the Dow 30, but for sure in the S&P 500. Most people associate large companies with reduced risk, especially the risk of total failure, and this is of course true.

Large companies have more options if their business(es) run into trouble. They can borrow money relatively easily, they can restructure operations, they can spin off poorly performing divisions, they can make acquisitions to shore up weak divisions, they can hire turnaround specialists, etc. Big companies fail too, just not very often. This is the reason the S&P 500 is the most popular index, worldwide.

Usually these are companies whose stock has done extremely well, and the outlook for their earnings is positive. Momentum buyers move in, and professional managers fear that their performance will fall short of their peers, if they do not own it. An additional reason is simply name recognition, especially for foreign buyers. People buy familiar names in the same way that they vote for the incumbent. They shy away from unknown names.

Business channels on TV give coverage to very large companies almost exclusively, because they want to appeal to the most number of viewers. This results in additional crowding into frequently recommended stocks,

The issue however is that as more and more investors buy a stock, the P/E or multiple (the number of times the price per share exceeds the per share earnings) keeps rising and becomes above average or far above average. <u>The number of buyers has crowded out and overwhelmed the number of sellers.</u> In order to justify buying these stocks you may have to discard normal P/E considerations, hold your nose, buy, and hope the momentum keeps going. Amazon is a good example of a crowded trade today with a P/E of 75. Investors expect future earnings to increase, due to increasing market domination.

Opportunities for long term returns may be better by looking beyond crowded trades. What does this mean for an ETF investor? You hold an overweight position in the S&P 500 because it's a backbone of US growth. However, in deciding on the balance of your portfolio, you might give greater attention to mid-caps and small caps, which will trade at more reasonable P/E's because they are less crowded. These stocks are sometimes referred to as "under the radar", although no NYSE stock truly is. Value investors also look for low P/E's, which they believe have more upside potential, or in other terms, a better risk/reward relationship.

Takeaway: Crowded trades are crowded for a good reason. These reasons may be justified, and they may not. Will Netflix continue to dominate the streaming of entertainment, or will Disney begin to reduce their near monopoly? If you are a buyer of ETFs, you will already own a large position in the mega companies because most ETFs are capitalization weighted, and therefore own larger positions in larger companies. If you look at the top ten holdings of many mainstream ETFs, you will see the FAANG stocks at or near the top of the list. So, to achieve diversification, it's necessary to own ETFs which focus on the less crowded company categories, including mid and small cap ETFs. Is any company worth 200 times earnings? No one knows, but we can say for certain that <u>all</u> trends eventually will come to an end.

TRADING ONLINE

Stockbrokers charge very small transaction fees online, most around $5-7 per trade. However, if you need assistance in making the trade, it will be classified as "broker assisted" and the fee with jump to over $30. So best to do it yourself, and it's very simple. All brokers have different platforms, however they are simple to use, and have lots of links where you can clarify something you don't understand. Do it once or twice and it will become second nature.

If you are buying it will tell you how much cash you have available, and also tell you if you have entered a trade which exceeds your available cash. Remember that generally it takes three days for you to receive the cash from a previous sale.

Initially it will ask you which account you wish the trade to be made from, a tax deferred or taxes paid account, and this is a good time to consider if you are selling, whether there will be a tax consequence of the trade, and also if you will be foregoing an upcoming dividend by selling before the "record date". (see previous section)

After entering the security you wish to trade, and the amount you wish to buy or sell ("sell all shares" will also sell your fractional shares), you will need to enter the order type. There are a number of order types, and if you become more interested in trading I recommend you explore the different choices. Usually you will be entering a market or limit order.

> **Market** - The sale will take place at the market price. Right now, if the market is open. If the market is closed, it will occur as soon as the market opens.
>
> **Limit** - the trade will take place only if the stock reaches a specified price, set by you, and for the time period you enter. Limit orders are explained in more detail in the following section.

If you are entering a market order when the market is closed, be aware that stocks may not open at the price it closed at when the market was last open. Events which have occurred while the market was closed may push the opening price either up or down (based on the direction of pre- open trade volume). If you are concerned that the price may be significantly different when the market does open, you may want to wait until the market is open, when you will know the price you will get. Long term traders will not care about these relatively small price movements from day to day and will enter a market order.

If you are entering a limit order, this means you do not want the trade to occur unless the stock has hit a certain price, up or down. If the stock is selling for $25/share and you want to buy it, but only if the stock becomes available at a lower price, say $22, you enter into a limit order to that effect. If you want to sell that same stock, but you think it may be trending up in the near term, you may enter a limit order to sell when, if, it reaches $27.

The most obvious risk here is that the trade may never happen. If you enter a buy order below the market price, and the stock keeps going up, your order may never execute. You will be asked on any limit order how long you want the broker to keep that order open. If you wanted to buy but only at a lower price, you may be OK with never having bought - but if the price keeps rising you will be seeing all the gains you missed out on by entering a limit and not a market order.

The more common unwanted consequence of a sell limit order is one that is placed "to protect your downside". The stop loss order is common. Active traders often enter a stop loss order for every stock they own, especially if they are apprehensive about a possible market pullback, or in a near term decline in the stock they are buying. You decide how much of a price decrease you will tolerate before you will want to sell. A decrease of say 5-10% is common. There are a couple of concerns here.

First, if the whole market drops precipitously and quickly, for some non-fundamental reason, like for example a significant geopolitical event, your sell order may execute, after which the market returns to normal - only now you no longer own it. You have been "stopped out". This can also happen when for technical, unknown reasons, the market has a flash crash - everything goes down, then recovers, usually the same day.

I learned the negative consequences of the stop loss order when I was in an investment club. We set stop loss orders for all our holdings, usually at about 8-10% below market, as many experts suggest you do. We only re-visited the holdings at our meetings, every month.

At a meeting, when we discussed our investment in XYZ, someone might mention that it was still above our purchase price, despite some negative events. We then might discover that we no longer owned XYZ, we were stopped out when Russia invaded the Ukraine (or some other unrelated event). We now had a recognized loss, and we therefore did not benefit from the subsequent recovery in the stock price. During periods when the market went down quickly, large portions of our portfolio were eliminated, leaving us only with realized losses. If by the time you realize you have been stopped out, and the market recovers, in order to buy the stock back you may have to pay more than you originally paid.

The lesson here is that the market is volatile. If you set the stop limit too close to the existing price, ordinary volatility will cause it to execute. On the other hand, If you set the stop considerably below market, you may decide if it's that low, you don't want to sell at that much of a loss - you'll just be patient and wait and hope it recovers. In both cases the stop may not work to your advantage.

Active stock managers almost always enter limit orders, trying to capture near term price movements to maximize their return. Jim Cramer, the well-known stock guru, said he thought entering a market order was stupid. As a long-term investor, I couldn't disagree more. What difference does 50 cents or a dollar a share matter when you expect to use this money 30 or 40 years from now?

Since ETFs are a basket of companies, their price movement will be less volatile day to day than individual stocks, therefore placing limit orders is chasing insignificant amounts. The broader the index is, the less volatile it will be. For example, an ETF of large cap stocks will be much less volatile than an ETF of a single foreign country, or a highly specific company grouping. (As for example, the worst ETF in the first quarter of 2019 was BDRY - <u>Breakwave Dry Bulk Shipping</u>, down 48%)

> ***Takeaway***: If you are a long-term investor investing your retirement money, capturing short term price changes is not meaningful. Buy what you think is a good investment and sell what you think has a poor future. Be mindful of any tax or dividend consequences of your trade, and whether the market is open, and use "market" orders. If you are fearful of a significant downturn in what you are buying, instead of setting a stop loss order, don't buy it. Either buy something else, or wait until you are comfortable that it is a sound decision. I have found that waiting until the next day to make a trade, often results in seeing the issue somewhat differently, and I was glad I waited.

LIMIT ORDERS

A limit order is an order to buy or sell a stock but only if it reaches a specific price. You are telling your broker that if the stock, or ETF, reaches a certain level, then buy it or sell it. It is the opposite of a market order, which executes immediately if the market is open (or executes when the market opens the following day).

When you enter a trade you will be prompted to select what type of order it is, market or limit, and if a limit order, how long it is to remain in force. If the stock of ETF reaches the level you set in, the trade will happen automatically, and you will receive a notification that your limit order has executed.

A limit order is not guaranteed to execute. A limit order can be executed only if the stock's market price reaches the limit price. While limit orders do not guarantee execution, they help ensure that an investor does not pay more than a predetermined price for a stock or does not hold on to a stock falling in price.

Depending on the direction of the position, a limit order is sometimes referred to as a buy limit order or a sell limit order. For example, a buy limit order that stipulates the buyer is not willing to pay more than $30 per share, while a sell limit order may require the share price to be at least $30 for a sale to occur. A stop loss order is the opposite of a take profit order: It is left to ensure that if the stock falls to the level you have set, an automatic sell order will execute.

Most commonly a limit order is placed when an investor has decided he would like to buy a certain stock or ETF but would like to do so only if the stock drops in price to a certain level. Investors might say, I like so and so but I want to buy it only if the price goes down to $X. So, he enters a limit order. If the stock never goes down to that level, no purchase ever occurs. You can place a time limit on the order, or have it be "good until canceled".

Perhaps more common is the stop loss order, discussed above. You may decide that if the price drops by 10% or more, it means something seriously negative has occurred, and you want to sell before the situation becomes worse.

Normal market volatility however can cause some terrible consequences. In the first half of 2018 the market has become terribly volatile, with the Dow falling or rising 300-700 points in a single day. Our current President can sink the market by 500 Dow points with one ill-considered tweet. If this happens, and you have set stops on all of your holdings, you may find that your entire portfolio has been sold, and your portfolio has been reduced to 100% cash.

Worse, if the market drops unexpectedly by a large amount, such as it does to major negative news events, and then recovers within the same trading day, you will have sold out at a low price, and if you wish to buy back the stock you will have to do so at a higher price, guaranteeing you a realized loss. When you read about a flash crash, where stock prices drop precipitously for no known reason (and then recover rapidly), the crash is magnified by stop loss trades executing automatically.

Say you buy a stock (or ETF) at $20 and set a stop loss at $18. The President tweets he may put tariffs on Chinese goods. Your stock drops to $17, and your sell order executed. The Whitehouse then says it will be a very limited action, the market recovers and the stock goes to $19. When you look at your email that night you will find out that you sold at $18, realized a $2 loss, and if you wish to buy it back you will have to pay $19. If the stock then goes up for the reasons you anticipated when you first bought it, the stock could rise past $20 before you realize what has happened, and to buy it again means you would have been much better off to not have sold.

A stop loss order can guarantee a loss, if you enter it at the time you make a purchase. If you had done nothing, you might have no loss or even a gain if the stock recovered. If you set the stop loss very low, it may stop a larger loss, but it also guarantees you a large loss.

Takeaway: A risk of using limit orders which execute automatically is that if you do not have the time to review your portfolio very day, you may experience unintended results.

You can use limits and stops for ETF orders however the need to do so is questionable at best, and I see no reason for doing so. Because you have a basket of stocks in your ETF, if one company does very poorly, or even files for bankruptcy (where if you owned that particular stock you might have wanted a stop loss order), it will not affect your investment materially.

On the buy side if you decide to take an ETF position it means you expect it to do well over time, and if the price rises it does not mean you suddenly want to sell and take profits. It's best to sell an ETF only when you have made a conscious thoughtful decision to exit the investment for fundamental reasons unrelated to market volatility.

ROTATION

Rotation refers to the collective movement of investors from one group of stocks to another, based upon a change in sentiment from one sector to another. Individual Investors move their funds around every day, however when large dollar movements in the stock market as a whole occur, over a period of months not days, it is a sign that investor sentiment is changing.

If for example the stock of financial companies begins to fall because of increased selling (or reduced buying) while the stock of industrial corporations is rising, this rotation might indicate that investors have shifted their expectations of the future for these two groups. It may be, for example, that interest rates are falling and seen as continuing to fall, which is viewed as harmful to financial company's profits, while these lower rates are expected to help the industrials profits due to lower interest costs. Market analysts and pundits watch for rotations closely because not only does it give us some insight into current collective market sentiment, it also may be detrimental to your own investment portfolio if you are on the wrong side of these rotations.

These rotations can only be identified by viewing past history, because daily price movements are mostly random. So it's a look back at where investors seem to be increasing their positions, and decreasing others.

Let's say you think banks are going to do well going forward, so you have over weighted them in your portfolio mix. Professional investors who are following and charting the market and the Federal Reserve's actions however have noted that interest rates have started to decline, and they think rates are going to continue to head lower over the next 6-12 months. Therefore, they have decided to reduce their bank holdings, and their selling lowers bank stock prices. You may be right about the longer term future of bank profits, but you begin to lose money because of the rotation which is occurring.

The stock market goes up and down with the collective expectations of people (and computers) and if the bulk of investors are moving in one direction while you are not, it won't matter who's right. You will experience reduced returns, or losses while this rotation takes place.

If you take a position in your portfolio which is at odds with overall market sentiment, you may be OK if you wait long enough for the market to correct. However, during that time, you will have had below market returns. Since professional investment managers are evaluated at least quarterly, they do not have the luxury of waiting out the segment downturn, so they will make an immediate change (this is one reason why active managers end up with a high portfolio churn rate). If you are only concerned about the very long term, like 20 or 30 years, none of this will matter because market rotations and business cycles will wash themselves out in that span.

The good growth of the US economy, low unemployment, regular job growth, and tame inflation has helped most US stocks in recent years, but not all. Brick and mortar retail stores have been hurt by the movement to online sellers like Amazon. Many have filed bankruptcy, and some forecasters expect malls to have 25% vacancy by 2020. The retailer's that remain have to re-invent themselves or die. The movement of consumers, led by millennials, to buying online did not happen overnight. Those that saw the rotation toward online buying and sold the brick and mortar stores, and overweight online sellers did well.

Takeaway: If you are interested in investing enough to follow your portfolio say, at least monthly, it pays to watch for these rotations. Fortunately, these shifts do not occur often. They used to happen slowly, however computers and very low transaction fees have sped this up. Trying to play the momentum in a particular stock is foolish. You have no idea when it will turn against you. However, when market momentum involves an entire business segment going up or down over a period of time, it may be wise to adjust your portfolio weightings accordingly, or be willing to wait for a period of years for the cycle to reverse.

RE-BALANCING

Rebalancing is the process of realigning the weightings of a portfolio of assets. Rebalancing involves periodically buying or selling assets in a portfolio to maintain a previously established level of asset allocation. (Don't forget to keep a record of what your asset weightings were set at). Generally, but not always, rebalancing pertains to asset classes, like stocks vs. bonds.

For example, say an original target asset allocation is 60% stocks and 40% bonds. If the stocks performed well during the period, they may have increased the stock weighting of the portfolio to say 70% for example. The investor may then decide to sell some stocks and buy bonds to get the portfolio back to the original target allocation of 60/40.

"Rebalancing" as a term, has connotations regarding an even distribution of assets however, this is perhaps a poor choice of words - there is no need to "balance" anything. It simply means bringing your asset weightings back to the original level you previously set.

Numerous historical analyses show that re-balancing will produce better returns over extended periods. The reason is partly related to the regression to the mean discussion above. Asset categories that have outperformed for a period have a higher probability of pausing and returning to average returns. Conversely assets categories which have done poorly have a greater probability of going up and also returning to the mean. When rebalancing, you will sell the winning categories and buy the lagging categories. This sounds counterintuitive, however rebalancing gives investors the opportunity to sell high and buy low, taking the gains from high-performing investments and reinvesting them in areas that have not yet experienced good growth.

The benefits of rebalancing are reinforced by investors and computer driven asset managers using a regression to the mean strategy, and also contrarian investors, and value-oriented investors.

Rebalancing also increases diversity. For example, should the value of stock (or ETF) X increase by 25% while stock Y only gained 5%, a large amount of the value in the portfolio is now tied to stock X. Should stock X experience a sudden downturn, the portfolio will suffer higher losses. Rebalancing lets the investor redirect some of the funds currently held in stock X to another investment, be that more of stock Y or purchasing a new stock entirely. By having funds spread out across multiple stocks, a downturn in one will be partially offset by the activities of the others, which provides a level of portfolio stability.

While there is no required schedule for rebalancing a portfolio, most recommendations are to examine allocations at least quarterly. It is possible to go without rebalancing a portfolio, though this would generally be ill-advised.

Based on changes taking place globally and in the business world, you may find your previous allocations are no longer optimal. Active investors like me, make portfolio re-allocations often, sometimes monthly. In that case a quarterly rebalancing may not be necessary. If you have not visited your portfolio in the last three months or so, then compare your today's asset percentages with your target percentages and make trades to bring you back to your plan. Your broker may have an automatic program for rebalancing you may wish to consider.

In former years brokerage firms used to charge relatively high fees to buy and sell securities, based on the dollar size of the transaction, and portfolio changes could become very expensive, if done often. With the advent of computers, and the lack of need for human involvement, fees are now nominal and no longer dollar size dependent. At most firms, any size trade is about $5, so there is no need to be concerned about making frequent portfolio changes. Transaction fees are no longer a deterrent to adjusting your portfolio allocations.

Most mutual funds providers rebalance their funds quarterly. When they do this, they will cause asset classes to move toward the mean. For example, after a period of falling stock prices, funds will buy stocks, with the proceeds of bond sales, which results in stock prices being pushed higher.

> *Takeaway*: ETFs follow an index so they do not rebalance. You, however, will want to rebalance your ETF portfolio periodically to reduce the weighting of assets which have risen beyond your planned level, and vice versa.

BUYING AND SELLING CONSIDERATIONS

There are a couple things to think about when buying and selling investments.

One is the tax consequences of your trade, if any.

Your broker's web page will ask you which account you want to make the trade in. Of primary concern is whether the account is in a taxable account, where you have already paid the taxes on that money, or in a retirement account where the taxes have been deferred like an IRA. Once money is invested into an individual retirement account, including a Roth, there are no tax consequences for trading securities within the account as long as the money remains in the same account.

Just like a checking or savings account, there are no tax consequences to moving money into or out of a regular, taxable brokerage account. However, there are numerous transactions that can occur within a brokerage account that can result in taxation. The most obvious is if you sell a security, whether it's a stock, bond, mutual fund, exchange-traded fund or any other capital asset. These types of assets generate capital gains (or losses) depending on the difference between the amount you paid and the amount you received after a sale.

Even if you don't sell any of your stocks or bonds, you can have taxable events in your brokerage account. When stocks pay dividends, that payout is taxable, even if you automatically reinvest the dividend into additional shares of stock. The same is true of bond interest, or dividends you get on a money market or savings account. All of these types of income are taxable in the year in which you receive them, whether or not you take the money out of your account.

Before entering a sell transaction, ask yourself if this trade will trigger a taxable gain or loss, based on what kind of an account it's in, and if a capital gain is involved, whether it is a short term (under 1 year of ownership) or a long term gain.

For most people the long-term capital gain tax rate is 0-15%, depending on income level, and 20% for high income earners. The short term capital gain tax rate is equal to your ordinary income tax rate or 0-37%.

It's not wise to make investment decisions solely because of the tax consequences, however you might want to place the trade at an appropriate time.

For example, If it's near the end of the year, you may want to sell something in which you have a loss, because the loss can be used to offset gains you have realized during the year (and also up to $3k in ordinary income). Conversely if a sale will trigger significant capital gains, you may want to postpone the sale into the next calendar year, so as to push the taxes into the next year.

If a capital gain is involved you will need to consider the tax rate, whether you have losses with which to offset the gain, and whether you might want to hold off selling until it will be classified as a long term gain (If you have some short term shares and some long term shares you can designate which you are selling - otherwise your broker will choose your longest held shares by default).

If the trade is from an IRA, Roth IRA, or other tax deferred account there will be no tax consequences, so you will not need to be concerned about taxes at all.

If you want to get rid of something you have decided is an unwise investment, make the sale and forget the tax consequences. What you decide to own going forward is more important than the tax consequences.

Another consideration in selling a security is the date dividends are scheduled to be paid. If there is no urgency connected with making a sale, check to see when the stocks "record date" for dividends is. The shareholders on that date will be entitled to receive the dividend or distribution, declared by the company. Consider whether you will be forgoing the dividend if you sell now, and whether you might prefer to sell after the record date has passed, so you will still receive the current dividend.

The payment date of the dividend does not matter. If you are a holder on the record date, and sell it before the payment date, you will still receive the dividend. If the amount of the dividend is small, you may decide it's not worth postponing your sale.

> *Takeaway*: Before you click on "execute this order", take a moment to think about whether there will be tax or dividend consequences of this transaction.

BUSINESS CYCLES

Life itself can be described as a series of cycles, no matter what you are describing. Things and people rise and fall, begin and end (except Keith Richards). One speaker at a lecture I attended, said the meaning of life was, and then he turned to the chalkboard and drew an up and down  repeating wave pattern. You can debate this, but what you can't debate is business cycles themselves, because they are constant and enduring. When they will change direction, how long they will last, and how deep they will be are not known, and forecasters are often wrong. Business cycles are a complex topic, but we should go over some basics here.

The business cycle is caused by the forces of supply and demand, the availability of capital, and expectations about the future. Here's what causes each of the four phases of the growth and contraction phases.

Expansion: When consumers are confident, they buy now. They believe their job is secure, job availability is positive, and they feel comfortable borrowing to make purchases. As demand increases, businesses hire new workers. This increase in consumer income, further stimulates demand. A little healthy inflation can trigger demand by spurring shoppers to buy now before prices go up. A healthy expansion can suddenly turn into a dangerous peak. It happens when there's too much money chasing too few goods. It can either cause serious price inflation or an asset bubble.

Peak: If demand outstrips supply, then the economy can overheat. Investors and businesses compete to outperform the market, taking on more risk to gain some extra return. This combination of excess demand, and the creation of risky derivatives, created the housing bubble in 2005. You can always recognize a peak by two things: First, the media says that the expansion will never end. Second, it seems everyone and his brother is making tons of money from whatever the asset bubble happens to be.

Contraction: A contraction typically ends in a recession. Three types of events trigger a contraction - a rapid increase in interest rates, a financial crisis, or runaway inflation (causing the Fed to increase interest rates). Fear and panic will replace confidence. Investors sell stocks, and buy bonds, gold, and the U.S. dollar. Many consumers lose their jobs, sell their homes, and stop buying anything but necessities. Businesses lay off workers, and hoard cash.

Trough: Consumers must regain confidence before the economy can enter a new expansion phase. They must see job opportunities and believe that things are getting better. We measure this with a consumer confidence index survey. Central banks help this recovery process with lower interest rates which encourages borrowing to make purchases such as cars and houses. Governments can also help this process with increased purchases, reduced tax rates and expansionary policies, although it often moves so slowly that these measures are usually late in coming and end up being incorrectly timed.

When the economy is expanding, certain pressures build up in the reverse direction which ultimately causes the expansion phase to end. Conversely, in a recession, the same occurs, causing the retraction to end. One simple example; in a recession people stop buying new cars as often, their existing car gets older and older, and eventually becomes a financial burden to maintain. Their total household debt gradually is reduced as time passes with no new borrowing. Eventually consumers bite the bullet, borrow, and buy a car. Somewhere people who build cars are put to work, who then have funds to make purchases. 70% of all US purchases are made by consumers (Gov't and business are the rest) and recessions only end when consumers start spending again.

There are certain categories of stocks which are likely to do better in an economic expansion, and vice versa. Investors try to anticipate these business cycles so they can adjust their holdings accordingly. Hardly scientific, professional investors try to start adjusting their holdings approximately 6-9 months before the business cycle enters a new phase. It's nearly impossible to do. It's often said that economists have predicted nine of the last 4 recessions.

You will do better with your savings if you pay attention to these economic changes. Most of this is common sense. If a recession is starting, it's best not to own luxury goods companies, for example. The only problem is that no one has been able to accurately predict when business cycles are moving into the next phase.

An economic recovery has been going on since the very deep 2007-08 recession, added by low interest rates. Corporate earnings have slowed down in 2019 and other signs of slowing have emerged. Does this signal a coming recession? When? 2020? 2021?

Most investors are currently staying strongly committed to equities, happy to ride the wave of expansion. However, investors in 2019 have become much more risk averse, shifting to low yielding bonds and buying defensive stock categories such as consumer durables, REITs, and utilities.

Takeaway: It is very hard to predict business cycles. History shows that there are no reliable "predictive" indicators, despite how many articles you read which make claims that certain indicators are "flashing red". I think these articles are mostly written as "click bait" - draw readers in and then bombard them with ads. Since we don't really know what's going to happen, it's unwise to make major changes to your investments - lighten up in some groups and add to others.

For example, if economic conditions appear to be worsening, you may benefit by reducing consumer discretionary and high beta groups and using the proceeds to add to your defensive groups like utilities, REITs, health care, and bond surrogates. Don't make drastic changes like reducing exposure to zero unless business or economic conditions there are very poor or highly unstable. For example, as an active investor, I have reduced my exposure to Great Britain to zero pending a conclusion to Brexit and cut way back on Europe until Trump decides not to tariff imported autos, which are critical to Germany. ETFs allow you to allocate investments to exactly where you choose.

BETA

The term "beta" is simply an arithmetic measure of a stock's volatility, by measuring its sensitivity to the movement of the overall stock market, which is determined by regression analysis. The S&P 500 is usually used as the benchmark. The beta of the S&P 500 is expressed as one (1.0). The beta of an individual stock or ETF is based on how it performs in relation to the index's beta. A stock with a beta of 1.0 indicates that it moves exactly in tandem with the S&P 500.

If a stock's performance has historically been more volatile than the market as a whole, its beta will be higher than one. For example, a stock with a beta of 1.2 is 20% more volatile than the market. So if the S&P 500 rises 10%, a stock with a beta of 1.2 would be expected to rise by 12%. Of course, beta works both ways. If the S&P 500 falls 10%, a stock with a beta of 1.2 would be expected to fall by 12%. The higher a stock's beta, the more volatile it is.

While a stock's beta measures its volatility, it does not necessarily predict direction. A stock that performs 50 percent worse than the S&P 500 in a down market and a stock that performs 50 percent better than the S&P 500 in an up market will each have a high beta.

If you are the type of investor who is easily rattled by market volatility, you may want to seek out investments that have a lower beta. Conversely, if you are seeking potentially higher returns in exchange for higher risk, higher beta stocks may be overweight. Most utilities stocks have a beta of less than 1. Conversely, most high-tech, Nasdaq-based stocks often have a beta of greater than 1, offering the possibility of a higher rate of return, but also posing more volatility. A common period for measuring beta is 3 years.

For example, as of July 2018 the PowerShares technology ETF QQQ (NASDAQ), has a beta of 1.2 when measured against the S&P 500 Index. Vanguards VWO ETF (emerging markets) has a beta of 1.08. Vanguards VPU ETF (utilities) has a beta of .17.

Volatility and risk are not the same thing. They are related to each other and often the terms are used interchangeability, which is incorrect. Volatility is one aspect of risk. Risk is best measured by return. High yield bonds issued by weak companies carry greater risk, and so the return is higher. However, HYG, the popular junk bond ETF, has a beta of only .12. See for example: HYG

> ***Takeaway***: Since most people do not like to see the value of their investment portfolio going up and down like a yo-yo, they equate this with risk. Each of us has a different sensitivity to volatility, and you must invest so that sleeping at night does not present a problem. When making investment choices look at the beta - investments with numbers above one move up and down by greater than the S&P 500, and numbers below one move less. Remember that volatility is only one element of risk. The beta for a security or ETF is listed on the summary page at Yahoo.com and under Performance and Research on Fidelity's website.

ALPHA

"Alpha" is another common term you may encounter if you are researching actively managed investments. Unlike beta, which simply measures volatility, alpha measures a portfolio manager's ability to outperform a market index. Alpha is a measure of the difference between a portfolio's actual return and the return of its benchmark index.

For example, if a mutual fund returned 10% in a year in which the S&P 500 rose only 7%, that fund would have an alpha of 3 (%). Conversely, if the fund gained 10% in a year when the S&P 500 rose 15%, it would earn an alpha of minus 5 (%). The baseline measure for alpha is zero, which would indicate an investment performed exactly the same as its benchmark index.

Generally, if you were investing in a mutual fund or other type of managed investment product, you would seek out managers with a higher alpha. Alpha and beta are based on historical data.

Seeking Alpha is a euphemism for beating the market. As discussed in this paper, beating the market over an extended period (after expenses) is a rare and elusive event, and pursuing this goal is a fool's errand. With an ETF you buy the index instead of trying to beat it.

RELATIVE STRENGTH INDEX

The Relative Strength Index or RSI is a momentum indicator that measures the magnitude of recent price changes, to determine overbought or oversold conditions, using historical share price data to arrive at a value. It is primarily used to attempt to identify <u>overbought</u> or <u>oversold</u> conditions in the trading of an asset, or of the market as a whole. The index takes the average gain of up periods during the specified time frame and divides it by the average loss of down periods during the same time frame. The default time frame is 14 trading days. The index value ranges from 0 to 100.

Traditional interpretation and usage of the RSI is that values of 70 or above indicates that a security or a market is becoming overbought or overvalued, and therefore, may be primed for a trend reversal or corrective pullback in price. An RSI reading of 30 or below is commonly interpreted as indicating an oversold or undervalued condition that may signal a trend change or corrective price reversal to the upside. Traders use extreme values of the RSI as a buy or sell indicator.

The RSI is nothing more than a momentum indicator for the time period being used. It's a technical indicator based solely on historical evidence. Historical price information is not a reliable predictor of future price movements. If the market as a whole has an RSI above 70, it indicates buying has been especially strong over the time period used, and a reversion to the mean has become more likely.

Computers making buy/sell decisions use RSI as one of their inputs. A long-term investor does not have to be concerned about the RSI, but an RSI around 30 may indicate a favorable entry point to put some idle cash to work.

MARKET PULLBACKS, CORRECTIONS and RECESSIONS

"Pullbacks" are somewhat loosely defined. The term is generally used to describe a price reduction in a stock of 5 – 10%. This triggers an increase in trading volume, as investors reassess their positions – bargain hunters move in and buy, holders of a stock may decide to sell at the reduced price and move on, long term investors largely ignore these aberrations.

A "Correction" is defined as an overall market or stock reduction in prices of 10% from the recent high. In the last 100 years, these happen, on average, once per year (however we have had 2 in 2018). The Dow Jones Industrial average used to be used to measure a "market" correction, but now most use the S&P 500, a better indicator of the overall market. Corrections do not last long, 72 trading days on average or about 3 months, but have been shorter in recent years due to traders "buying on the dip". Most investors do not panic over a correction and are willing to wait it out. Traders look to buy at reduced prices.

A "<u>Bear Market</u>" is defined as an overall market or a stock reduction in prices of 20% or more from the recent high. Bear markets average <u>15 months</u> in length and happen statistically every 3.5 years. In the last 50 years (1968) there have been 6 bear markets as measured by the S&P 500. The longest period in history <u>without</u> a bear market was 120 months (1991-2001). As of July 2018 we have had 111 months without a bear market. Bull markets do not end merely because of their age - it takes an economic event for that to happen. The average decline in the stock market in a bear market is 35%, so these are serious. Bouncebacks have been quicker of late, due to value buyers, contrarians, and buying on the dip.

Many investors panic in a bear market. It's too painful and too long for them to do nothing, so they sell some or all of their holdings, which or course prolongs the downturn (I hate those guys).

A "<u>Recession</u>", is defined by economists as two or more consecutive quarters of GDP contraction. Over the last 50 years, they average 10 months in duration and happen every 5 years. The last US recession was 12/07-6/09. Bear markets do not always culminate in recessions, but usually do.

Historically recessions have been caused by:

- External shocks to the economy such as the OPEC oil embargo or a world war;
- Asset bubbles which burst, such as the 2000 dot com crash, or the housing/subprime mortgage crash of 2008;
- Unsustainable price increases causing severe inflation, together with interest rate increases by the Fed to rein in inflation.

Sometimes it is difficult to identify a single underlying cause, and there may be evidence it was caused by normal business cycles.

The biggest fear of a stock market investor is a recession. Stock prices will decline materially, pretty much across all sectors, and possibly for an extended period of time, as company earnings decrease. The shock of seeing your savings drop by as much as 50% is enough to frighten anyone. Whenever we have one, a number of non-professional investors will leave the equity market and not return. The pain is too great.

It's recommended to watch the indicators enumerated below closely, because the consequences of doing nothing can be painful. The consensus is that the stock market anticipates changes in economic cycles by about 6 months, which is not a precise number, but more of a subjective guess.

If economic indicators indicate a recession is likely or imminent, the market will start dropping about 6-9 months before it actually occurs. For the same reason, the market will start climbing about 6 months before the recession comes to an end. By the time you're in a recession it's too late to do anything about it, so you need to know the signs that a recession may be coming.

Economists often refer to the big four recession indicators, they are:

1. *Decreasing or flat Industrial Production. Companies are cutting back the volume of goods they produce.*

2. *Declining or flat Personal income. The total dollar personal income in the country – what people are earning, has plateaued or is decreasing.*

3. *Decreasing or flat non-farm employment. An increasing unemployment rate or a reducing trend in hours worked.*

4. *Decreasing or flat real retail sales. Total sales adjusted for inflation.*

All of these variables are reported on by the government at different times of the month. These changes take place gradually, so you don't have to stay tuned continuously, but make a note to read about these factors from time to time. The obvious trigger for your doing so is the release of the US unemployment rate, which always makes front page reading. If a recession is starting to look probable, you will see lots of articles discussing the factors above.

Monthly ups and downs to all these factors are normal, as are business cycles. These result in bull and bear markets. As a long-term investor, you need to be able to tolerate these cycles. However, when you start to see consecutive declines in any of these factors for 3 months or more, it is time to pay closer attention, as a recession may be looming.

A fifth possible indicator of an oncoming recession is a flattening, or an inverted yield curve. The yield curve refers to interest rates graphed versus the years to maturity. Typically, short-term interest rates are lower than long-term rates, so the yield curve slopes upwards, reflecting higher yields for longer-term investments. Higher long-term rates take into account future economic growth, inflation, and risk. For example, a one-year loan has a lower interest rate than a 30-year mortgage.

An inverted yield curve occurs when short-term interest rates exceed long-term rates, which may signal worsening economic conditions in the future (but also may not).

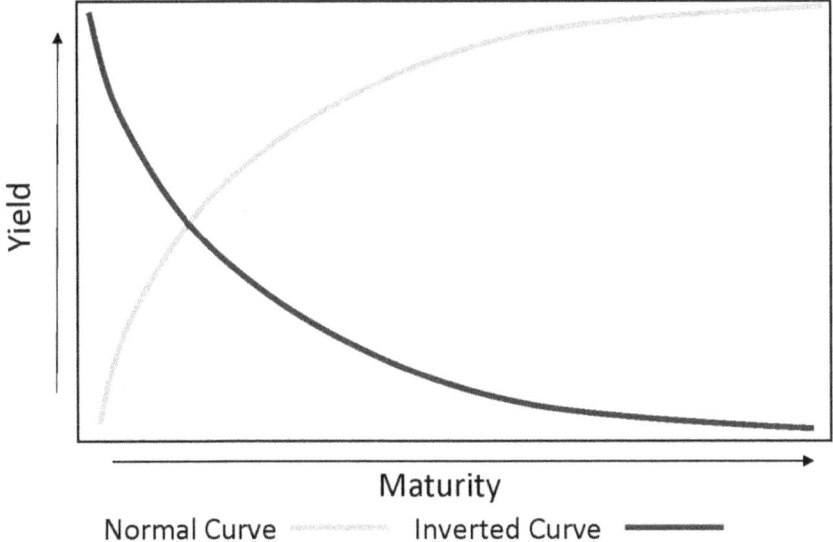

From an economic perspective, a flattening or inverted yield curve is a noteworthy event. An actual inversion in certain bond maturities is occurring as of this writing (5/19).

Many analysts attribute this to the Fed's unprecedented tightening measures, and historically low interest rates in other countries, as opposed to an oncoming recession. Despite this flattening, we are experiencing strong fundamental growth in our economy.

Since our economy in mid-2019 is presently moderately strong, with an unprecedented low unemployment rate, no recession is seen as likely in the near term, hence the debate continues as to what the flattening yield curve is telling us, if anything. If you would like to read further see: Inverted Yield Curve

If a recession looks to be on the horizon there are things you can do to reduce risk and minimize (not eliminate) your losses without dumping all of your investments. See "Reducing Risk"

MARKET TIMING

Market timing is a strategy where you attempt to maximize your overall return by selling all or most of your investments when prices are deemed to be too high, and you believe prices are highly likely to decrease materially going forward, and then re-invest those funds at a future date when you believe prices have bottomed, and are going to increase going forward.

The term applies to wholesale moves in and out of the market by selling investments and holding cash instead, as opposed to moving in and out of a particular stock (trading).

The determinant of whether prices are high or low is often determined by the average price/earnings multiples (see section above). As to whether the stock market is going to be headed higher or lower is in the eyes of the beholder. But for most of us it is an expectation we reach after reading and listening to experts discuss what is going on with our economy, and the thousands of variables which affect it.

When the list of problems or obstacles the economy faces becomes much longer, or seemingly greater than the positive influences, investors become gloomy, and start predicting dire consequences ahead, such as the probability of a recession.

As one market timer put it, "those who get out first, get out best" meaning those who sell at the beginning of a downturn will get higher prices than those who don't reduce their holding until after a serious downturn has already occurred. Unfortunately, no one knows when these market movements will occur, so this expression has no meaningful value. (There are a lot of unemployed fund managers who believed this).

The problem is that there are always doomsday prophets, who enumerate the serious political and business problems which are present, and it's difficult to ignore their advice to sell, for fear of being wrong.

The practice seems intuitively simple and logical. If you're a smart person who pays attention to the state of our economy, corporate profitability, the level of stock market prices, and all the geo-political factors which affect business earnings, you reason that I should be able to anticipate <u>major</u> overall moves in stock prices, both upward and downward.

Fear is often the primary motivator here. You have your life savings invested in stocks and bonds. Your greatest financial fear is to lose this money, which is critical to your being able to have a comfortable retirement. When the doomsayers start talking about huge future risks, the first inclination is to sell everything and move into cash.

Unfortunately, it's like a carnival game. Market timing looks easy to do, but it's quite impossible, and many studies have shown how poorly market timers do.

Overall market timing, where you move wholesale into and out of the market, cannot be done successfully. Market timers will have terrible returns, or losses. The reasons for this are many, but people continue to do it. They may believe that they can time the market, or they may have simply become panicked after reading a prognostication that the market is heading into a dark tunnel. A recent study done by Wells Fargo Investment Institute (Mar 15 2019) corroborated the results of several previous studies. It found that investors who remained fully invested in their assets for the long term received a much higher return - 7.61% since 1989, a 30-year span. Investors who were not invested on just 10 of the best market days had their return reduced to 5.1%.

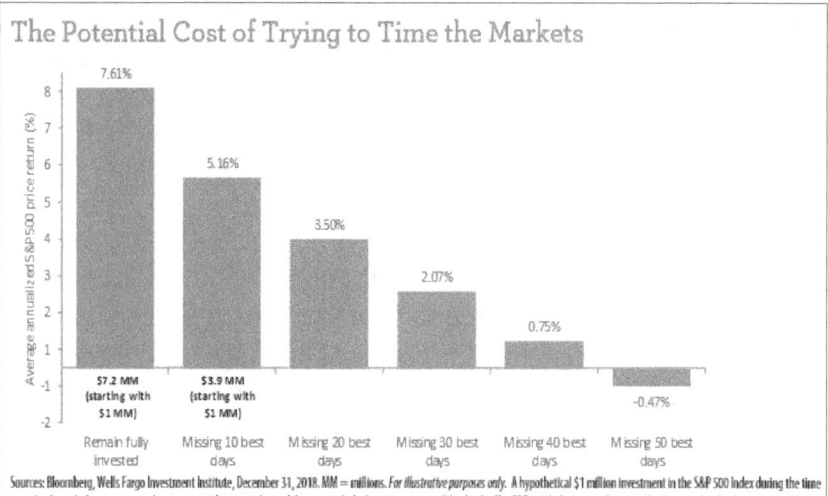

The primary reason it doesn't work is that no one can predict the future. The strategy requires you to identify not only the price peaks, but also the valleys—doing even one of these is impossible.

Also, the market will experience large price increases on a very small number of days each year. If you are not invested on those few days, your return will drop significantly. The drop off in return is startling, sometimes reducing an up year's gains to losses. Obviously, no one can predict when these huge up days will occur.

The data shows that market timers do not stay invested a long enough period of time to reap the rewards that the market can offer more disciplined investors. The data also shows that when investors react, they generally make the wrong decision.

Professor and Nobel Laureate William Sharpe wanted to identify the percentage of time a market timer would need to be correct to break even relative to a benchmark (index) portfolio. He concluded a market timer must be correct 74% of the time to outperform a passive portfolio at a comparable level of risk. Subsequent studies have concluded that market timers need to be correct between 70-85% of the time to outperform a comparable passive portfolio, validating Sharpe's work.

Professional market timers also lose. A recent study by Mark Hurlbert in April 2018 analyzed the results of over 60 professional market timers, over the two large price increases and corresponding drops in the first three months of 2018. <u>The timers had it completely wrong, being highly invested at the peaks (when they should have been sold out) and being invested minimally at market bottoms (when they should have been invested heavily).</u> They bought high and sold low. They thought they could predict the future - the most common investing mistake there is.

If you have what you believe to be enough uninvested cash so you can survive a market downturn of say 12 months without having to sell, then you can ride out a downturn if it does occur (as many of us learned in 2008-09). Also, market declines have been getting shorter and shorter as astute investors start buying when prices have declined significantly.

Takeaway: Market timing can be looked upon as the bad result of a reasonable investing strategy, which is taken to extremes. If market risk appears to be high and/or stock prices are at a very high level based upon historical price/earnings multiples, it may make sense to reduce risk somewhat, and build up your cash reserves - but not to sell out.

Trying to follow strategies like selling in May and going away, and the thousands of other similar market timing adages (even if they don't rhyme) is foolish and will reduce your total gains. These adages are true sometimes and sometimes they're not. Since you don't know which will happen, you end up uninvested during periods of market growth.

Everybody makes mistakes. This is an unpredictable environment. Shift weightings, not wholesale changes, and your mistakes will be measured and not catastrophic.

Investment gains are maximized by the amount of time you are invested, and market timing reduces the amount of time your funds are at work for you. Time in the markets will always beat timing the markets.

REDUCING RISK

The best investing strategy is to establish a diversified portfolio, contribute to it on a periodic sustained basis, and then re-visit it monthly, or at least quarterly, and make changes you believe make sense based upon economic conditions. You revisit your investments and increase the weighting or decrease the weighting (sometimes to zero) of each investment choice, recognizing that normal business cycles are inevitable. This process however becomes much more important and critical if an economic recession is approaching.

It has become popular to describe the collective mood of investors as "risk on" or "risk off". When the market is described as risk on it means investors, collectively, are increasing risk by buying equities because they see the market positives outweighing the negatives going forward, lifting prices. Good economic news or an absence of negative news, leads to higher prices and momentum traders exaggerate the upward trend.

When the market is described as risk off, it means investors are reducing risk by selling equities because of the fear of lower prices. This fear may be caused by political uncertainty, negative economic reports, excessive market volatility, companies reporting reduced earnings, or just about any serious negative news. If investors collectively sell equities they will accumulate cash, which they may hold, or they may invest in one or more of the so called "defensive" asset categories, which are deemed to be less risky, and usually hold their price level, or decline less, during market downturns.

A recession, or more accurately the fear of a recession, is the ultimate risk off period. Stocks will go down a lot and for an extended period. Therefore, is it very important to adjust your portfolio if one is expected (Recessions are predicted much more often than they actually occur). If you believe the chances of a recession are high, say more than 50%, within the next 6-9 months you should take steps to reduce risk.

One way of reducing risk is too do some selling of riskier investments, and less volatile investments such as those with betas greater than 1.0, and to increase your level of cash or near cash. Conversely, when price/earnings multiples are low and/or the economy is gaining strength, it makes sense to put a greater proportion of savings to work, decreasing cash and perhaps moving into some higher return/higher risk categories, like smaller companies for example.

You will do better if you make these changes <u>gradually</u>, as your expectations are either borne out, or found to be incorrect. Making wholesale changes in a short time span is discouraged by most financial advisors. Gradual changes reduce volatility and can be a lifesaver if you make an incorrect choice.

Overweighting lower risk/lower return assets will not eliminate reductions in principal but will reduce them. (Remember these are only paper losses unless you sell and "take" the loss). In the recession of 2008, arguably a much worse event than the 1929 crash, the S&P 500 lost 50% of its value, REIT's lost 65%, and high yield bonds lost 30%. Bank of America, my former employer, saw its stock fall from $55 to $4, as no one knew how much the bank's mortgages were worth. (The bank's purchase of Countrywide Mortgage, and its portfolio of uncollectable mortgages, nearly sank the bank). The only asset class which did not decrease in value during that recession was US government bonds.

<u>Here then, are some suggestions to reduce risk:</u>

1. <u>Increase cash or cash equivalents</u>. Increasing cash is the same as not investing, so you do not want to overdo this. Cash doesn't go down, but its buying power goes down as inflation marches on. This is especially a problem today because cash in a savings vehicle like a bank CD pays very little. Read the "Cash" section of this paper and think about increasing your safety funds – but not more than 25 or 30% of your total savings. Another choice is "near cash", which are funds held in low risk, low return vehicles such

as a short-term bond ETF. There are a number of choices here - see ETF Choices.

2. <u>Reduce stock holdings and increase bond holdings</u>. When the economy is growing reasonably, bonds produce low returns and are at risk of principal losses if interest rates are increased. However, if the economy is slowing down or has entered into negative growth, stocks will drop in value by significant amounts as a result of reduced business earnings. Also, the Fed will probably reduce interest rates to stimulate growth, which will cause bonds to increase in value. For the seven years following the '08-'09 financial collapse, bonds have benefited from artificially low interest rates set by the Fed. Consider a portfolio with a higher proportion of bonds than equities, but only do this if the chance of a near term recession is high according to most analysts.

3. <u>Increase diversification</u> as much as possible across various asset classes. By dividing your portfolio up into several small diversified segments, your losses will be mitigated. Include:

   a. Own all <u>size</u> companies, large, mid-cap, and small (but less small because they are weaker companies)
   b. Own <u>Real Estate</u> - REITs
   c. Diversify <u>geographically</u> - Worldwide
   d. Diversify by <u>industries</u> including utilities
   e. Own varying bond types – Government, Corporate, municipal, and ultra-short bond ETFs.
   f. Own varying asset types – such as preferred stock, low volume ETFs (SPLV)

4. <u>Move stock holdings into defensive categories</u> (besides holding cash) including bonds, preferred stock, consumer staples, dividend stocks, low volatility (beta) stocks, value stocks, REITs, utilities, and healthcare. Healthcare stocks have long been thought of as a defensive category because the demand for healthcare remains relatively constant even in poor economic conditions. However many, including myself, consider healthcare a growth

industry as well, as demand for healthcare increases largely due to an aging population. Thus, healthcare has both growth and resistance to economic contractions, making it my favorite market sector.

5. <u>Reduce consumer discretionary ETFs</u> - where consumers may postpone purchases, such as autos, durable goods like appliances and furniture, leisure products, travel related companies (airlines, hotels), restaurants, and especially luxury goods, especially boats and jewelry.

6. <u>Reduce investments in growth categories and move the money into value</u> categories.

7. <u>Reduce high beta and increase low beta investments.</u> The ETF SPLV (low volatility) has a beta of .68.

8. <u>Sell any leveraged or inverse ETFs</u> you own, which magnify gains and losses by 2 or 3 times. I don't recommend these in any market, as they increase volatility. The market is quite volatile enough in my view, without doubling or tripling it.

9. <u>Sell anything classified as high or above average risk</u>. I would include high yield debt, debt of foreign sovereigns, equities in weak foreign economies, collateralized debt, collateralized loan obligations, crypto currency, hedge funds, private company investments, foreign exchange currencies, stock options, IPOs, venture capital, high yield REITs, and penny stock.

DO NOT – sell everything. Do not sell short, which is a trading strategy where you realize gains if the investment goes down. Selling short is for day traders and professionals who watch the market continuously. Similarly, do not invest in ETFs that short the market.

If you make some of these moves, remember to start unwinding them not after the recession is over, but when the worst seems to be over. Remember professional investors are always focusing forward and trying to anticipate economic changes, so expect the market to start turning up 6 months before the recession is officially over. The cost of selling one ETF, and buying another is only $10, so the expense of making changes is microscopic compared to the losses you may mitigate or avoid.

Do not think of this as a massive project, or you will put it off. As you begin to hear more and more commentary concerning a slowing economy, gives some thought to making gradual changes to reduce risk as outlined above. You can make trades in the evening while relaxing at home. They will execute at the market open. (Fidelity will give you a warning if you do this. They want you to understand that the market may open higher or lower in the morning, therefore your trade may execute at a slightly higher or lower price than its previous day close. The difference may be important to day traders, but not to long-term investors.)

VOLATILITY

Stock market volatility has soared in 2018. Triple digit gains and losses in the Dow have become common. This is not healthy for the average long-term investor. Wild swings convince many small investors that the stock market may be too risky for their life savings. Surveys show that many investors have become disillusioned with stocks due to this volatility, and have gone exclusively into bonds or cash, which as highlighted often in this paper, produce meager returns, and in periods of increasing interest rates, actual negative returns - before even considering inflation.

The economic recession of '07-'08 has taken its toll. Huge swings in the Dow and flash crashes haven't helped either. A recent study from Bankrate found that 30 percent of millennials (those aged 18 to 37) say cash is the best place to put money you won't need for 10 years or more. Just 21 percent of those 38 and older say the same. Less than a quarter of millennials cited investments in the stock market as the No. 1 way to <u>store money long-term</u>, even though <u>that's what experts recommend</u>. Close to 77 percent favor other options, including cash, real estate, gold and bitcoin (which decreased 73% in 2018). My guess is they heard their parents talking about lost savings.

A large part, if not most of this volatility is caused by the huge volume of shares being traded by computers buying and selling, independent of humans. No one knows how much of the share volume is being traded today by robots, but estimates are at least 40% and perhaps as much as 80%. Some quant funds focus on very small daily changes in prices and make money by doing high volume trades. Day traders thrive on this increased volatility, and love to see swings of 300-400 Dow points in a day. Their computers, using immediate price and volume data, predict movement and then execute high volume trades to capture price movement within minutes, and in some cases, seconds.

All of this is particularly offensive and disturbing to the average long-term investor. It galls me to see my life savings getting whipped around by trades which have absolutely nothing to do with fundamental investing. Even worse, to hear high frequency traders bragging about how much they are making due to increased volatility.

Unfortunately, there is absolutely nothing that can be done about this, and it's probably going to get worse. The holy grail of stock trading has always been a fool proof method of buying and selling, and computers, loaded with algorithms, take this concept to the next level.

The owners of the stock markets themselves benefit greatly from the increased volume, so they have no interest in making changes. Whenever there is a "flash crash", where stock prices crash in one day or hour because of runaway computer trades, a NYSE spokesperson will say they are looking into the issue and will advise of future corrective measures. In fact, no corrective measures are ever taken – it would reduce their profits. The so-called circuit breakers, which stop trading at certain levels, are placed so high that they are almost never activated.

On Feb. 5th 2018 the Dow average dropped by 1,175 points or 4.6%. The S&P 500 was down 113 points or 4.1%. The circuit breakers did not kick in because the <u>first threshold for halting trading is drop of 7.1%.</u> In other words, the stock market has to go into utter freefall before a circuit breaker is tripped. The owners of the stock markets make millions on days like this.

Therefore, we have to live with this "new world", which requires an increase in patience, and a stronger stomach, which the younger generation seems to have trouble with - understandably so.

The fact remains that stocks are the only liquid means of obtaining a return of 8-10% per year, and the vast majority of people, young and old, need to earn more than 2 or 3% on their savings in order to not outlive their nest egg. Companies keep pushing out older, higher paid employees to cut costs, while at the same time our life expectancy keeps getting greater.

If you become troubled about this, take a look at a very long-term chart of the S&P 500 like this one, and gain some comfort seeing how remarkable this index has performed when daily changes are ignored.

S&P 500 Large Cap Index – 90 Year Historical Chart

You can also benefit from not looking at the market each day, something which I have trouble doing.

The increase in high frequency computer trading does produce some benefits - such as an increase in market liquidity, lower transaction costs, and also by reducing buy/sell spreads (brokers profit spreads), which is some consolation. Lastly, embrace passive investing using indices, where daily activity is of less concern to you.

> *Takeaway*: Stock pickers say investing in averages means you'll never do better than the average. Fortunately, the averages, particularly the stock market averages, have done quite nicely as the chart above shows - producing returns consistently greater than the rate of inflation, when measured over time.

III. INVESTMENT CHOICES
CASH

People used to refer to cash as an investment. When money market funds used to pay interest rates of 5% or more, that classification would be accurate (and may still be again someday). Then, you could say you were 60% in stocks, 30% in bonds and 10 % in cash, which had a real return (and low risk). However, since our Federal Reserve, and the Central Banks around the world have been trying to stimulate their economies, they have lowered interest rates to zero or below zero in some countries (Japan, Germany), and as a result, today cash either has had no return whatsoever, or such a low yield it will not measurably affect your return. The return on cash, in 2019, is so small it should properly be classified as a non-investment" or "withheld investment." It essentially represents money you have chosen not to invest.

Since the Fed began raising rates in Dec 2016, the return on cash has risen, as major bank CD's are approximately 2.5-2.9% (1/2019).

Uninvested cash that you do not need from day-to-day, falls into two categories - <u>timing,</u> and <u>safety</u>. <u>Timing</u> means you have held back investing money to wait for a better time to buy. Perhaps you think stock prices are too high, or a down-turn in prices is coming. Maybe you have this money because you sold something you thought had reached a peak in value, so you could buy it back later at a lower price, or perhaps buy something else in the future. This is a conscious decision to wait before investing this money, which you intend to deploy at some point.

It may make sense to increase cash somewhat if the market has reached a very high level (see price earnings ratio) which you believe may possibly be unsustainable. In this way you can reduce your loss if prices retreat, and also <u>provide cash for future buys</u>. This action is a strategic un-weighting, a risk reduction, not a sale of all or much of your entire portfolio.

The second category for holding cash is <u>safety.</u> You need to have a reserve of cash for emergencies and unexpected expenses, or worse, a reduction in your income or loss of employment. In the future you may be able to take out loans to cover these expenses, however if you have lost your job you may not qualify for a loan, and also obtaining a loan in the future may come with a high interest rate. So the issue becomes how much cash do I need, and how can I keep this amount as low as prudently possible, since it will not return more than 2% at best.

Having an open line of credit, like a home equity line of credit (with no annual fee), is recommended to reduce cash needs. This is because if something bad happens, you may not be eligible to borrow at that time. Companies like USAA do not charge any annual fees for a home equity line. (There are initial fees, including the appraisal). These lines of credit have variable interest rates and you do not want to have a large balance on one when interest rates are rising, if possible. If you do not own a home, a credit line on a credit card can help. The negatives are that if you do use it, the interest charges will be very high, and further, the credit card company can reduce your credit line at any time.

Note: Under the Fed Tax reduction passed in early 2018, interest on home equity loans is no longer deductible unless it was used to "buy, build, or substantially improve your home". How that is determined is beyond me, since money is fungible, making unclear its source or use.

However, the most important reason to hold cash for safety is so you are not forced into selling your investments, especially tax deferred investments like 401(k)s, to raise cash for expenses, during a down market. This cannot be over emphasized. When people have serious financial problems, caused for example by terrible health care costs, a common solution is to start selling investment savings. If the market happens to be in a pullback at that time, you will be wiping out previous gains, or possibly realizing losses. To preserve your returns, you must sell when the market is favorable.

Markets will always have downturns or pull backs, and it is true that they are actually needed, and are therapeutic for the market - 5-10% pull backs are going to happen, even if the economy is doing OK. This is often necessary to flush out speculators and eliminate bubbles. It's very important to weather these downturns without selling.

How much cash should you hold for safety? This is a very difficult question to answer. A lot depends on your life situation, your job situation, your family, your health, whether you have equity in a home, whether you have an open credit line and whether you might be called upon to help pay for health care for a close relative. I think cash to cover normal living expenses for 6 months should be a minimum, with some open credit available, 9 months is better.

You can always sell stocks and get cash in 3 days. Stock downturns are lasting for shorter periods in recent years, which is fortunate, so a downturn of 5-10% should be over in one or two months. A bear market, a decrease of 20%, happens infrequently, thank goodness, but these downturns take longer to recover – perhaps 6-12 months.

Downturns have shortened, that is, a recovery in prices has come faster in recent years, because of the popularity and success of the "buy the dip" strategy. In a market which is moving up, the only way to do better than the overall averages is to hold some cash back for purchases when prices have declined. These purchases push the market back up, and hopefully you will have a gain. This strategy is very popular right now, especially since the market has been going up fairly steadily since March 2009. Professional money managers always retain some "dry powder" to take advantage of market pullbacks, as a way of improving their return performance (and their subsequent salary bonus).

If you absolutely have to sell shares in a down market, you can deduct some of these losses from any capital gains you may have. (In down years, your capital gains are probably zero, however).

GOLD (and precious metals)

Gold is a commodity, but it needs to be discussed separately because of its unique value characteristics. Its price is determined like all commodities by supply and demand. Unfortunately, the supply and demand for gold is impossible to determine.

The demand for gold is affected by individual consumers, manufacturers, investors (for gold funds) and sovereign countries for their currency reserves. Countries hold large amounts of gold and sometimes buy or sell large quantities of gold, but do not reveal doing so. If they disclose that they are buying gold, its price will increase, increasing the cost of their purchase, and vice versa. (As I write this Venezuela is selling gold because of serious economic crises there). Sovereign buying/selling is the largest single factor affecting the price of gold, yet you won't know about it until after the fact. Other factors like the gold buying season in China, for use in jewelry and manufacturing are not significant.

Recently with the advent of gold trust ETFs such as GLD and IAU have affected the overall demand for gold, as gold moves in and out of favor with investors and hedge funds.

The demand for gold breaks down as follows:

1. As a form of currency; largely a subjective, immeasurable factor from people or countries who fear the collapse of paper money.

2. As a hedge against inflation. Inflation is not the rising of prices; it's the reduced value of paper money. When inflation is high, people and countries buy gold which is less vulnerable to inflation than paper money. When inflation numbers are reported higher, gold usually rises as investors look for a store of value.

3. As a commodity used for the production of jewelry and other industrial applications, where it is used sparingly because of cost. This factor is relatively small.

4. As a hedge against falling stock prices. Gold and stock prices usually go in opposite directions, but not always. Having some gold can off-set stock declines.

The supply of gold is also difficult if not impossible to measure. Interruptions in mining operations, like miners' strikes, or political problems within a mining country, will affect prices somewhat, but not usually over extended periods. Other problems cloud the supply picture. If a mining company finds a large deposit, they will not disclose it, for fear prices will drop.

The worst feature of gold, by far, is that there is absolutely no way - none - to determine what the fair value of gold is. Attempts to value gold by comparing it to other variables, such as a certain multiple of the price of silver, have proven of no value. Analysts will often say it is undervalued or overvalued based upon a chart of past prices; however, this is absolute guessing. Price charts are of absolutely no worth in valuing gold.

Price is driven by fear more than anything else, and secondly inflation. Gold prices in the short run will go up when news of increased inflation occur, on news of increased economic growth (which can lead to inflation), and when the Fed increases interest rates (also signaling increased growth and inflation). No one knows whether the price will go up or down over longer periods, inasmuch as there is no way to value it.

Like other commodities, gold produces no income, and has no dividend, leaving its value open to conjecture.

The fear theory is that if a significant new fear hits the market, for example Trump threatens to take military action against North Korea, or starts a worldwide trade war, investors may be spooked. They may sell stocks, which will fall, and hoard cash or buy things that do not fluctuate with the value of paper money, like commodities, including gold.

The easiest and best way to own gold in my opinion is to buy the ETF IAU or GLD. Do not buy an ETF of gold miners, or gold mining companies. These are extremely volatile, moving as a multiple of the movement of gold, and have produced very poor returns.

Owning gold outright, like buying coins and putting them in a safe deposit box, involves storage costs, and is cumbersome to buy and sell, making it illiquid. Also, when you buy and sell, the dealer takes a significant profit on the difference between wholesale and retail price.

Be aware that when a gold ETF such as IAU is sold, your gain is subject to a 30% Federal tax, called the "Collectables" tax rate. If you do buy it, plan to hold it and/or only buy it in an IRA (where no capital gains are taxed – because taxes happen only when funds are withdrawn).

Because of the relatively high price of gold, now $1420/once, a number of smaller investors have resorted to silver seeking affordability. The price of silver has steadily trended lower since 2011, and now at $14 (5/19), it has not been a good investment. Investors have largely given up on silver as an investment.

Many people have subjective feelings about gold because of the fear that something bad might happen, and owning it provides some sort of psychological comfort, akin to putting money under the mattress.

It provides some diversification, as gold and stocks usually move inversely, however when you hold a small amount, say 5% of your portfolio, the effect on your total portfolio in dollar terms is small. Also because of its high absolute price, a significant gain of say $20/oz. only affects your investment balance by 1.5% or so, which doesn't help much. Further, gold does not always move inversely with stocks, because of its relationship with the value of the dollar.

Over the years I have owned a small amount of gold for diversification and added IAU into my portfolio in early 2018 as inflation was moving higher and Trump was possibly starting a trade war, which among other things will increase inflation in the US.

> *Takeaway*: Gold is an asset which is impossible to value moves up and down capriciously, is unpredictable and not understandable, and whose supply and demand is not determinable, but which may partially offset declines in a stock portfolio. In my view this is not such a great place to invest your life savings. Gold behaves more like a trading asset, where investors buy when global fear increases significantly, like the fear of a Middle East war, and then sell as those fears subside and the price of gold decreases. If you decide to add gold to diversify, I would buy IAU at perhaps 3-5% of your total. IAU and GLD are virtually the same except for the expense ratio – GLD is .40%, IAU is .25% (but their performance is the same). Do not, however, buy gold because you have determined it is undervalued, because that is the current definition of fool's gold.

ENERGY

Energy seems like a good place to invest because everybody needs it; people, businesses, and governments. Seems like a no brainer, yet investing in energy has been a minefield for several years, and for several different reasons. Any discussion of energy requires looking at its components.

Coal – Coal is a dying industry. Everybody knows it except Trump. The fantasy of "clean coal" has been proven to be unattainable because of prohibitive, uneconomic costs. The final straw dropped in 2017. A huge attempt to build a clean coal plant by The Southern company in Mississippi was abandoned in mid-construction. This plant was supposed to be an industry model for future clean coal plants. The runaway costs of the plant meant that the cost of the electricity produced would be cost prohibitive. The plant is being converted to natural gas, which is cheap and plentiful. Coal will disappear, first in the developed countries, and eventually in undeveloped countries. An investment suicide.

Wind – The wind industry is very small and fragmented. There are only 100K employees in the US, primarily in 5 western states. It will grow, but at present there is not enough investment choices to provide diversification as there are too few players. So far these companies have struggled financially, while some foreign companies have done better (Norway for example). Wind energy production has been flat in California, which was once the leader, since 2012. Texas has the most, and the Midwestern states are also growing.

Who doesn't like wind? It's free right? Unfortunately, like everything else there are difficult obstacles to growth. To build a farm you need large tracts of land (or sea rights) in a location with a strong and steady wind every day and be able to overcome existing land restrictions - which can be daunting. You must find financing for expensive towers and overcome resistance from environmentalists who raise a number of objections, such as ruining natural views and damaging bird populations. Also, a problem is maintaining supply when the wind stops, as current electricity storage solutions are expensive and limited in scope.

Perhaps the biggest obstacle is that the cost of the electricity produced, which is still high, especially compared to plants fueled by abundant and cheap natural gas. Solar energy production, which can be much cheaper, is a tough competitor, except in desolate areas with constant wind, and less sun, like Scandinavia. These issues make wind energy problematic and with insufficient diversification for the average investor. Large existing utility companies seem to have the best chance of success in this field.

Solar – The solar industry in the US is also very small, only 375K employees (4/17). Solar installations are growing very rapidly, both consumer and business, and the percentage of power produced by the sun is growing daily. Investors poured into solar companies in recent years expecting huge returns - it seemed like a no brainer. Get energy for free and then resell it. But unfortunately, it has been a disaster for them, for a number of diverse and unrelated reasons.

As of mid-2017 5 major companies have filed bankruptcy. Tesla may have saved Solar City from the same fate by buying it. Stock prices have cratered. Among the issues: Extremely low priced panels imported from China have wiped out the panel producers profit margins, demand from China has fallen off significantly (reasons unknown), fears that Federal tax credits will be reduced or eliminated (this has not happened, credits recently renewed), intense competition by installers has reduced profit margins, and investors fear existing panels may become obsolete as new more efficient panels are being developed (this has already happened). The cost of solar electric production still requires subsidies to be competitive (to cheap natural gas) and the payback period is quite long at about 10 years.

Meanwhile governments, federal and local, have been inconsistent, and in some cases harmful by creating laws and regulations which hinder growth. For example, allowing utility companies to charge solar users infrastructure fees, and higher rates (than non-solar customers). Also, reducing or eliminating "net metering", where solar users bill electricity back to the utility (the utilities don't want it). Utilities themselves have been unfriendly to solar while pretending to support it, for fear they may someday become obsolete.

A somewhat new issue being faced, in states like California, is that on sunny days the electricity produced using solar panels results in a surplus, with inadequate cost-effective storage technology available, the electricity must be sold at a loss, or is lost permanently.

As a result of these and other issues, solar investors, and companies, have suffered greatly. Someday these issues will be worked out, however for now the risks are too high for the average investor.

<u>Oil</u> – Oil is so dominant in the energy industry that it makes all other components insignificant. If you try to diversify and buy an energy ETF, like the biggest and most popular, XLE, your result will mirror the oil industry 100%. Exxon makes up 22% of that ETF, and all 10 of the top 10 holdings are oil companies. This is not really energy ETF, as it is an oil ETF. The stock of oil companies correlates 100% to the price of oil, no matter how hard the companies try to diversify and uncouple their stock price from the price of oil. Worse, the price of oil is virtually impossible to predict.

Like all commodities, the price of oil varies with supply and demand. I believe as a fossil fuel which is damaging to the planet, its long-term use will decline, eventually to close to zero, but not in our lifetime. Its use will go on for decades because most of the world runs on oil. It is cheap to pump out of the ground, and it is plentiful. Massive infrastructure in the industry has been built over the last 100 years, including wells, cargo ships, refineries, pipelines, storage facilities, retail locations, etc., which will guarantee cheap oil for many years. According to BP, the world has enough proven oil reserves to last until 2050, with no new finds. More than ample supplies have been supplemented with technological advancements like shale extraction, sand oil capture, and horizontal drilling.

Humans have become very good at finding and extracting oil out of the earth. At the present time we have more oil than we need. OPEC is cutting production to reduce excess supply, however, we still continue to have somewhat of a glut.

On the demand side, worldwide demand is still rising, but at a decreasing rate. This is because large undeveloped countries, which rely on oil for industrialization, are offsetting reduced demand in developed countries. In the future, albeit very gradually, growth in demand will be reduced by the growth of renewable energy, abundance of cheap natural gas (which burns cleaner), an increase in the use of electric motors in transportation, and the push by governments, environmentalists, and those concerned about climate change, to reduce the release of carbon into the atmosphere. Utilities are converting plants to cleaner natural gas as fast as economically possible,

As an investor, oil, and all of the related industry has been very poor for several years. The price has been going down since 2014 when it was about $100/barrel to the present level of about $53 (6/19). This decline has taken down the stocks of every oil related business with it, including drillers, transporters, storage firms, oil service and supply companies, and refiners. In June 2014 XLE, the largest energy ETF (primarily oil), was $101/share, today it is $61/share (6/19) - while the S&P 500 has gone up 46% in that period.

The problem for investors is that the price of oil is too volatile. The price of oil will continue to go up and down due to short term supply and demand imbalances, OPEC decisions, imposition of tariffs on oil producing countries, and a host of other factors which are not foreseeable, especially when geopolitical disputes occur. There are many investment firms which specialize in forecasting the oil industry, and they have all failed in this endeavor. The landscape is littered with investment banking companies like Morgan Stanley and Goldman Sachs which have incorrectly predicted a rise in the price of oil. Recently a number of firms have had to throw in the towel and conclude that predicting the price of oil is a fool's errand.

Takeaway: More than ample worldwide supplies and reserves, combined with downward pressures in demand due to incentives to use cleaner renewable power such as solar and wind, look to continue a poor long-term outlook for oil and all of the companies in this industry.

Many financial pundits are recommending energy investments today, in large part because they have declined so much, and their P/Es are low because of so much selling. This may be a good trading strategy but not a good investment strategy. My personal view is that oil, a fossil fuel, will gradually become the coal of tomorrow, and as a slowly dying commodity, should be avoided as a long-term investment. There are many who think prices are so low it is a time to buy. I am not one of them, especially if you're investing money for 20 or more years into the future, and not interested in short term price behavior.

XLE the largest energy ETF was $63 on Nov. 1, 2010 - as of June 25, 2019 it was $63. Nine years of no gain. Dead money by any measure.

INTERNATIONAL INVESTMENTS

The world economy is about $80 trillion. Numbers vary, but of that amount, the US is about 24%, Europe is 22%, China is 15%, and Japan is about 6%. If you invest only in the US you are excluding about 75% of the world GDP.

It's not quite that simple however, as large US companies do a large portion of their sales overseas. The S&P 500 does approximately 40% of its sales in foreign countries. Further complicating matters, foreign companies often build their products in the US, especially autos, to lower transportation costs, whereas US companies often outsource their production to lower labor cost countries. To not invest outside the US is missing an opportunity to diversify your portfolio and reduce risk and volatility.

History shows that the greater your diversity of portfolio, the better you'll do. Owning international investments is part of that diversification. It is generally recommended that in normal worldwide economic environments, it will improve your long term returns to have a significant portion of your portfolio in foreign country assets, the percentage depending on the strength of foreign economies, vis-à-vis the US. If US stocks are increasing more strongly than other countries, you would overweight US and have less overseas, perhaps 15%. If the US is declining or growing slowly, then you may want to increase foreign investments up to perhaps 25-30%.

Investments could include stocks, bonds, commodities, real estate, etc. However, for non-professional investors like us, our knowledge of market conditions overseas is limited. Do we really know enough about what's happening to commercial real estate in France, or whether Greece is able to fully pay its bond debt when due? We don't, so these areas are best left to professionals who specialize in certain countries or asset classes. Therefore, it is wise for us to stay with equities, common stocks of large companies, where local economic conditions are less relevant.

The worldwide economic situation however is rarely "normal", whatever that means, but if we stay abreast of world news, we will have at least some knowledge of which countries are experiencing healthy growth and which are in an economic recession (negative growth). Since as discussed, ETFs spread risk by owning the stock of many companies, you can maximize your returns by making investments in countries or larger geographic areas which are experiencing good economic conditions and minimizing or eliminating investments in countries experiencing economic downturn.

In 2018, Europe had begun to slow down, taking stocks with it. The reason is not clear, perhaps the fear of reduced central bank stimulus, or perhaps Trump tariff's effect on corporate costs. In previous years, Investors had moved into European stocks, where P/Es were lower than in the US, and the European central bank had reduced interest rates to zero, however, pessimism seems to be growing. Countries who export significantly to the US, especially Germany, are vulnerable to tariffs, and Germany has been the greatest source of economic strength in Europe in recent years.

Concern still lingers over economic conditions in certain countries where governments are struggling to repay large debts caused by years of government deficits. When interest rates increase to more normal levels, the interest cost on government debt will increase, making the deficits even higher. This often results in increased taxes, which hurt consumers and businesses alike. Countries which currently have these issues include Greece, Italy, Ireland, and Spain. England is doing OK however no one knows if Brexit, leaving the European Union, will hurt it significantly, if they ever achieve that aim.

For these reasons I would strongly advise against buying the bonds of a foreign government. If a sovereign government discloses that it will not meet, or perhaps have trouble making payments on its bond debt, the value of those bonds will fall precipitously and overnight.

Trump's attempt to reduce trade tariffs unfavorable to the US by threatening to withdraw from all of the existing trade agreements the US has previously agreed to, is creating nightmares for investors. No one knows when and how these trade wars will end, assuming they do. During these acrimonious trade negotiations, the stocks of many countries have fallen significantly, including China, Mexico, Canada, and Europe - primarily those countries who sell a significant amount of goods to the US. European ETFs like EZU, VGK, and emerging markets ETFs like FXI and EEM have fallen significantly. Some by 25%. (I have taken the drastic step of totally selling these and other international ETFs until the trade matter is somehow settled). Will Mercedes, Audis, BMWs, and Volkswagens have a 25% tariff if sold in the US? We have no idea, however the consequences of that creates an unsatisfactory level of risk for Germany, and any country with significant exports to the US.

The Far East has gone through a period of solid growth, including China, Australia, and New Zealand, however a slowdown is presently occurring. Commodity producing mines, which are a large part of the economies of Australia and New Zealand, have seen a downturn as construction in China has slowed from too fast to still strong. China is still the fastest growing country in the world, which argues for investing there, however when growth moderated from 9-10% to 6-7%, investors grew cautious and stock prices stalled. Stock prices there had been rising again as investors adjusted to the more reasonable growth rate of about 6.2%, however the tariff wars begun by Trump in 2018 have resulted in a horrible decline in Chinese stock prices. The level of risk is too high and stock prices have been plunging there.

It is generally not wise to reduce diversification through full reductions in asset categories, however the trade war which is presently ongoing is unprecedented, and the unpredictability of events is bad for business in several respects. China is bearing the brunt of the tariff war.

Japan had been in an economic slump for decades because of an aging and declining population. Their birth rate is only

1.4 babies per woman, and if a couple only produce 1.4 offspring, the population will decline and age (also immigration is weak). Consumer spending had been weak because of this. ETFs have been formed to allow investment in the Far East but <u>excluding</u> Japan such as EPP (which I have owned). Japan's Fed has taken drastic measures, reducing interest rates to below zero, and the economy has begun moving up again and their stock market has been achieving new highs. India looks to be moving into solid growth fueled by a large population, education, and outplacement income from the US. However, the country has a very long way to go to improve per capita GDP up to levels in developed countries.

These generalizations will obviously change, so it is suggested you read international business news from time to time to stay informed, if you have international investments. Bloomberg on TV and online does a great job of this. Since no one knows which countries or geographic areas will do well or poorly over extended periods, the solution is to almost always have some international exposure, but to overweight strong economic areas, and underweight weak economic areas, and avoid the problematic countries altogether.

That said however, the Trump administration is creating havoc in worldwide stock prices and investors and businessmen are in the dark as to the outcome. There has been a decline in international stock prices as described above, as investors have decided to reduce this exposure due to the additional risk which is now present.

Worldwide economic conditions generally change very slowly, as economic cycles are in the 3-5 year range in general, so there is no need to address portfolio changes every month. The Trump tariff wars is an unprecedented exception to this rule. To those with significant international exposure, a review should be done to evaluate the new risks posed by this reckless, one-man policy.

Normally it would be wise to go over your holdings quarterly to see if you want to make some changes. Changes are now very cheap to make, and quick and simple online. Sell something and buy something else and your transaction fee is only about $10. To be conservative, as a non-professional, buy ETFs which include only large companies in prospering countries or regions. Also, I would avoid bonds, commodities, and real estate in foreign countries unless you have above average familiarity and understanding of the country.

Buying stock ETFs in a single foreign country, like only Germany, or only Australia is not recommended for a retirement portfolio. Any investment based on a single foreign country will result in more risk because of a lack of diversification, and therefore will be more volatile, up and down. Better to pick a broad-based region ETF, such as Pacific or Far East or Europe. There is also all-world ETFs like Vanguard's VEU which excludes the US, which is an easy way to add international exposure, without drilling down further.

The U.S. has outperformed all other markets since the recession of 2008 primarily because of high tech company expansion. This will not last forever. The US is expected to continue to do well for the next couple of years, but it is likely that at some point other regions will perform better. This, if only because the US stock prices are at an all-time high (mid 2019) and other countries stocks are priced lower, and considered better buys as determined by their average P/E ratio. This is not meant to suggest chasing international stocks as a trader. As noted earlier, international investments add diversification, which has proven to increase long term portfolio returns.

Takeaway: Long term portfolios should have a portion in international investments. How much that should be is arguable. Recommendations usually start at about 15-20% and go up to as much as 50%. I think 30% is a reasonable middle ground, which I would increase or decrease as circumstances dictate. In light of the very serious trade was currently being conducted by Trump, many countries equities are suffering badly, and I have lowered that percentage accordingly.

If you already have investments in countries being significantly hurt by Trump's trade wars, I would not sell them. These issues will be resolved eventually, either by Trump or the president(s) who follow him. Economists all agree that the more trade the better, for both economies, and this logic will eventually prevail. Also, there will be a gain to stocks in those countries when an agreement is eventually reached with the US. I just hope I live long enough. Some of the issues in this trade war are not just economic but have national security implications (like Huawei for example) and this will mean the issues are not likely to be resolved completely or quickly.

EMERGING MARKETS

The classification Emerging Markets (EM) was initially intended to include countries whose economies were not fully developed. Presently 25 countries are categorized as emerging (by MSCI). To see a complete list go here: https://www.msci.com/market-classification. Largest among the countries in this classification is Mexico, Brazil, Russia, China, India, and South Korea.

Many investors choosing an emerging market ETF may not realize that the MSCI index many of these ETFs follow is very highly concentrated in just five countries - China 30%, So. Korea 15%, Taiwan 12%, India 9%, and Brazil 8%, total 74% - leaving only 28% for the rest of the world. There is nothing inherently wrong with this, only that investors choosing popular ETFs like EEM or VWO need to be aware of where the exposure is concentrated. If you buy a China ETF such as GXC, you will have a very large overlap.

This classification was supposed to be for countries with smaller and weaker economies, however, to include China and South Korea in this list, no longer makes sense. My guess this inclusion will be changed at some point. Samsung, for example, one of the largest companies in the world, being classified as an emerging market stock is wrong and misleading.

This investment category has historically been associated with greater risk and greater volatility, in both directions, and therefore not suitable for conservative long-term portfolios. I would not be comfortable investing in Columbia, Turkey, or Peru, however ETFs not only spread this risk among many countries, but also concentrate primarily in stronger and larger economies like China, South Korea, and India, and as such reduce risk to levels acceptable for a portion of a long term portfolio.

Reasons for choosing emerging markets include a favorable population age distribution. As of 2020, developed nations will have three people of working age for every person age 65 and up, according to United Nations figures. By contrast, in the developing world, there will be 7.7 working-age people for every senior—a far more favorable dependency ratio and a key reason emerging markets will enjoy faster economic growth over the next few decades. Developing economies have young, large, fast-growing working-age populations, plus they don't have the financial burden of supporting substantial numbers of retirees.

Another reason to own emerging market shares are price earnings multiples. P/Es of companies in these markets are about 25% lower than those in the US, attributable to less stable governments, less stable currencies, lower per capita GDPs, more challenging economies, and less transparent accounting practices (using different standards than our US GAAP accounting standard). This disparity became even more pronounced when US stocks started to hit record average price earnings ratios in 2018 and '19 as a result of a 9-year bull market.

This lower EM multiple is seen as creating an opportunity for above average returns, (especially for investors with a value focus) and the EM sector has become more popular with non-professional investors. These countries may have more upside for economic growth simply because of their smaller size, than more mature economies like our own, which grow more slowly in percentage terms, due to the laws of large numbers.

On the negative side, is a startling statistic from a recent *Financial Analysts Journal* article: Over the two decades through 2017, China's real per capita GDP grew 8.2% a year—but its stock market's real return was just 0.7%. Because of stock dilution, there's sometimes scant connection between a country's economic growth and its stock market's performance. This dilution happens when companies issue new stock which dilutes the existing shares,

Very low bond yields are also a factor in investors seeking sources of better returns elsewhere. Investors are increasing their attention to the BRIC countries (Brazil, Russia, India, and

China) which are seen as possibly having better opportunities for strong economic growth which will improve domestic corporate earnings. (Because of its conflicts with the US, and the economic sanctions imposed by the US, Russia's economy is in serious difficulty, and risk there is no longer acceptable).

The strong performance of EM stocks was abruptly halted in Jan 2018. This because Trump single handedly started a trade war with many foreign countries, most notably China. Unfortunately, the concentration of EM ETFs in China has devastated their returns. Concentrations of any kind increase risk, and sadly it came home to roost in 2018 with this unanticipated trade war between the US and China.

The risk of owning EM stocks is now (6/19) significantly above average and until the tariff issue is resolved, I recommend committing no new money here. The largest ETF, VWO, recovered somewhat in the first half of 2019, up 12%, as the Whitehouse tweeted that trade talks were moving along. If you already own it, I would not sell and take losses, as eventually something will be worked out, although we may be talking years.

If you want to add a portion of your portfolio in this sector, perhaps 5-10%, the easiest and safest way is to buy a large, highly popular ETF. When choosing one, scroll down to a list of the 10 largest holdings to familiarize yourself with the type of companies held, and which countries they reside in. You will recognize many of the large and stable companies listed, including mobile phone companies, utilities, banks, consumer product companies, etc. The most popular ETFs in the US are Vanguards VWO ($64B) IEMG ($59B), and EEM ($32B), which are normally average risk choices in this space, with a predominance of large companies in the more stable growing countries.

A strong argument can be made for eventually having a significant investment exposure in China, because it has the highest economic growth rate of any country in the world. Their economy is shifting from mostly exports to internal consumption, a favorable development, and their recently slower growth rate (6.2%) is actually healthier and more sustainable. Senior party leaders have endorsed capitalistic economic practices, in spite of being a communist country, and have taken many steps to stimulate growth while placing regulations to reduce the risk of asset bubbles.

A number of other emerging market countries are also affected, although not as significantly. The wide differences which exist between the US and China in trade issues argues for a prolonged period of disagreement, perhaps years, and perhaps extending into the next US political cycle.

The largest China ETF, FXI, includes China's 50 largest companies, however the much smaller GXC has done significantly better, has a lower expense ratio (.59 vs. .74 %), and includes 350 companies. I prefer GXC. Bear in mind that any Chinese ETF will overlap significantly with any other emerging market ETF.

If you add emerging markets to your portfolio you must be prepared for volatility which is greater than US stocks. ETFs like EEM and VWO will take a downward move whenever there is a financial crisis in one or more of these countries, and people start to talk about the crisis spreading to other countries.

Within the last four years there have been flare ups involving Italy and Greece, and recently in Turkey, Russia, and Brazil. These stocks will move downward as investors sell and ask questions later. Foreign banks are especially vulnerable to these sovereign problems over worry about the inability of some companies to repay bank loans. If the currency of a country falls significantly, as Turkey's Lira has, any debt which is owed in another currency, such as dollars, will become a much larger obligation. US banks with large overseas loan books are also vulnerable, such as Citibank.

Government level financial blowups in emerging markets have a much greater negative effect on the bonds and currencies in those countries, than they do on corporate stock prices. This is one reason buying foreign company bonds or currencies is not recommended for a non-professional investor.

> *Takeaway*: It makes sense to own a relatively small portion of a long-term portfolio in emerging markets. Not only for reasons of diversification, but population demographics, lower P/Es and higher growth rates in those countries. Volatility is higher, as is risk, and country concentrations in most ETFs, especially China, increase risk. For these reasons I would not commit more than 5-8% of your total there.

ANNUITIES

Annuities are contracts to receive a fixed payment, usually monthly, often for life, usually from an insurance company, in exchange for an upfront cash payment to them. I dislike annuities, as do most financial advisors, for a number of reasons. Included among these are the fees associated in buying (sometimes to pay sales agents), whether the contract is "fair" financially to the recipient, whether the party paying out will fulfill its obligation, the "loss" if you die prematurely, the one-sided legal contract language, and that when you die, nothing remains for your beneficiaries, unless you accept a lower payment for a reduced survivor benefit.

The insurance company has to build into their price/return calculation a net profit for themselves, must build in a return to pay for all of their overhead and administrative expenses, and must build in a cushion in case the market turns against them. They use a contract containing numerous pages of very small print - all written by their attorneys to their benefit, and your disadvantage.

In general, it is generally not advisable to give anyone money up-front, for a possible return or benefit to be received later, which is exactly what an annuity is. Your life situation may change, they might default, etc. However, with annuities, the greatest drawback is you will receive less of a return on your money than if you had invested it wisely.

Insurance companies love annuities, because they receive all the money up-front, will pay it out in small amounts over many years, can invest the money in long term higher yielding investments, like real estate, and operate under a contract with you written totally in their favor.

Insurance companies employ professional salesman to sell annuities. They receive substantial commissions and continuing fees, because the profit for the insurance company is high. The salesmen, who are often dealing with people one on one, are supposed to outline all the benefits as well as the shortcomings of these contracts, but I don't have to tell you which information is likely to be left unmentioned.

You must be highly skeptical of annuity sales pitches. Most likely you will not learn about the shortcomings until after it's too late. As with any product where the sales commission is high, the salesperson is highly anxious to make a sale. Under these conditions they will spend most or all of their presentation on the advantages and talk as little as possible about the disadvantages - it's only human for them to do that.

Insurance companies are continually coming up with new investment products which sound great. One of these is the Fixed Index Annuity, where they are attempting to capture the popularity of indexed investments. It promises asset protection on the downside, stock market participation on the upside, and a lifetime income stream. As you may have guessed it's not a great choice. There is no such thing as a high return with little or no downside risk - but it sure sounds good. If you are tempted by one of these presentations, say," I'll get back to you" and Google "advantages and disadvantages of (whatever the product is called)".

Regardless of the product structure, insurance companies have to cover their administrative overhead (they have lots of employees), cover their marketing expenses (advertising and sales), provide a profit for themselves, and provide a cushion in case the market turns against them. You get what's left.

Many companies who owe pensions to former employees decide to out-place this obligation with an insurance company, or other service providers. If you are owed a pension, you may be offered a choice between a lump sum payment and an annuity. The annuity usually will have a matrix of various benefits and terms. If you chose the annuity you will receive less by making this choice than you would by investing the lump sum funds reasonably yourself.

If the lump sum offer is fairly determined, it is advisable to take it, and invest it along the guidelines outlined in this paper. One problem is that you are not an actuary, and you will have no way of determining if what they are offering you is fair. The methods used in computing them are extremely complicated, and as you can guess, they favor the company.

There's not anything you can do to change the amount they are offering you anyway, so it is what it is. However, by taking the lump sum you will have the freedom to invest it as you wish, and when you die, your beneficiaries will inherit the balance.

Not every advisor agrees on this. They point to the myriad number of bad things which could happen if you do your own investing vs. the certainty of an annuity. They include choosing bad investments, the market turning against you, the possibility of your cognitive decline in later years, and dying and leaving investing decisions to your spouse. They recommend taking a reduced annuity payment with a survivor benefit for your spouse.

I would argue that you will receive a greater income by investing the lump sum in a mindless and relatively low risk ETF such as the S&P 500 on the equity side, or the Vanguard total bond ETF BND, on the bond side. That way the power of compounding will work for you instead of the issuer.

You might also invest the funds in a three-part ETF split. For example, a 45/40/15 split as follows - 45% S&P 500 (VOO), 40% Total bonds (BND), and 15% international stock (VXUS), and then leave it alone.

The annuity is better suited to someone unwilling to assume any risk of volatility, does not wish to be involved in financial matters, and is willing to accept less for the pension they earned.

There is no shortage of information written about annuities, which you can access on the internet. If you do, make sure the source is not biased.

Takeaway: In my view, Insurance companies should be used for insurance - not for investing. I know that any product they offer is going to be more favorable to them than it is to me, otherwise they would not be offering generous commissions to their agents for selling them. Also, I know that their lawyers have written the pages of fine print for their benefit, and I wouldn't understand them even if I read them.

TARGET DATE OR RETIREMENT OR LIFE FUNDS

Target Date funds, also called Retirement funds, or Life Cycle funds, are a simplified way to invest by buying one fund which is tied to your expected retirement date. For example, if you are 50 years old, plan to retire at age 65 (who knows this anyway?) you pick a fund 15 years into the future---so as of 2017, you would pick 2032, or the closest year available, probably 2035. The fund picks investments for you, increasing the proportion of bonds as you approach retirement age. As a concept, there is nothing wrong with these plans. As you age you want more a more conservative portfolio. In practice however these plans have had several problems, and worse, their performance, collectively has been very poor. Here are some of the problems.

1. Today, people live decades beyond their retirement date. The date you retire is not the date you wish to give up on the appreciation of equities. With these funds you will end up with a very high proportion of bonds, both in the early years, and also in the later years. This is because of outdated investment "rules of thumb" which assumed a very high proportion of bonds for retired people – 70-100%. This is now a flawed concept. <u>Bond returns are currently too low, around 2.5%, to provide for decades of retirement income.</u> It worked when people only lived until their early 70's, less than 10 years after retiring at age 65, and bond yields were closer to 5%. The Vanguard 2015 fund for example, with 6 years remaining, is up to 38% bonds.

2. These funds are not tailored to your life situation or your risk profile (see Risk Profile). They attempt to satisfy the risk tolerance of an "average" investor, which may not be you. Some people are much more conservative than others, and your portfolio should reflect this. People who have a large amount of investable funds can afford to have more bonds. People who have many years to live and a modest amount of funds, cannot afford to have assets earning only 2.5%, especially in periods of high

inflation. These funds do not include, or exclude, investments particular to your personal views or preferences. In short, they are a one size fits all, good for baseball hats, but terrible for portfolio investing.

3. Letting someone else pick your investments for you assumes you are not capable of making your own choices. Before ETFs this had more justifiability for persons with very little interest and knowledge of investing. ETFs now provide a highly diversified, transparent, and easily understood why to invest.

4. Fees for these funds have decreased due to customer demand for lower cost funds, however their expenses still exceed ETFs by a large margin. <u>They averaged .66% in 2017</u> vs. ETFs which are generally between .05% and .25%.

5. Historically, these funds have done poorly. I believe the reason for this is many of these funds use actively managed mutual funds (both Fidelity and Schwab) and have a high proportion of bonds. I attribute this to poor execution. When these funds were started, bonds were returning 5%, as was cash in money market funds. No one saw the Fed reducing rates to zero for close to a decade, so the funds were not set up to accommodate significant changes such as this.

If you want something extremely simple which you don't have to look at often, consider a Vanguard low priced index fund, such as the Vanguard Balanced Index Fund or the Vanguard Life Strategy Fund - and use a further into the future date like 2050 to lower the bond allocation.

Some financial providers have attempted to correct the problems associated with target date funds, but I believe you should pass on them unless you have absolutely no interest or desire to manage your own investments. You will do better picking your own investments, tailored to your likes and dislikes, and adjusting it from time to time based on changes in the world, and also changes in your life situation. For investors who do not wish to spend any time developing their own portfolio, a Robo advisor is a better choice. It is tailored to your risk profile, and can be customized to meet your needs (see Robo Advisors).

Similarly, a "Funds of Funds" is a fund which merely chooses a collection of other funds to invest in. The original idea, to create a simple one stop shopping fund, to increase diversification while also maintaining a target profile, has essentially been replaced by ETFs which do the same thing only cheaper. The returns of these funds have been poor, and you will end up paying redundant expense fees - those of the fund itself, plus those of all the underlying funds - wasted money.

> ***Takeaway***: Target date funds seem like a good idea but are generally too conservative for most people, have sub-par returns, above average expenses, and are a one size fits all concept. If you are looking for a super simple long-term strategy which you can forget about, go to "Some Portfolio Recommendations" near the end of this book.

IPOs

IPOs are initial public offerings, where a privately owned company decides to go public, and issue shares for the first time. These are usually smaller companies in their infancy, who often have no earnings, or losses, but have what is believed to be a promising future. There are exceptions. Sometimes a struggling company is taken private, bought out by a private buyer, and when the business begins operating profitably, it does an IPO. Some companies have grown large before going public, like Uber, and Lyft.

IPOs get a lot of attention on Wall Street and on business TV channels, because there are many investors who like to take a chance on these companies, by "getting in on the ground floor". They are hoping the company catches fire, and they make huge profits quickly.

Unfortunately, the failures outnumber the successes by a large margin. Buyers often dump their shares during the first day of trading to take advantage of the buzz and attention. Some shareholders are prohibited from selling until a "lock up" period expires. When the lock up period ends, increased selling will likely occur, pushing prices down. After a few days or months when reality sets in, share prices drop, and only recover if earnings start increasing for real.

Facebook was an exception where everyone knew that their very high number of users would eventually result in huge earnings, which it did. Most of these companies however are soon forgotten. This is truly gambling not investing, where early investors see the company as a possible candidate for being acquired. You can do equally well at roulette. These stocks have obviously no place in portfolios held for long term retirement savings.

COMMODITIES
(Gold and Oil discussed elsewhere)

Historically commodities, the product itself, not companies who produce commodities, were invested in only by professionals. The companies which need those commodities to stay in business had experts on staff that bought and sold commodity futures contracts to ensure future supply and also to hedge against large price increases. High volatility in prices, and the need for specialized expertise in a particular commodity, precluded the average investor. Oil or cotton markets, for example, were followed only by a small number of specialists and floor traders who worked at that exchange. The price of aluminum, nickel, copper, wheat, corn, lumber, or oil, was followed only by the people in that business. Investors didn't want 10 tons of wheat dumped on their front door.

Over time investors began to see that a profit could be made by taking the "other side" of the trades taken by companies which were only interested in securing a future stream of commodities at a fair price, to keep their business operating.

Investing in commodities, again, the actual product, not companies who deal in those commodities, is considerably more risky than investing in companies. Companies, taken as a whole, generally make profits and grow. Unsuccessful companies will go out of business. Stocks taken as a whole go up in value 80% of the time over long periods, which means that the value of your investment is very likely to go up if you wait long enough.

This is not true of commodities. Their value is dependent on the demand and supply conditions existing at that time. If more than enough supply exists, the price will not go up, and could go down for very extended periods. Worse, future prices are not predictable, period.

The market establishes the value each day based upon actual sales transactions, however there is no way to determine if this price is high or low. Professionals make forecasts of supply and demand and analyze historical price chart patterns, which have the same reliability as palm readers. If you hear someone predicting the future price of oil or gold, roll your eyes.

About the only thing you can conclude, and this is not helpful, is that when the major economies in the world are growing their economies, demand for most commodities will increase. Unfortunately, that doesn't help, because if companies figure out how to produce more of a commodity, prices will move lower.

The best example of this being the technology of getting oil and gas out of shale deposits by cracking the earth with injected sand, combined with advanced horizontal drilling technology. For the first time ever, the US can now produce more oil and gas than it needs.

ETFs which include companies which are dependent on, use, or deal in a commodity became a vehicle for average investors to "play" this market without resorting to futures contracts, which are best left for professionals. It created another way to diversify their portfolio and/ or take advantage of what they believed were profit opportunities. ETFs offered a way to not only spread risk among different companies in a single commodity, but to buy one ETF which included many different commodities, usually called material ETFs.

Investing in the actual commodities themselves, through futures contracts, has a number of issues. They have no dividends, no income, and no earnings. Because they have no cash flow they are impossible to value arithmetically. Anything which produces cash flow, like a company or an office building, can be valued by discounting the future cash return into a value today. Also, raw materials have to be stored and secured. They are very volatile in price and have produced poor returns over extended periods.

From 1991 – 2017 annualized returns of commodities were only 2.2%. They were down 6.5%/year over the last 10 years and were down 5% through mid-2017 (a lot due to oil). Meanwhile the companies who deal in these commodities are subject to the risk of availability and prices which may turn against them.

China's rapid growth, caused by the industrialization of such a huge population, resulted in massive building of all types – buildings and infrastructure. China became the dominant buyer of commodities worldwide and so prices followed suit. Prices soared for all types of commodities - concrete, steel, copper, etc. and investors piled in (including me). Materials ETFs such as VAW, XLB, and IYM became popular. With ETF's you could buy the commodity itself, or companies which produce and sell that material. Both categories track closely together. Early investors in these ETFs did well, however the situation has changed markedly for the worse.

China started to slow down from the 9-10%/year range to the 6-7% level. Stories started appearing that construction in China was not only overbuilt, but severely overbuilt in certain types, such as apartment buildings. An 11/18 report noted that 20% of Chinese homes were vacant, a staggering 50 million apartments. Worse, it turned out China had been stockpiling huge quantities of certain commodities, such as copper and steel. Orders for materials were canceled and prices plunged. These types of scenarios have frequently played out in the past, but China had become such a huge proportion of total sales its effects were terrible. Mining companies all over the world had to shutter facilities, and it became evident that during China's rapid growth period, their suppliers had overbuilt their capacity to produce. Worldwide gluts appeared, and prices cratered.

In hindsight commodities have not been a great choice for the average long investor in recent years. Much of this is because of declining oil prices, but it was also caused by China. China overbought commodities and stored them, and also built up too much infrastructure to produce these natural resources. This resulted in worldwide gluts of many commodities and dumping at below cost prices.

Besides having poor long-term returns, commodities have been shown as a poor source of risk diversification. That is, correlations show owning them had very little positive effect in reducing downturns in the stock market. If world economies are not growing, stocks and commodities are both affected negatively, and therefore both will decline together. If world economies in general are growing, as is the case today, and China is not retrenching, you may wish to hold a relatively low weighting of these assets – perhaps 5%.

If you pick an ETF which includes the stock of companies primarily engaged in commodity production, you will get some diversification, but if the overall stock market declines, so will these stocks. You would obtain better diversification by investing in the commodities themselves, however all of the ETFs created so far have significant technical problems, therefore at this point I do not recommend them.

Another risk with commodities is created by the dollar. Since we price most of these commodities in dollars, if the dollar goes up, commodities (priced in dollars) will have to be priced lower, and vice versa. So, in addition to trying to gauge the future supply/demand picture for a commodity, you also have to factor in the movement of our currency - an additional layer of difficulty and risk.

What had been a worldwide global recovery in 2017 and 2018 had many experts predicting commodity prices to move up significantly in 2018, based upon increased demand for raw materials caused by this worldwide economic growth. At the start of 2018, many pundits chose commodities as the investment of choice for the upcoming year. These experts could not have been more wrong.

Developed markets outside the US began reporting weaker economic growth, even as US growth marched ahead strongly. This became known as the world economic uncoupling. Why this happened is not clear, however Trump's tariff wars was certainly part of the problem. Commodity prices started falling in mid-2018 (except for oil which went the other way). Also contributing was a stronger dollar caused in part by the Fed continually pushing interest rates higher. The stronger dollar has reduced prices of commodities sourced in emerging markets.

Takeaway: Investing in commodities, even though sometimes being inversely correlated with the stock market, is perhaps too problematic for the average investor, especially if reviewing your portfolio often is not desired. Worse, the ETFs which presently exist to capture commodity values based on futures contracts, have technical flaws and have very high expense ratios.

The very broad based and often quoted Bloomberg Commodity index which tracks 22 different commodities, is at 79 today (7/22/2019) vs. 118, 5 years ago, a decline of 33%, and its 1-year return is minus 5.1%. This performance hardly encourages one to invest. If you believe commodity producers will prosper, buy an ETF of the companies that are in that business, such as VAW or XLB, and recognize that this will probably not diversify your portfolio of common stocks.

BONDS

A bond is a debt security, similar to an IOU. It is a loan, where the funds are raised by selling securities to investors. The issuer of the bond may be a government, municipality, or corporation. The bond usually has a fixed interest rate, also known as the coupon, but may also have a floating rate, where the rate floats above a stated benchmark rate. The term of the bond varies depending on the purpose. The issuer of the bond pays the stated interest to the holder (usually through the broker network) throughout the life of the bond, and is obligated to repay the principal, or face value, or par value, at maturity.

Bonds come in all types, sizes and configurations. Investors buy bonds as a relatively stable, low yielding investment, which provides a continuous source of income to them, at a fixed (usually) interest rate. The investor may buy and hold an individual bond until maturity or sell it to another investor. More likely he will buy into a fund which holds bonds, or an ETF of bonds, of the type, maturity, and category of issuer they are interested in holding. If you have enough funds, you can buy individual bonds through your broker, and hold them until maturity.

Private independent bond rating agencies such as S&P and Moody's apply a grade to bonds to indicate its credit quality. These evaluations give buyers a way to evaluate a bond issuer's financial strength and ability to repay a bond's principal, and interest in a timely fashion. Bond ratings are expressed as letters ranging from "AAA," which is the highest grade, to "BB", "C" or "D", which is the lowest grade. Different rating services use the same letter grades but use various combinations of upper and lower-case letters to differentiate themselves.

Investment grade refers to the quality of a company's credit. In order to be considered an investment grade issue, the company must be rated at 'BBB' or higher by Standard and Poor's or Moody's. Anything below 'BBB' rating is considered non-investment grade. A rating of 'BB' or lower it is known as "junk", which means the probability that the company will repay its issued debt as it comes due is deemed to be speculative - having some doubt.

When I was younger, bonds had stated interest rates, the coupon, in the 4-5% range. Because of their stability and steady source of income they were a significant percentage of most investor's portfolios. Studies showed that portfolios with bonds in them did better over the long term because bonds continued to pay interest even when stocks were in a downturn, and generally, but not always, bonds and stocks move in opposite directions.

Bonds reduce the highs, and also reduce the lows of the sometimes volatile equity (stock) market. This "averaging" effect lowers overall yield, but also reduces risk. This combination has historically been recommended to all investors, but with older investors having a much greater proportion of bonds - as much as 80% or more for a person 65 years old. This age-old philosophy is outdated and needs to be retired in the dust bin.

When our Federal Reserve, along with most central banks around the world moved to force interest rates down in order to stimulate economic growth in 2008, the coupon rates of bonds went down accordingly. Bond interest rates got so low, and continue to be so low, that they barely, if at all, exceed the inflation rate. If the rate of inflation exceeds your bond interest rate you are have a portfolio which is decreasing in buying power. If you retire at 65 and live until 85 your money probably won't last long enough. The rate of inflation, even when it is low - the government says it's about 2.0%, (a disputable figure) – the effect over decades is very damaging to a fixed income portfolio.

I believe anecdotally the inflation rate is actually higher than the government reports. The government's methodology is biased, as the government saves billions in national debt interest when interest rates are low. Also, the realized rate of inflation is different for different people depending on their age and station in life. Do you have kids entering college? Are you buying your first house? Do you have a serious illness?

It's hard not to notice much higher prices everywhere you look; healthcare, college, the dentist, the grocery store, car parts and repairs, houses, etc. The increasing cost of things is pervasive and unrelenting. Also, inflation rates are largely expected to increase in the future, as a result of several factors including wage cost pressure, due to extraordinarily low unemployment, tariff wars, and worker shortages. Wages have increased very slowly since the '08 recession and are now showing signs of upward pressure. This is happening with both lower paid workers (higher minimum wages) and skilled labor, where shortages are growing.

The Trump trade war will cause consumer prices in the US to increase significantly as so much of our manufactured goods are imported, especially from China. Only 9% of the US workforce is now engaged in manufacturing, a number which moves relentlessly lower each year.

If inflation in the US returns to the historical levels of the past 50 years, as I believe it will, the meager coupon on bonds will present an even greater problem for long term investors as buying power will decrease. Meanwhile bond yields are being held in check, in part, by foreign buyers who face yields close to zero in many countries. Those buyers will have to expose themselves to currency risk however, as our bonds will have to be converted to their own currency at some point.

BOND TYPES

Government bonds – When issued by the US government they are called treasury bills (mature days to 1 year), notes (under ten years), or bonds (up to 30 years).They carry the full creditworthiness of the US, and have low interest rates because the issuer is believed to have essentially zero credit risk (the risk the issuer can't repay at maturity). They represent the lowest risk bond available.

The ten-year US bond is often used as a benchmark to indicate the overall level of rates on US gov't debt. Today the interest rate on a ten-year bond is 2.1% (6/19). If you bought this bond you would receive 2.1% each year in interest but not receive the principal back for ten years. You could however sell the bond. Most people do not buy individual bonds, they buy bond funds, mutual funds, of bond ETFs. If they want their principal back it is easy to sell.

Corporate bonds – Bonds issued by corporations for business purposes. Most people buy them in a bond fund or ETF where risk is diversified. The interest rate will depend on the creditworthiness of the issuer, which is a measurement of inherent risk. Investors rely on credit ratings given to corporations by rating agencies like Standard and Poor's, Moody's, and Fitch.

If you are interested in high quality bonds, they are called "investment grade" and have ratings from AAA down to BBB. Speculative bonds are rated from BB+ down to B-. Substantial risk bonds are rated CCC+ down to C, and bonds in default are rated D. Any rating below CCC is very speculative and to be avoided. Average long-term investors will want to stay with investment grade bonds. The average interest rate on investment grade corporate bonds is about 3.5% (6/19). The huge corporate bond ETF LQD with $34B invested has a yield of 3.5% but is up 9.3% YTD because of falling interest rates (6/19).

50% of all corporate bonds categorized as investment grade are rated BBB, the lowest investment grade. If interest rates rise and corporations have increased interest expense, some of these companies could see their rating decline 1 level into BB, or junk. This may also happen if our economy weakens and some corporations experience lower profitability, and have a greater difficulty meeting all debt obligations when due.

High Yield bonds – Also called "junk bonds", these are bonds issued by corporations and rated "BB" or lower and have a higher credit risk and therefore have higher interest rates. The term "junk bond" is a poor label, making it sound as if they are worthless. However, many investors allocate some portion of their portfolio to these bonds, known more accurately as "high yield" bonds, as a way to increase their average yield.

When the interest rate on US and investment grade bonds dropped to their current levels - equal to or marginally above the rate of inflation - many investors decided to invest in more risky bonds to get a higher return. Bonds rated BB as of 6/19 carry average interest rates of 4.5%. Rates for junk bonds used to fall in the 6-8% range, however the entrance of more buyers seeking higher yields has pushed the yield down, to where many investors consider the return too low for the risk being taken. Buying a BB or lower rated bond singularly would be very risky, but in a large fund or ETF where defaults are averaged into the total, they can be an acceptable risk for a small portion of your portfolio.

Over the past 15 years, high-yield bonds have delivered returns virtually on par with the S&P 500 Index of large-cap stocks, but with much lower volatility. Better still, in recent years, the default rate on high-yield bonds has averaged just 2% a year, compared to an historical average closer to 4%. A "default" defined as when a bond issuer fails to make a scheduled payment. This performance has encouraged many investors to own these bonds, however rising interest rates can be a problem for the issuers of these bonds, especially if the economy slows and corporations earn less profit and have less available cash flow to repay debt.

A problem with junk bonds today is their elevated prices. Because so many investors have been chasing yield with bond rates so low, investors have poured into these bonds, raising prices and lowering yields. The result is that the return you earn is considered by many to be too low for the level of risk you are exposed to. In other words, you are not getting enough of a return for the risk you are taking. HYG, the popular 18 billion dollar ETF of junk bonds has a 7/19 yield of only 5.3%. Worse, I doubt very many buyers of this ETF have an understanding of the creditworthiness of the underlying company debtors. I worked in subprime corporate lending my entire career, and most of these debtors are very weak, if not precarious financially.

If our economy begins to slow and corporate profits show signs of moving lower, I would recommend reducing significantly, or exiting this asset class.

<u>Convertible bonds</u> - A convertible bond is essentially a corporate bond with an embedded equity option which enables the holder to exchange the bond for a fixed number of shares at a time of his own choosing, subject to certain restrictions. They have features of both stocks and bonds. This unique aspect of these bonds allows companies to pay a lower interest rate than they normally would have to but allows individual investors to maintain higher potential for price appreciation should equity prices rise. For this reason, <u>convertible bonds</u> tend to exhibit a stronger correlation with equity markets than bonds, and may not make great investments for investors who are seeking ETFs that are <u>uncorrelated to their equity holdings</u>.

According to <u>a Merrill Lynch study</u>, convertibles provided 70% of the upside potential of a company's common stock, on average, while providing much higher protection on the downside. The price of convertibles demonstrated smaller losses than the stock in all but one month over the study's duration. This suggests that while these types of securities are generally correlated with their underlying equity shares, they offer investors a safer alternative that might be ideal in shaky markets.

There are some disadvantages to convertible bonds as well. Should equity markets sink, it could leave investors "out-of-the-money" with no hope of converting into equity. Further, some convertible bonds have a 'mandatory' conversion feature forcing the owner to convert the bond into stock no matter what the price is at the end of the bond's life. Convertible bonds can be used to reduce risk by reducing equity holdings and adding convertibles - a half step toward bonds.

Municipal bonds – These are bonds issued by local states, cities and counties, for the building of roads, schools, and infrastructure projects. They are backed by the taxing authority of the issuing government unit, or sometimes the revenue from the project itself (like toll roads). They carry very low interest rates because the occurrence of defaults is very rare.

In most cases, but not all, the interest you receive on these bonds is not taxable income at the Federal or State level. Interest rates depend on the credit rating of the issuer, and the length of the bond. Rates fall in the 1-3% range. These bonds are often held by wealthy investors who are in high income tax brackets but are also used for "widows and orphans" funds which require very low risk. The return on a municipal bond is increased by a function of your tax bracket - a 35% tax bracket lifts your effective return on a 2% bond to about 3%.

Treasury Inflation Protected Bonds - Treasury inflation protected securities (TIPS) refer to a treasury security that is indexed to inflation in order to protect investors from the negative effects of inflation. TIPS are considered an extremely low-risk investment since they are backed by the U.S. government and because the par value rises with inflation, as measured by the Consumer Price Index, while the interest rate remains fixed. Interest on TIPS is paid semiannually. TIPS can be purchased directly from the government through the Treasury Direct system or by buying an ETF such as TIP.

Because the semiannual inflation adjustments of a TIPS bond are considered taxable income by the IRS, even though investors don't see that money until they sell the bond or it reaches maturity, some investors prefer to get TIPS through a mutual fund or ETF. TIPS usually carry interest rates lower than other government or corporate securities, so they are not necessarily optimal for income investors. Their advantage is mainly inflation protection, but if inflation is minimal or nonexistent, their value is less. Many recommend these ultra-conservative securities, but I don't because their yields are very low.

Takeaway: Bonds are used by investors to reduce risk, diversify their total portfolio, and to provide a steady source of income. There is no evidence that would indicate what the best level of bonds to hold is, although most advisors assume the proportion is higher as you grow older. Bonds are seen as a way to be cautious, and investors buy more of them when scary political or economic events happen.

However, the return on bonds is very small and may fall lower than the rate of inflation. Bonds also have significant interest rate risk when interest rates increase, which many are not aware of, or don't fully understand - discussed below.

BOND RISK and INTEREST RATES

Most people have read that bonds are much less risky than stocks and that if you are a cautious investor you should buy bonds and not stocks, or at least much more in bonds than stocks. This stems, I think, from the basic understanding of what a bond is. If you buy a bond and wait until maturity, you will receive your full principal back, (assuming there is no credit default), plus you will have received a fixed interest rate while it has been outstanding.

However, the value of a bond is inversely related to interest rates. If rates rise, the bonds value will decrease. If rates fall, bonds will increase in value. This is because investors will discount a bond portfolio if its yield is less than current market yields. If you were to sell the bond, before maturity you would experience a loss of principal. A buyer would prefer to own a more recently issued bond having a higher rate or coupon. Since the interest coupon on a bond is small at say 2-3%, the principal loss may wipe out all of your interest income, and possibly more.

This is what has happened in 2018. For example. Vanguard's total bond market ETF, BND, declined 3.7% through 10/18 compared to its average yield of 2.7%.

Popular core bond funds often follow the Bloomberg Barclays US Aggregate Bond index, such as iShares core US Aggregate bond ETF AGG. Funds that follow this index have a duration of about six years, considered an intermediate term bond duration. This means **when interest rates rise one percentage point, the index's bond prices will fall 6%.** I wonder how many buyers of AGG were aware of the materiality of this inverse relationship. AGG has fallen 4.2 % over the last year (10/18).

Many investors are unaware of this risk to principal, and are told that to avoid risk, buy bonds with investment grade ratings, with the belief that their principal is 100% safe. However, If you wish to avoid a loss of principal if interest rates go up after you purchase a bond, you must buy

<u>individual bonds and hold them to maturity, not buy a bond fund or ETF.</u>

If you go in to your broker and buy individual bonds, and hold these bonds to maturity you would not experience a loss of principal if interest rates rise, and this is what many larger investors do. The broker will set up a ladder of varying maturities, but you will need $100-200K at a minimum to do this. The problem here, however, is that by buying individual bonds you become exposed to default risk - the risk that the debtor becomes unable to repay the bond. If you decide to buy individual bonds in order to avoid rate risk, it is wise to stick with strong debtors, such as large US banks.

If you own an individual bond, a principal loss would only happen if you needed to sell before maturity, and interest rates had risen since you bought it. If you hold an individual bond to its maturity, you will receive the full principal (absent a default) however you will have a below market return investment for the entire period you held onto it, if interest rates had risen.

The issue is that the vast majority of non-professional investors do not buy individual bonds and hold them to maturity. They buy bond mutual funds or ETFs, which are constantly buying and selling, replacing older bonds, and the market value of the fund, is computed and reported each day. That value will go down if interest rates are rising, and vice versa.

The inverse relationship between a bonds value and interest rates is arithmetical, and a function of the maturity length of the bond. The longer the maturity the more the inverse effect will be. This is why in an increasing interest rate environment; advisors recommend you buy short term bonds to lessen, but not eliminate, the diminutive effect.

When a bond fund sells a bond at a loss because of increased interest rates, it replaces it with a new higher rate bond. The higher rate on the new bonds, over time, will offset some or all of the loss on the old bond. However, at the time of the sale at a loss, the value of the assets in the fund will decrease.

Say you purchase a 2.5% individual bond maturing in 10 years. Interest rates then rise. The market value of your bond goes down. You have a choice - sell it at a loss (realize the paper loss) or hold it until maturity where you receive your full principal back but will have held an investment with a below market return doing the entire period. If the term of the bond is short, the loss of yield is less. If instead you buy a bond fund or ETF and interest rates rise, the NAV of your fund, or price of your ETF will decline, however the fund will be adding new higher yielding bonds, which will offset the decline.

If you want to understand this concept more fully, take a look at this link: <u>Bond vs. Bond Funds.</u>

> ***Takeaway***: Bonds are thought of as a safe investment, however bonds decline in value when interest rates increase. Buying a bond fund in an increasing interest rate environment will result in a loss of principal value, which may exceed the interest yield of the fund. Bonds are less volatile than stocks, increasing or decreasing in smaller increments, and many see this as reduced risk. You can reduce this reduction in value due to interest rate increases (but not eliminate it) by buying only short-term bonds, say 2 years or less in duration.
>
> Conversely, in a decreasing interest rate environment bonds will gain in principal value. It makes sense to lower your bond allocation if rates are rising steadily and increase your bond allocation when rates are declining. This is one reason investors are so focused on Federal Reserve rate changes.

BONDS vs. BOND FUNDS and BOND ETFs

A great deal has been written about whether active or passive (index) management is more appropriate for a bond fund. This is because the vast majority of investors own funds, not individual bonds. You will find differing opinions on this subject. These are my views after quite a lot of research, which I did to decide on the best way to invest my own savings.

Bonds trade differently than stocks, and active managers argue that passive investing in bonds has shortcomings. They list the difficulty in achieving efficiency, which is the closeness of the fund's performance to the performance of the underlying index. They also point to weighting issues, where large issuers of bonds will become overweight in the index. They note that passive funds will have to buy more of upgraded bonds, in effect buying when prices are high. They note the difficulty for a large fund to obtain some bonds which are thinly traded and less liquid. Lastly, they point to active bond funds which have outperformed their passive counterparts.

The last point, the performance, is all that really matters to an investor. Who really cares about the technical issues involved, at the end of the day, whatever performs better, after management fees are subtracted, is better. Generally speaking, since there are always exceptions, the bottom line is that <u>actively managed bond funds are not able to outperform their passive counterpart by enough of a margin to pay its higher management fees</u>, over the long term.

Across virtually every subcategory of bond funds, the active strategies trail the indexes just like their equity-fund counterparts, according to the S&P Versus Active Report, SPIVA, from S&P Dow Jones Indexes. Active bond fund managers have difficulty overcoming the effect of their higher fees, in part, because yield differences between bond categories is smaller than for equities.

While there will always be a number of actively managed funds that outperform in any given year, over time index funds tend to come out on top primarily due to fees. The gap between the two types of funds is large enough that the difference compounds over time. Also, the market is very efficient, so that it's extremely difficult for a manager to deliver consistent outperformance over the long term. Per Morningstar, "In general, actively managed funds have failed to survive and beat their benchmarks, especially over longer time horizons."

Perhaps most discomforting is research into actively managed bond funds which outperformed their passive benchmark. It found that managers had achieved that performance by taking a position in riskier bonds such as junk bonds which carry a higher yield, and also by going out further in time on the yield curve, which has higher yields but greater risk. Passive funds are restricted to only the type of bond and duration contained in its index.

With some types of bond funds you will notice that most of the offerings in that space are actively managed such as ultra-short ETFs, such as NEAR. If you are unsure about choosing, you can use the Yahoo Finance chart tab to enter any fund or ETF symbol and select a longer period like 3 years or more to evaluate its performance. Remember that bond performance from 2008 through 2016 was enhanced by super low interest rates and returns since 2016 are being held back by rising rates.

To address the need for small investors to have a way to invest in a bond ETF without the risk to principal, a relatively new type of ETF called a fixed term defined maturity bond has been developed. You purchase a maturity date, such as 2022, and the fund buys corporate bonds maturing in that year, holds them to maturity, starts selling them in advance of maturity, and remits funds at maturity to the holders. This combines the benefits of bonds—monthly income, final distribution at maturity, as well as control of portfolio maturity, yield, and credit quality—with the advantages of ETFs—broad diversification, liquidity, transparency, convenience, and cost-effectiveness. This gives you much the same effect as a broker prepared ladder. If rates rise your yield will still stay at the level at which you purchased it, but you will avoid any principal loss.

If interested in these investments read about the offerings of Bulletshares by Guggenheim at: Guggenhem Investments.

BONDS – My View

Because of the very low yield on bonds today, together with the interest risk outlined above, I am not a fan of bonds. For most of us, bonds do not yield enough to provide for 25 or more years after retiring. However, because we are afraid to lose any of our hard earned savings, we respond to those who tell us bonds are safe and stocks are risky, by investing in bonds.

Consider this: Highly regarded financial authority Jeremy Siegal of the Wharton Business School studied stock and bond returns from 1871 to 2012. He found stocks outperformed bonds in 96% of all 20 year holding periods between those years, and stocks outperformed bonds in 99% of all 30-year periods in that time span.

When interest rates are rising, as they were from 2008 through 2018, investment advisors say "be cautious" in buying bonds. What they mean euphemistically is, any bonds you buy are going to go down in value so you better buy very short bonds because they will go down less. It seems to me that not buying bonds at all in this environment makes greater sense.

If you want to reduce risk in an equity portfolio there are steps you can take, as outlined herein, without resorting to bonds. Even if interest rates are steady, the low yield on the bonds barely, if at all, exceeds the rate of inflation. It won't be that long before $10 will buy one loaf of bread or one jar of salad dressing.

If interest rates stabilize and/or start to decrease, or the economy begins to slow down, I recommend adding some bonds for the diversification they provide. Some stock categories called pseudo-bonds or bond surrogates – stocks with high dividends in slow growth, stable industries such as utilities, have become popular among those not wanting to own bonds when the Fed is raising interest rates. However, their stock price will also go down if interest rates rise, as will real estate investments.

Without bonds in your portfolio you will have somewhat greater volatility, and you might not like this. You will have to be patient, and not be frightened into selling equities during a downturn. This is easy to say, but it is very difficult to watch your life savings shrinking in value for weeks or months. Some people will lose sleep and you may find you do not have the stomach for a portfolio exclusively of equities. However, if you are more interested in getting a better return, you will need to have primarily stocks and less bonds.

It has been especially trying in 2018 and 2019 because of the chaos in the White House, where too much is said and done based on impulse and not planned out thoughtfully, where advisors are totally ignored, and fired for disagreeing with the president. The stock market is affected negatively by uncertainty. Businesses postpone buying and expansion plans until the business climate is more clear.

Computers, programmed to buy the dips, have reduced the extent and the duration of stock market pullbacks in recent years. If our economy begins to show signs of falling into a recession, of falling job growth, and an increasing unemployment rate, for example, the downturn could take over a year or more to recover. In that event, consider moving a greater portion of your investments into bonds when these events start emerging. If the Fed decides to lower interest rates to stimulate the economy, bonds will increase in value somewhat.

Takeaway: Bonds are unexciting, their return at present (6/19) is so low they offer no protection against inflation, they will reduce volatility at the expense of return, and their price will move inversely with interest rates. They generally, but not always, move inversely to stocks, mitigating both upward and downward swings. They make the most sense when the economy is beginning or in recession and equities may do poorly because corporate profits are weak, and the Fed is decreasing interest rates to get the economy going. Bonds can be a more acceptable investment when coupon rates are higher, like 5% or more - they were in double digits in the 1980's.

With the 10 year US gov't bond at only 2.1% (6/19), interest rates are extremely low in historical terms. To get a higher return you need to go into higher risk investments like high yield bonds, for example. Looking out 10 years or more, it's more likely that rates will be higher than lower, as will rates of inflation. Unless you believe you may need to access your savings within the next year or two, it's hard to make a case to own bonds today.

PREFERRED STOCK

Preferred stock is a senior form of common stock. It is classified as equity, not debt, on the company's balance sheet, however as an investment it performs very much like a bond. Unlike bonds they usually have no maturity date, and theoretically remain outstanding permanently. In practice however companies periodically exercise their call option and pay off their preferreds and issue a newer series to replace it.

In a liquidation preferreds are paid before common stock, but after bonds.

When you buy them, you are purchasing an equity share in the company. Preferred stock has a periodic dividend which must be paid before common stock dividends are paid. If the company is cash poor it can suspend the dividend, however, this almost never happens because the company then must suspend all common stock dividends as well.

"Preferreds" can increase in value if the company does well, similar to common stock, if they have a convertible (into common stock) option. They tend to be issued by companies at the very high end of the credit range, like banks, and also at the very low end, like private or pre-public companies which do not have the strength to borrow funds at reasonable interest rates. Each issue is rated by the bond rating agencies, so you will know the financial strength of the issuer.

Each issue has unique characteristics which contain provisions such as when shares may be "called" (when the company pays them off) or converted, where investors may convert their shares into common shares under certain conditions. Preferreds have no voting option, unlike common stock, however this is little or no concern to most minority investors, who rarely vote their common shares anyway, since the major shareholders control voting majorities. Minority shareholders should not expect their vote to have any effect on the outcome.

Preferred stock carries a yield substantially greater than a bond. Institutions are large buyers of preferreds due to tax advantages. Preferreds are popular with older well-off individuals, who are not interested in taking common stock risk, prefer a less volatile investment, have enough money to not need significant capital appreciation, and most importantly, enjoy receiving generous dividend payments. They receive a yield significantly higher than a bond without taking significant equity risk.

The weaknesses of preferreds include: upside gains will be lower than the common stock, their price is inversely interest rate sensitive, their dividend is fixed, and some companies with a weak balance sheet may offer these because issuing common stock is not financially practical.

A common criticism of preferreds is the callable feature. If interest rates rise the company will not call them, leaving investors unable to take advantage of the higher rates. Conversely, if interest rates fall, the company calls the preferreds and then issues new ones at a lower rate saving them interest expense. Thus, the investors' high rate return is terminated. In practice this happens relatively infrequently for a variety of reasons, and investors accept this shortcoming as the yield they receive is much higher than a bond.

Preferreds are referred to as bond surrogates, not a bond, but act like them, especially regarding interest rate changes. Actually, they are more like a bond than a stock. You can own them through an ETF (which will have a somewhat higher expense ratio than most ETFs) or buy a particular issue directly through your broker. For example, you can buy the Bank of America BAC-B issue paying 6.0% today, callable 2023. These trade daily and the market price varies.

Over the last 10 years the popular ETF of preferreds, PFF, has remained flat in price; however, it has a very high dividend of 5.7%, which triples the return on government bonds. You may consider this a near cash investment, a slightly higher risk and a fairly good return, and more stable than common stock. If interest rates are rising, as they have been since

12/16, the principal value of preferreds will decrease somewhat, but not significantly.

No single holding in PFF represents more than 2% of assets, thus offering good diversification. The expense ratio of preferred ETFs is somewhat higher than common stock ETFs. PFF has an ER of .47%.

> ***Takeaway***: Preferred stock is one way of diversifying by buying a hybrid - half stock, half bond security. It is generally considered a low risk investment when issued by large corporations. It comes with a relatively high yield, will appreciate somewhat if the company's stock does well, and is less volatile than common stock. It will be somewhat inversely related to interest rates. The lack of voting power is of no real significance. Replacing equity with preferreds is one way of reducing risk if signs of an oncoming recession increase.
>
> The two popular ETFs of preferreds, PFF and PGX are highly diversified, and contain primarily large bank preferreds, and represent a relatively low risk for a 5.9% yield. Both have appreciated considerably in 2019 because of falling interest rates (PGX by 11.2% through 6/19). Rising interest rates will negatively affect preferreds in the same way as they do bonds.

HEALTHCARE

I am a strong believer in healthcare as an investing choice and I am overweight this segment in my portfolio considerably, more than any other sector. The reasons for this include: an aging US and world population, a virtually non-discretionary purchase absent of shopping for price, the disconnect between prices and what people actually pay, and the growing belief among world populations that healthcare should be provided to everyone as a basic right, not dictated by your financial wealth, or lack thereof.

I consider healthcare a permanent core position for your portfolio, regardless of the growth rate in the economy. Recently the political argument over what kind of healthcare program we should have in this country and what role the government should play in holding down price increases has whipsawed prices both ways. However, increasing populations, which are aging in most large developed countries, will increase the demand for healthcare services worldwide.

Statistically you will spend 80% of your entire life's healthcare bill in the last two years of your life. This is documented. It is primarily due to the very high cost of treating cancer and other grave diseases, which are terminal if left untreated. Therefore, as the population of the world ages, healthcare demands increase exponentially. Most of us don't seriously consider not being treated because of staggering costs, regardless of our insurance status or financial means. We go ahead and hope we can find a way to pay for it somehow, perhaps with family help. We also don't usually shop around to find some cheaper treatment, or some cheaper drug. (Doc, have you got anything cheaper that maybe won't kill me?) No one wants their tombstone to read, "He thought the cheaper drug would work".

Because of Medicare, Medicaid, other insurance programs, and HMO's and PPO's, we find ourselves somewhat insulated from staggering healthcare bills. You have little hope of understanding the billing process. You skip to the bottom line, see how much your share is, swallow hard, and start figuring out how you'll pay the total patient share.

As people begin to demand governmental help with escalating healthcare costs as a human right, it is likely that more people will eventually come under a plan of some sort, where taxes are used to subsidize costs. The result will be more people getting treatment. It will take years, but I am assuming that as much as none of us want to have a welfare state, healthcare must be part of a developed nation's obligations to its inhabitants.

Healthcare touches everyone, which includes voters. Politicians are going to be pressured to provide some sort of a plan, or face removal from office. The huge cost and the complicated web of existing services and plans will cause this effort to move slowly, and plans will probably come and go, like the Affordable Care Act, however whatever plans or programs evolve, companies who provide healthcare products and services will benefit.

US companies sell a huge proportion of sales internationally, and in many cases have a great deal of pricing power (sometimes too much), which also makes them favored investments.

An investment issue, however, is that many of the businesses in this sector do not make good investments, in my estimation. Let's look at the five major healthcare segments. (Note: these views are mine and many will disagree).

<u>Health insurance companies</u> - like United Health, Humana, Aetna and Cigna. These are very difficult to understand companies. Their plans keep changing and are not understandable, people are constantly switching plans annually, they are subject to intense criticism for overcharging and/or overbilling, they are monitored by the government, and they have hundreds of lawyers trying to reduce any payouts they make. Their billing statements are like a smoke screen, and they engage in numerous sub-contracts with other companies which kick back money in certain cases.

None of this is transparent to the customer. I frankly don't trust them. They describe "great" plans and have long contracts with endless small print nobody reads, all designed to make it look great but not pay you as much as you think, especially if your healthcare becomes very expensive. I would only recommend investing here for people who have worked in the industry and can understand if it has a profitable future. I also do not like their moral conundrum: Do we reimburse very sick people for staggering health bills? I leave this sector for people who think they can understand its business issues.

Pharmaceutical companies – Like Pfizer, Merck, Roche, and Bayer. These companies live and die depending on the success of their drug research. The 10 year or more process of finding effective drugs, going through years of trials, determining their effectiveness and commercial suitability, gaining government approval, obtaining patents, and then going to market is daunting. No one knows which if any of the drugs in the company's pipeline will ever succeed and actually come to market (85-95% do not). In order to pay for all of that, they have to charge exorbitant prices for all "new" drugs and hope that their patent protection holds long enough for the product to be financially successful. They also use loopholes to extend the life of their patents so they don't end up as generics. They also make money by buying small companies who own exclusive rights to a drug, and then increasing prices.

There is a bipartisan effort in congress to force drug costs down, and no one knows where that will lead. These companies also face constant public criticism for overcharging on life saving drugs needed by severely sick people and are also highly vulnerable to class action lawsuits potentially costing billions, for drugs which end up harming or killing people. In my mind this is another impossible to understand business from the outside. The stocks of these companies have done poorly. Pfizer's stock, highly touted by many managers, was $35/share in 2002 – today it sells for $36. Merck is down 13% in the last year – in the last 5 years the stock has gained 107% vs. the S&P 500 which is up 248%.

Hospitals and Nursing Homes - These companies struggle to break even despite a huge demand for their services. They receive 85-90% of their revenue from the government via Medicaid and Medicare, which is always revising its schedule of payments downward. Hospitals perennially operate at a loss because of very high operating overhead, and end up needing financial assistance, such as charitable contributions, to continue. The American Hospital Assoc. reported today (8/21/18) that on average 30 hospitals a year are closed down in the US, and the trend is worsening, especially in rural areas. I do not want to invest in a business which has so much difficulty achieving profitability.

Nursing homes attempt to make a profit by hiring employees at the low end of the wage scale and giving patients poor service or neglecting their needs. It's no wonder we don't want to put our loved one's there. They often have to resort to cheating (overbilling the government) to make up for their losses, and also by over-charging those patients who do have the ability to pay. I am sure there are reputable and well-run homes, but their track record on average is poor enough for me to avoid investing in them. Taking advantage of the sick and elderly is capitalism at its worst - another necessary evil.

Biotech or biomedical companies – Like Gilead, Amgen, Celgene, and Biogen. This group is a subset of the pharmaceutical sector and has many of the same risk issues as that group, but more so, as they tend to be smaller, with fewer drugs undergoing research. The offset is a huge financial payoff if a drug is effective and patentable. Some consider this field the future of medicine, including the exciting field of immuno-oncology, where your own immune cells are injected to cure cancer. The overall performance of this sector has been quite volatile, down 10% over the last year (6/19) but up 20% in the first half of '19. This is a high risk/ high reward sector, and therefore extremely risky if picking individual companies, however an ETF spreads that risk out. If interested, consider XBI, which I own, a popular, low cost, highly diversified, $5B ETF, where no one company exceeds 3% of the total holdings. (IBB, a popular choice, is too concentrated - the top 5 holdings equal 40%)

Medical Equipment, Devices, and Supplies – This is my favorite investment group. Unlike the healthcare categories above, they are simple to understand companies who make and sell everything you see in a hospital except the drugs. Their products are essential for healthcare providers, and this leads to considerable pricing power. Their customers rely heavily on these companies for their products but also their expertise. A great deal of these products fall under the disposable supply category, which results in continual re-orders, and more and more products are becoming disposable (to reduce infections). US companies lead this industry and sell approximately 50% of sales overseas. There is a very limited selection of ETFs available. I own IHI for larger companies, and XHE, which is equal weighted. Both of these ETFs have done extremely well.

If you decide to buy a broad based healthcare ETF like the popular XLV or VHT, and you look at the top ten holdings, you will see that they are heavily weighted toward pharmaceuticals and include companies in all five of the categories above, most of which I do not care for.

They also have a large concentration in Johnson and Johnson, which is highly diversified, but has an enormous litigation risk element. Johnson and Johnson is a popular holding. It is large and very diversified. However, the enormous risk element to companies which sell healthcare products was realized by J&J when the risk of cancer from talcum powder turned into thousands of lawsuits, with some settled for huge dollar amounts. This underscores the risk in investing in individual companies.

FINANCIALS

Financial stocks account for 15% of the S&P 500 (12/18) and include commercial and investment banks, insurance companies, credit card companies, mortgage finance, consumer finance, specialized finance, stock brokers, asset management and custody, corporate lending, financial investment, real estate investment trusts (REITs), as well as companies engaged in real estate management & development.

This is a broad sector, and although you can invest in a very broad brush ETF such as XLF, the most popular, I do not recommend that. I would recommend looking at the individual businesses within the sector and choosing investments there, because these businesses have highly divergent characteristics, and therefore respond and act much differently.

Banks tend to do better with higher interest rates, but REIT's do worse. Credit card companies follow consumer spending as well as credit default rates. Insurance companies are very diverse, and must be analyzed by the particular business segment they are primarily in, such as property and casualty, auto, life, healthcare, commercial insurance, pension management, etc. Whereas Visa and MasterCard are not even classified in this segment, as electronic payments companies are in Information Technology.

When asset managers refer to the financials they are usually talking about banks, which are the largest industry in this sector. However, the only proper way to evaluate this sector is to focus on the underlying businesses and invest accordingly.

Generally speaking, I would favor banks in periods of rising interest rates, and vice versa, however their plodding growth rate will never result in outstanding equity performance. Banks historically have relatively low P/E's and are sometimes seen as value stocks, but this is not correct. The low P/E is reflective of a stable industry usually growing by no more than mid-single digits annually and are sometimes compared to utilities. The big commercial banks have already reached the 10% of market share (measured by deposits) allowed by law therefore they can no longer buy other banks. M&A in banking has to be confined to the regional banks, although not much has been happening recently.

I prefer to stay away from insurance companies for reasons listed under Sectors I Avoid. I do not favor credit card companies (the credit lenders, not the e-payments companies like Visa and Mastercard) because of cutthroat competition and the tendency to move into subprime borrowers. I favor REIT's as a way to diversify, but not in a period of rising interest rates.

I do not think it imperative that you participate in this sector specifically. If you own large cap index-based ETFs you will have enough ownership through them. Large and regional banks are very safe, credit wise, and are likely to benefit from rising interest rates which made them popular as of mid-2018, however their stock prices have not moved appreciably since 2017. I believe the banks offer better investment opportunities in preferred stock and bonds, which have default rates near zero, than buying their common stock.

Traditional banks are also being challenged by a number of growing so called "fin-tech" companies, which are finding new ways of assisting consumers and business with their financial needs.

> **Takeaway**: The Financial sector contains a number of different businesses which perform differently and cannot logically be grouped together for investment purposes. Broad ETFs like XLF include highly different businesses. If you are interested in financials, consider owning ETFs which focus on particular industries which you believe will do well going forward. Remember that if you own a large or mid-cap company ETF, you will already have exposure to the financials. Also, because banks have below market P/E ratios, they will be overweight in any value oriented ETF you might own (like VTV or MGV).

REAL ESTATE INVESTMENT TRUSTS

Over many decades, REITs have been one of the best long-term asset classes for investors to build income and wealth over time. REITs have increased by a compound growth rate of 10% between 1972 and 2018.

A REIT is a type of security that invests in real estate through property and trades on major exchanges like a stock. Some REITs invest in mortgages rather than real estate, however these mortgage (mREITs) are generally considered to be too risky for a typical investor.

REITs provide investors with an extremely liquid stake in real estate, whereas if real property is owned outright, it is an illiquid investment, which sometimes takes months to sell. REITs receive special Federal tax considerations and typically offer high dividend yields. Equity REITs invest in, and own properties - mortgage REITs invest in mortgages on real property. REITs can be bought and sold easily, and generally correlate inversely with stocks and bonds, therefore they provide a measure of diversification. REITs provide an investment vehicle for real estate that is comparable to a mutual fund, allowing both small and large investors to acquire ownership in real estate ventures, own commercial properties such as apartment complexes, hospitals, office buildings, timber land, warehouses, hotels and shopping malls.

All REITs must have at least 100 shareholders, no five of whom can hold more than 50% of shares between them. At least 75% of a REITs assets must be invested in real estate, cash or U.S. Treasuries, and 75% of gross income must be derived from real estate. REITs are required by law to <u>maintain dividend payout ratios of at least 90% of their taxable income</u>, making them a favorite for income seeking investors. REITs can deduct these dividends and avoid most or all tax liabilities, while the owner/investors are individually responsible for income taxes based on their own personal tax situation.

Some REITs will invest specifically in one area of real estate such as hotels, office buildings, shopping malls, or apartment buildings. Some invest in a specific region, state or country. Others are more diversified. There are several REIT ETFs available, most of which have fairly low expense ratios. The ETF format can help investors avoid over-dependence on one company, geographical area or industry.

REITs are generally viewed as a convenient way to capture real estate growth, diversify your portfolio, earn strong dividend yields, and move the income tax responsibilities to the individual investor. A major weakness is that they are vulnerable to rising interest rates, which directly affect real property values. As mortgage rates rise, the all-in cost of buying property rises, lowering demand, and possibly selling prices. You should underweight this group when mortgage rates are rising, and vice versa. There are also ETFs for international REIT's, which is another source of diversification. The problem with international REIT's is that real estate is highly dependent on location and geography, and most of us are not familiar with those factors outside the US.

REITs require a strong, active, and knowledgeable management team, who can successfully buy and manage real estate having a favorable cash flow, at economically supportable prices, and also obtain mortgage financing at reasonable interest rates. Therefore, investors primarily rely on the REITs past performance as a measure of management strength. Unless you have particular knowledge or have researched the past performance success of particular REIT managers, you would be best served by choosing an ETF of larger well-established companies.

A large diversified REIT such as Vanguards VNQ is very popular as a one size fits all, or you may be interested in drilling down to particular property types. For example, because of the shift by younger people to buying online, mall vacancies have increased recently to 9% (10/18) leading some to believe the US is "overstored". With vacancies increasing, you may wish to avoid this sector. Meanwhile the relentless increase in the prices of single-family houses has caused a flood of new apartment construction, increasing vacancies (4.8% July '18), however if people cannot afford a house, demand should continue to be strong for rental units over the longer term.

REITs are sensitive to interest rates in general, but more so to long term interest rates. In 2018 short term rates have risen, however long term rates have remained relatively flat, leading to a flattening yield curve (see Market Pullbacks).

> *Takeaway*: To be diversified it makes sense to have a portion of your portfolio in REITs. If you have an interest here in a particular real estate segment, go to ETF.com and search for a list of ETFs to choose from in your property type, like apartments for example. If you don't want to drill down by property type, consider a broad ETF like VNQ. It will increase in value somewhat slowly, but over time should earn 10% or so. I would suggest perhaps 6-10% of your portfolio be in real estate.

TELECOM

This is an area I know little about, and I don't fully understand how the business is changing, so I have stayed away as an investment. The playing field is moving and changing because of major changes in consumer preferences, as phones are used less and less for calling someone. Major carriers are looking to expand their universe to include media and entertainment by way of acquisition, and it's becoming harder to classify these companies.

Verizon was a preferred provider due to coverage and clarity, however they started to lose customers to plans with unlimited data because of streaming. Major costs of building out the latest technology have been accompanied not by higher prices for their plans, but instead lower prices caused by price wars with smaller companies seeking market share. The demise of landlines, the switch to everything mobile, and the use of mobile as a source of entertainment means companies have to reinvent themselves, and often.

There's extremely little diversification in the industry – Verizon and AT&T account for 45% of the largest ETF VOX, and the next largest holding is Century Link (whoever that is). Lastly, many believe these companies are becoming like unregulated utilities, with nominal growth prospects. This is evident when their price moves correlate with the utilities. Twenty years ago, AT&T stock was $40, five years ago it was $34, today it's $33.

Buyers are only motivated by a very high dividend. AT&T stock has a yield today of 6%, whereas corporate bonds have an average yield of only 3.5% (6/19). They moved these companies into the Communication Services sector, which doesn't make sense to me.

A small industry with an unknown future. Not my cup of tea.

VANGUARD FUNDS

As of today, Vanguard has become the largest fund and ETF operator with 5 trillion in assets under management. Investors are moving to their index funds because of their outperformance over long periods, and low fees. In June 2019, Vanguard became the second ETF issuer—after BlackRock—to cross the $1 trillion mark for ETF assets under management.

Vanguard offers a total of 80 ETFs, the largest of which is the Vanguard Total Stock Market ETF (VTI), which has $116 billion in assets under management. As of 6/19, Vanguard had eight ETFs included among the top 10 funds for inflows, with the Vanguard Mid-Cap ETF (VO) pulling in more than any other U.S.-listed ETF, with inflows of more than $2 billion.

Their guiding principle is extremely low fees, and on that score, the asset weighted average of all Vanguard ETFs expense ratios as of 6/19 is an almost unbelievable .10%. This means that for every $10,000 invested your annual fee will be $10. Also, they have no hidden fees, and do not delve into higher risk assets to improve yield.

I would not choose Vanguard however, as a broker. They have almost no retail offices (19 locations worldwide), so there is no one to sit down with if you so desire. Fidelity is an excellent broker, trades are only $5, their website platform and research pages are excellent, and there is no fee for merely signing up. The majority of the funds they manage however, have performed poorly - in large part because of their slow adoption of passive, low fee indexed ETFs - they still primarily offer actively managed funds. (They are slowly changing as high cost mutual funds go out of favor). I would recommend Fidelity as a broker, and when choosing ETFs, always include Vanguard as one of the choices in your comparison.

Vanguard has offerings in all of the basic fund categories, however in some cases they might not have exactly what you are interested in. These might include specialized areas, where you want to exclude certain market segments, or want an "equal weighted" ETF (see Diversification). For example, you may want to invest in the Pacific Rim, but exclude Japan, which had been a poor performer over the last 20 years (doing better now). Vanguard may not have such a choice. For the average investor, Vanguard will usually have what you need – good performance, common sense, nothing exotic, and low expense ratios.

I always like to compare at least 3 or 4 options when choosing ETFs, and It's not hard to compare them using Yahoo's chart option. You can add as many similar ETFs as you want and click on various time frames to see how each performs. To start the process, get a list of possible choices on ETF.com, by searching for the type of ETF you are interested in. They will give you a list arranged by assets under management. (The most popular ETF in a category is very often not the best performer).

If you are considering ETFs which follow the same index, chose the lowest cost option.

SECTORS I AVOID

Everyone has their favorites and "unfavorites" when it comes to investing. These are my least favorites, together with some of the business reasons why. It doesn't mean I'm necessarily right, but we all develop prejudices over our lifespan, usually because of unhappy previous results. There's nothing wrong with leaving some investments alone because of personnel biases. For my money, there are many better choices, with less risk exposure, than the following industries.

- Restaurants - They fall in and out of favor. They may do well for a while, but then start declining, with very few exceptions. They may achieve a reasonable base of customers, but investors are unmerciful and want growth. Investors focus on same store sales growth or lack thereof, ignoring that the existing level of business may be sufficient to generate reasonable profits. As restaurant chains become larger, growth of more than a couple of percent becomes very difficult. How many ways can sales volume be increased? Five years ago Subway was booming with their $5 foot long. Sales have been declining for the last four years without a clear reason. Try to think of the restaurants you know that have been successful for 10 years or more (mostly fast food). The industry is littered with failures, and most of them struggle to grow earnings. Stock prices are volatile. Business issues include, high overhead, availability of competent employees and turnover, rising minimum wages, vulnerability to food borne illnesses (Chipotle), franchise management quality, aggressive competitors, changes in consumer preferences, and an inability to control food cost.

- <u>Retailers -</u> Like restaurants, they go in and out of favor. E-commerce is killing the brick and mortar stores like book stores, and especially department stores, whose expenses are too high. The number of bankruptcies of major, previously successful chains, is a warning for long term investors. Many cater to groups of customers whose preferences are fickle—like teenagers and luxury buyers. Retailers are often concentrated in apparel, which is a market segment which has done terribly in recent years, for a long list of reasons we don't need to enumerate here. The list of apparel retailer bankruptcies is a long one.

    o The only segment which seem to have long term staying power is the off-price discounters, where they have embraced e-commerce - Ross, Marshall's, TJ Maxx, etc. The number of mass market retailers remaining standing is coming down to Walmart, Target, Costco, and Macy's - where did the rest go?

    o Investors expect a retailer to experience strong and/or increasing year over year same store sales growth. This is an unsustainable goal. At some point retailers are unable to get any more sales out of a store, and same store sales plateaus, or God forbid, goes negative. If it does, investors dump the stock. Costco is an example. With each store already doing a huge level of volume, achieving same store sales growth of more than 3 or 4% is extremely difficult. Investors, historically are not interested in stores not increasing same store growth by less than 5%. If you are a long-term retail investor, at some point same store sales will level off and the share price will drop significantly.

- o When the number of alternatives is reduced to a handful of choices, for example, Home Depot and Lowes in home improvement, perhaps they will have staying power. However, e-commerce continues unabated. Being the last survivor didn't help Toys-R Us. Will Best Buy as the last mass market electronic seller make it? I'd rather not guess. So far, retailers who have embraced and expanded their e-commerce platform have been chosen by investors, including Walmart, Target, and Costco. In my view retailers are more suited to stock traders than long term investors.

- <u>IPOs</u> - Initial Public Offerings are new stock issuances for previously non-public companies. They generate tons of publicity and buzz. Their initial prices are set high based on a favorable sales and earnings forecast prepared by the underwriter, which is receiving a huge fee to establish "fair value". IPOs often go higher initially as buyers are hoping to get in on the ground floor, but usually drop in price after the initial excitement wears off. High risk, high reward for the small number of companies which survive. These are suited for day traders placing bets and then watching the momentum play out.

- <u>Insurance Companies</u> - I stay away from this industry because I don't understand it, even though I have worked for one. Excluding life insurance companies, which provide a known benefit for a known price, it seems to me the only way they do well is by selling overpriced policies and then using lengthy contracts written in their favor, and lots of lawyers to escape having to pay out, or pay out as little as possible, in the event of a loss. Their administrative overhead is very large. When they do pay out, it's usually less than you expected to receive, and then they increase your premium rates and collect their money back. Their existence is based upon a negative concept - collect money from people up front, and then pay a small group of them as little as possible at some future date. To me, it's a necessary evil.

- o They increase their profits by taking financial advantage of their own customers—a backward concept. As a consumer you will need to buy certain categories of insurance, for your home, your car, for your life when you have young dependents, but there is no need to invest in them. There is also no need to buy investment products from them - you will do better elsewhere. Also it looks like global warming may be increasing the number and amount of losses incurred from weather disasters, which will impact property and casualty insurers. Any consideration in this industry must concentrate on the type of insurance products offered - life, property and casualty, health, long term care, annuities, pensions, etc. In their defense, people need insurance in several areas, especially health and property damage.

- Hospitals and Nursing Homes - These companies struggle to break even despite a huge demand for their services and very high prices. Also, there is too much reliance on the government for revenue, which is always seeking ways to reduce payments to providers. See also Healthcare.

- Pharmaceutical Companies - These companies, like Pfizer and Merck, spend millions on drug research, most of which ends up on drugs which do not work effectively (est. 90%). Drugs which do work have to be priced at gouge levels to reimburse years of research expense. Excessive price increases are common, and huge payments are made to keep generics from both being produced (prolonging the life of expired patents) and used (through agreements with distributors). Increased regulation of prices and practices seems inevitable - one of the few bipartisan issues in Washington. Instead of selling more at lower prices, they seem to prefer selling less at outrageous prices. It's hard to think of another industry which has been as punitive to their customers.

- o Remember Valeant Pharmaceutical? - They were so crooked they had to change their name (now Bausch Health) - and the Mylan Epipen increased 600% in 9 years. Pfizer's stock price is at the same price as in 2001, as is Merck's. If you want to invest in this space, I prefer biotech (ETFs only). The price of these stocks has edged up in '18 as investors move into healthcare ETFs which lifts all boats.

- Shopping Malls - As of mid-2018 shopping malls are doing poorly as e-commerce sellers like Amazon, replace department stores creating mall vacancies and mall closures. Many believe the US is overstored. One recent report forecasted 50% mall vacancy by 2020 which sounds high but who wants to bet their wrong? In contrast, apartments and condos are experiencing heavy demand and higher prices because home prices in the US have risen so high most young people cannot afford to buy a home. An oversupply of retail malls is resulting in a need for them to consider re-inventing themselves, like switching to warehouse or office space, however this will lessen value.

- Airlines – Investing in airlines, in my humble opinion, is a mistake, although Warren Buffett disagrees, God knows why. The industry goes through boom and bust cycles, and you need to guess when these cycles are beginning and ending. Airline results are continually whipsawed by two nemesis – oil prices – their biggest cost factor – and increased capacity. Increased capacity can be from existing airlines adding planes, or new competitors. The airlines have no way to control either of these issues. Nine airlines filed bankruptcy between 2003 and 2008. Almost every airline has declared bankruptcy at least once, including United ('02), Delta ('05), and American ('11). Look at the list of airlines 20 years ago and most names are gone.

- When ticket prices are up and planes are full, several new economy airlines are started. These startups become popular because of their lower prices, so the majors have to reduce rates, and try to compete using fare discounts – planes fly less full and profitability falls. They have recently resorted to charging for previously free things like bags of peanuts and use of overhead bins (good grief).

- The airlines habitually underpay their employees resulting in job actions and pilot shortages, one of which is happening now (2018).

- Lastly, this is perhaps the only businesses where the customers are treated terribly, and the airlines don't care – just fill seats, and charge for anything and everything. Drag people off flights, kill their pets, and make people sit on the tarmac for 8 hours – no usable bathroom. Most people hate flying not out of fear, but because of the hassle, and getting treated like cattle. What a terrible business.

We all need to fly and so demand is not the issue, but we do not need to invest in them.

- New businesses – This seems obvious but there seems to be an endless number of people willing to throw money at whatever seems to be the next fantastic opportunity - usually a tech "disruptor". If one of these new things turns out to be a success, so what? If you missed out on Twitter or Facebook, it's not the end of the world, you didn't lose anything. Include here Bitcoin, and derivatives, where there is no underlying thing of value, but merely a Wall Street manufactured way for investors to make bets on things which go up and down, like the VIX index. The street is littered with failures, like Gopro, which seemed, for a while, to be very promising business.

- Luxury Goods – I have a strong bias against companies which make and sell very high-priced consumer goods.

These companies usually overcharge relative to costs, resulting in huge gross margins, a euphemism for price gouging. They have to continually convince shoppers that their goods are somehow superior and are worth their higher price. Sometimes this is true, but often they take advantage of an uninformed public with marketing hype, and appeal to status conscious people. $5000 ladies' handbags and $3000 watches satisfy the lowest rung of human values in my view. This business is highly susceptible to economic downturns, including stock market declines, and is also susceptible to much lower priced knockoff products. Many businesses make outsized profits selling to the rich, which I prefer to leave for others to invest in.

- <u>Media</u> – The media landscape is going through a complete overhaul due to cultural change. As we all know cell phones, the internet, and the adoption of streaming as a way we access entertainment, news, sports, and politics is rendering previous business models obsolete. Newspapers and magazines and cable TV are disappearing. Established businesses like AT&T, Disney, Fox, and Comcast need to keep reinventing themselves through mergers, acquisitions, and asset sales. There are going to be winners and losers in media, I just don't know how to determine which is which. Will Disney or Comcast buy Fox? Will ESPN keep dragging Disney down or will they sell it? Will cable TV totally disappear? How can anyone know how this plays out? All of these large companies are represented in the capitalization-based index funds and this is enough exposure for my taste.

CHOOSING ETFS

Read this section to learn how to choose ETFs. This may seem daunting but after doing it a few times it comes easily. Every day, new ETF categories are created by fund companies who want to give investors a way to invest passively in whatever market segment or class of investment they believe will offer new ways to diversify your portfolio. New indexes are created by investment companies which are then used for ETF rule-based investing. Most ETFs follow the index as closely as possible (how closely they follow the index is called their efficiency) by buying every stock (or bond, or commodity) in the index if this is feasible. We now have an index for about every category of investment you can imagine. At the end of this paper I include a list of popular ETFs and one's I own or have owned.

One way to start is by Googling "Best _____ ETF", and fill in whatever type of company or sector you are interested in. Such as: Mid-cap, (mid-size) Stocks, Australian, companies, Energy companies, Short term Corporate Bonds, Gold, High Dividend Stocks, Real Estate (REITS), Chinese companies, Utilities, Healthcare companies, etc. You will come across articles describing and ranking specific ETFs by category. You can also do a search on ETF.com by ETF type and you will get a list.

Read descriptions written by reliable sources like ETF.com, Forbes, Morningstar, Vanguard, Wall Street Journal, and Fidelity, I don't recommend Motley Fool, Seeking Alpha, or The Street. Investopedia.com is good for basic understanding of terms.

After reading the descriptions of the ETFs listed, jot down the stock symbol of some you want to look into further, go to one of the stock research sites and enter the stock symbol in the search bar. I primarily use Fidelity (click research) Yahoo (go to Yahoo Finance), and ETF.com (free with email and I get their daily email which is very good). Each site provides similar information, just in a different format.

Fidelity is probably the most accurate, and also has the most detail, sometimes too much. Yahoo has an easy to use summary, easy tabs to specifics, and interactive charts. Fidelity is somewhat less intuitive, but also more current. ETF.com has better comparison charts, but they are spread out on different tabs.

Here's what you want to learn:

- What is it? Read the description of what the ETF's invests in, also called the profile. What index, if any, does it follow? Type of company, size of companies, location (country), etc.

- What is the expense ratio? This is the annual fee the investment company charges for management. For ETFs: 0 -.10 % (great); .10--.25% (good) .25 - .40 (OK) Over .40% (high). This is a most important factor for comparing similar ETFs. Ratios over .40% may be tolerable if there is no good alternative, such as China or an equally weighted ETF. History shows that when comparing ETFs and funds, the expense ratio is the <u>single most important factor</u> in determining performance over time, when comparing funds following the same or a similar index. However, a better performing index trumps a very low ER.

- What are its holdings? Scan the top 10 or more holdings to get a feel for what companies it holds. Are you comfortable with the list? Do they fit the intention you have?

- What are the concentrations (amount of diversification)? Under the holdings list note how much of the ETF is concentrated in the top few names. The major benefit of an ETF is to spread the risk among many companies. However, many ETFs end up with high concentrations, because the index requires them to, due to capitalization weightings, and this is a weakness.

    o For example, XLE is a large energy ETF. It is dominated by oil companies and Exxon is so large on a relative basis, that the ETF must hold 24% of its assets in Exxon. This is not desirable. Look at the % of the total the Top Ten Holdings represent. If the top holdings has a very significant share of the total, look for other alternatives. There are some ETFS that are "equal weighted" where each holding will have approximately the same weighting, like 2 or 3%. These are much preferred, although there are not many of them, and their expense ratios may be somewhat higher.

- How big is it? Bigger is better (usually). The AUM is the "assets under management". But don't assume the largest (most popular) is the best - it often isn't. Tiny ETFs may be less liquid, will have greater bid/ask spreads, and are subject to greater volatility. Moreover, why hasn't the fund grown larger? Very large actively managed funds have some disadvantages of size, however ETFs do not. If there is no large ETF for a category you want, sometimes you have to choose a smaller one (I have XHE ($540M) and PSCH ($943M) for lack of a good alternative). If you hold on to your investments rather than trade them, the size of the AUM is not as relevant.

- How many shares trade daily? Large investors need high volumes of trade activity in case they decide to sell (ie., are there enough buyers out there?). For small investors like us, this is not an issue.

- How has it performed? I usually leave the performance test to last. When I've narrowed my choice down to 3 or 4 ETFs, I go to Yahoo Finance (finance.yahoo.com) enter the ETF symbol in the search box, enter, and then click "chart", the second tab after Summary. You'll see a simple line chart for the period underlined at the top. The chart is not complicated by the daily range data in Fidelity which is unneeded. Click "comparison at the top of the cart, enter the symbol for the next ETF, click save and you'll see both ETFs graphed together. Enter as many symbols as you want. You can also enter a Index like the Dow or S&P 500 to see how your choices compare to it. I usually add the SPY for the S&P 500. Then gradually click on different time periods for the chart and observe how your choices did, at say 1 month, 3 months, 1 year, 2, and 5 years.

Vanguard has been the leader for conservative ETFs with very good performance and very low expense ratios. When comparing ETFs, it good to have at least one Vanguard ETF among your choices for comparison. Small differences in the ER are secondary to how well the ETF has performed. If two ETFs graph exactly together, that means they follow the same index. In that case chose the lower ER.

IV. YOUR RISK PROFILE

One of the first steps in developing an investment portfolio is to develop an understanding of your own tolerance for financial risk, and also the risk tolerance of your significant other. Any reputable wealth advisor will try to determine what you risk tolerance profile is before recommending investment choices, however more important is that you make this determination yourself. All investments go up and down in value, but some much more than others. If you go through a significant financial downturn, as many of us did in 2008, you will learn a lot about your own risk tolerance, and whether you need stomach acid blockers (like I do).

The infallible axiom of investing is that less risk provides a lower probable return, and more risk provides a higher probable return. If you think you have found a low risk/high return investment you are having a hallucination caused by mind altering substances, or a questionable brother in law.

We all sit somewhere on a continuum of investment risk ranging from the least risk or zero appetite for risk, say, on the left, and super aggressive risk, say, on the right. Where you are on this scale depends on your age, your genetic risk appetite, your income, how many dependents you have, how much you have already saved, your overall level of optimism or pessimism, your previous investing experience (such as huge losses on a bad investment), your health condition and health insurance situation, and I'm sure you can think of a few more.

All of us are a complex bundle of all of these factors, and it's important to understand where you are on the risk scale. <u>Everyone wants to be cautious with their savings – no one wants to lose money. But there is a financial penalty for being too cautious</u> – you might not make enough of a return to live comfortably and may run out of money in retirement.

Surveys show the number one fear of people in, or entering retirement is outliving your savings. This has become an enormous issue because we can reasonably expect to live to 85 or even longer, while corporate downsizing may end your career before you've even reached 65. You need to make healthy returns, but you also need to sleep at night.

Here is a brief characterization of the continuum of investment risk profiles. It's a bit simplistic but you'll get the idea.

- At the far left, super cautious individuals will hide money under the floorboards, put money in bank savings accounts or bank certificates of deposit, leave their money in a checking account (cash), or buy US government bonds. They tolerate 1 or 2% interest rates because they are deathly afraid of losing principal. They like owning gold and may put gold coins in a lock box. They may buy lottery tickets to alleviate their fear of having inadequate savings.

- Moving to the right, the next group still leans toward caution, but is aware that they must take some risk to get a better return. They buy some stocks, but mostly bonds. They may move up from US treasuries to corporate bonds (debt of US corporations) or municipal bonds and keep cash balances moderate. The stocks they buy are stable large "blue chip" companies like those in the Dow 30, utilities; consumer staples companies, perhaps banks and insurance companies, and stable companies paying good dividends like AT&T. The bonds they buy are Gov't bonds, investment grade corporate bonds, and utility co. bonds. This group is usually called "cautious".

- Wanting higher returns, and willing to tolerate market downturns, the next group has either 100% stocks or a high stock bond ratio like 70/30. Their bonds lean toward higher risk higher/return choices like longer term governments, less than investment grade corporate bonds (high yield or junk), or foreign bonds (gov't or corporate). Their stock portfolios lean toward rapid growth companies with elevated P/E's, often technology companies, international stocks, and emerging markets stock. They may invest in commodities, real estate, or mortgage lenders. They lean away from utilities and stable slow growth industries like food and beverage. This group is usually called "aggressive". Even though retired, I'm in this category, even though I'm not supposed to be.

- At the extreme right, high risk takers will buy stocks in small companies which have not made a profit yet, make loans to privately owned startup companies based solely on an idea, buy high interest rate bonds issued by third world countries or financially distressed corporations, invest in questionable schemes like buying into life insurance policies held by other people (viaticals), may invest in collectables like baseball cards, put money into crypto currencies, etc. They buy stocks on tips heard at cocktail parties, buy whatever is going up right now, probably are concentrated in a handful of individual companies, sell anything which doesn't go up right away, and probably own a motorcycle, and are thinking about trying base jumping where you dress up like a flying squirrel.

These generalizations are obviously an oversimplification, but hopefully they will start you thinking about where you are on this scale. In truth, we probably really don't know how much tolerance we have for a big drop in the market, as we did in '08 when the S&P 500 dropped 50%. That decline probably set the bar for the worst that could happen to the major averages, as our US financial system had essentially failed. Many have exited the stock market permanently after that happened, understandably so. The recovery since then has been remarkable, but many have missed it altogether. A lot has changed since then to prevent a recurrence, and I don't believe that will happen again, to that degree.

When your holdings go down in value it does not mean you have lost money, unless you sell and realize the loss. If you have invested wisely, your assets will recover, as long as you are patient, and don't sell out prematurely. It like having a mint '55 Chevy in your garage. Its value will wax and wane as collectors decide what's hot and what's not, but if you wait long enough, it will increase in value (inflation almost guarantees it).

Patience is very difficult when you see a statement from your broker showing your life savings has gone down significantly. If you are losing sleep because of a downturn, you may need to invest more cautiously, but keep in mind even cautious portfolios go up and down.

If your holdings have gone down, google a 50 or 100 year chart of the S&P 500. Its march upward is relentless when seen in long term perspective, and it will give you some comfort.

As you get older you will definitely move to the left on this scale. After retirement you can't afford a huge setback, which might have been tolerable when you were 30. On the other hand, most of us will need to take some level of risk to live comfortably. If you are rich you do not need to read this. Invest 100% in US bonds and go fishing.

What is rich? Obviously, it keeps going up due to inflation, but the larger issue is the exorbitant cost of healthcare in the US. Every day I read about people who thought they had enough saved for retirement, and then literally lost it all trying to pay for insane healthcare costs for cancer treatment, or nursing home costs.

Think about your response to this situation: Your life partner is seriously ill; the doctor says treatment XYZ may bring them back to health but it will cost $500,000. What are you going to say? Ah well doc, that's too much - do you have anything that doesn't work as well but is cheaper? My spouse's cancer treatments were $15,000 every three weeks, and her cancer was one of the least difficult to treat.

Most investment advisors suggest you hold more bonds than stock after age 60. I disagree, unless you either have at least $3 million, or more, where a 2.5% return will provide $75,000 for living expenses, or you have a very low maintenance lifestyle and you can somehow exist on Social Security or a work pension.

If you live off the grid, like in an Idaho cabin with solar panels, get water from a well, get around on a Schwinn, don't go to NFL games, don't have any unemployed kids, collect Social Security, and never get sick, bonds may work for you.

There is a serious fallacy about retirement. Someone started a rule of thumb that lives on, that your living expenses would go down by 30% in retirement. The reason being no commuting expense, no mortgage, lower clothing costs, lower taxes, etc. This may have been true many years ago but I'm afraid it doesn't work today.

House repairs and improvements and utilities stay at the same level, as do insurance premiums, automobiles, property taxes, and food (more if you eat out often). In your early retirement years (called your go-go years) you travel more, help the kids financially, probably treat yourself to a nice car, and maybe a vacation property, and in your later years, healthcare starts soaking up your cash, and inflation starts to take its toll. In my experience your living expenses will not change much in retirement.

It's not possible to generalize here because all of us lead such different lives, but anecdotally people I talk to say they spend less on some things, but other new expenses offset any savings, and they don't see much of a change in their total cost of living. Living in San Diego you say a small prayer before opening the water bill. (If you have a swimming pool fill it in with dirt and plant geraniums).

What all this means is that it would be nice to have so much money you can buy Gov't bonds and forget about capital appreciation like the cautious group on the spectrum. Otherwise you need to move to the right and join us folks over on the right.

There are a couple of Risk Assessment tools available on the internet where you can answer a bunch of questions and Walla! Your risk profile is magically revealed. I tried the one offered by Vanguard <u>Vanguard Risk Assessment Tools</u> and was disappointed. There were not enough questions, and it didn't even ask me my age. It recommended I have 50% in bonds, when in fact I had none at that time because of rising interest rates.

The robo advisor's websites also have risk questionnaires. I recommend you try one or two of these, they don't take much time, but they will get you thinking about what the issues are.

Do not forget to take into account your significant other, especially if you are investing their money as well as your own. If you are of different risk tolerance levels, split your funds into two parts.

Also consider splitting your savings into say three risk categories and establishing a separate brokerage account for each - it won't cost anything. In your cautious account go strictly with bonds (beware rising interest rates however), bond surrogates, and utility type stocks; in the core account go for domestic S&P 500 ETFs; and in the riskier account go for international, emerging markets, high yield debt, small companies, etc. Use only ETFs in each. This way you will always know how your risk profile looks. If want to dabble a bit in individual stocks which look good to you, set aside a small finite amount which you understand could drop by a significant percentage, or join an investment club which calls for a small enough contribution to be insignificant.

Some risk profiles talk about coming to grips with how much you can afford to lose. To me this is nonsense. No one wants to lose anything. It's more about patience. If the market pulls back significantly you will feel like you need to do something, to stop the reduction in your savings. But if the market has already gone down significantly, selling would turn paper losses into real losses. The best thing may be to do nothing. Remind yourself that you're a long-term investor, markets always come back, look at a 100 year chart of the S&P 500, and forget about the market for a while.

Unfortunately, markets don't recover overnight, and there's nothing you can do to hurry it along. The market will recover in a zigzag up and down pattern over months not weeks, and occasionally over more than a year. This is why patience is a key ingredient in measuring your risk tolerance.

Once you determine the level of risk you are comfortable with, you can establish a portfolio. You can make portfolio changes easily, because of changes in your risk appetite, risk assessment, or changes to your life situation, so don't think any of your choices are cast in stone.

V. STRATEGY- ASSET ALLOCATION

The strategy recommended herein is to use low cost ETFs to develop a highly diversified portfolio for long term investors. The object is to maximize your return without taking excessive risk, so your money will be there when you retire. This approach will not produce huge gains in short periods, and conversely, not endure huge losses. You give up the former to feel comfortable and protect your downside. Your overall return will be at least equal to average global returns, and if you make educated informed choices, you will exceed those returns. You set asset allocations at the outset, and review them at least quarterly, and make changes as you deem appropriate. You give up the belief that you, or anyone else, can pick individual stocks correctly over the long term, and your portfolio will outperform the vast majority of those who employ financial advisors, or use actively managed funds.

Your portfolio should be as diversified as possible. The asset choices are stocks (US or int'l), bonds (corporate, municipal, or gov't), commodities (precious or construction metals, oil, or agricultural), savings vehicles like CDs, and real estate (actual, or businesses which own R/E like REIT's). Everything else includes things most of us don't understand, cannot afford, or are illiquid, such as original works of art, antiques, collectables, and things which are rare or in finite supply like 1950's Porsches, and raw land. Since you will have likely have most of your money in the US stock market, you will benefit by choosing investments which usually move inversely with that market, or at least have a low correlation with that market (easier said than done).

One of the most difficult decisions is what proportion, if any, you should have in bonds. Almost every model will show an increasing proportion of bonds as you age. The problem with having a large proportion of bonds is well outlined in this paper - you may outlive your money because of inadequate returns. Rules of thumb commonly used for bond allocation also ignores the particulars of your life situation - how much you have to invest, the cost of your lifestyle, kids ages, health, parent's health, health insurance situation, your risk tolerance, the direction of interest rates, the direction of the economy, and what your time horizon for using the money is. Bonds decrease in value in periods of increasing interest rates, and inflation may reduce your rate of return to zero. As of mid-2019, average bond yields of 2.0% are about equal to the inflation rate of 2.0%, so no real dollar gain results.

The less you have saved the less you can afford to lose. As you increase your proportion of bonds, your volatility will decrease, that is downturns will be less severe (but still go down) and your return will also decrease.

To illustrate the difference between stocks and bonds since the recession of 2008-09, a portfolio of 60% stocks and 40% bonds, as many guides suggest, would have yielded 6.2%, vs. a 100% stock, S&P 500 return of 11%.

For the 12 months ending 8/31/18 the 60/40 portfolio would have earned 7.6%, vs. the S&P 500 return of 19.7%

For the higher return of stocks, you have to stomach pullbacks of about 10% approximately on an annual basis, and as much as 20% or more in bear markets, perhaps once every 5-10 years, caused by a recession or severe economic downturn.

Keep in mind that stocks tend to follow overall economic activity, up and down, while bonds fluctuate more with interest rate changes, in an inverse fashion. Stocks generally move inversely with bonds, but not always.

When interest rates increase to where you can earn 3-4% in a bank savings account or bonds have 3-5% coupons, that will argue for putting a larger chunk of your savings in bonds. As interest rates rise on bonds and saving vehicles like bank CD's, investors will move more of their funds from stocks into those vehicles to reduce risk, and the price of stocks may decline.

VI. PORTFOLIO RECOMMENDATIONS
(3 or 4 capitalized letters are ETF stock symbols)

- For a <u>small portfolio, say under $25k</u>, as you may have from a former employer 401(k). It's probably not worth over thinking your allocations. Perhaps:

  60% in the Vanguard total US stock market VTI

  40% in the Vanguard Global stock index (minus US) symbol VXUS.

  (Warren Buffett's suggestion: 90% S&P 500; 10% short term Gov't bonds)

- For a <u>portfolio of say $25-100k</u>, I would split it up into perhaps 6 pieces. Say:

  S&P 500 - 25% VOO;

  Europe or Euro zone (ex. Britain) - 20% VGK or EZU;

  Healthcare – 15% - IHI and XHE (7.5% each);

  Technology – 15% VGT;

  Emerging markets – 10% VWO;
  Corporate bonds - 15% LQD (as long as interest are rates not rising significantly).

- For a <u>larger portfolio which you don't want to have to look at too often</u> consider:

    US Stock – 45% - Large cap 20% VOO, midcap 15% IVOO, Healthcare 10% IHI

    Int'l Stock – 30% - Global ex. US 15% VXUS, Pacific 10% VPL (includes Japan), China; Emerging Mkts. 5% GXC;

    Bonds – 20%, 10% Aggregate bonds BND, 10% Corporate bonds LQD

    Real Estate – 5% VNQ

- A <u>simplistic ultra-cheap portfolio</u> you could look at infrequently:

    Total US Stock market - 45% - ITOT (ER .03)

    Developed World stocks ex. US - 30% SPDW (ER .04)

    US Investment grade fixed income (Corp., gov't., mtg backed) - 15% SCHZ (ER .04)

    Emerging Markets ex. Korea - 5% SPEM (ER.12)

    REITs broad selection 5% - SCHH (ER.07)

- Here's another portfolio offered by <u>Kiplinger, taking advantage of super low Vanguard fees:</u>

    S&P 500 - VOO 35%

    Mid cap - VO 10%

    Small cap - VB 10%

    International (developed markets) - VEA 17%

    Emerging Markets - VWO 8%

VI. PORTFOLIO RECOMMENDATIONS
(3 or 4 capitalized letters are ETF stock symbols)

- For a <u>small portfolio, say under $25k</u>, as you may have from a former employer 401(k). It's probably not worth over thinking your allocations. Perhaps:

    60% in the Vanguard total US stock market VTI

    40% in the Vanguard Global stock index (minus US) symbol VXUS.

    (Warren Buffett's suggestion: 90% S&P 500; 10% short term Gov't bonds)

- For a <u>portfolio of say $25-100k</u>, I would split it up into perhaps 6 pieces. Say:

    S&P 500 - 25% VOO;

    Europe or Euro zone (ex. Britain) - 20% VGK or EZU;

    Healthcare – 15% - IHI and XHE (7.5% each);

    Technology – 15% VGT;

    Emerging markets – 10% VWO;
    Corporate bonds - 15% LQD (as long as interest are rates not rising significantly).

- For a <u>larger portfolio which you don't want to have to look at too often</u> consider:

    US Stock – 45% - Large cap 20% VOO, midcap 15% IVOO, Healthcare 10% IHI

    Int'l Stock – 30% - Global ex. US 15% VXUS, Pacific 10% VPL (includes Japan), China; Emerging Mkts. 5% GXC;

    Bonds – 20%, 10% Aggregate bonds BND, 10% Corporate bonds LQD

    Real Estate – 5% VNQ

- A <u>simplistic ultra-cheap portfolio</u> you could look at infrequently:

    Total US Stock market - 45% - ITOT (ER .03)

    Developed World stocks ex. US - 30% SPDW (ER .04)

    US Investment grade fixed income (Corp., gov't., mtg backed) - 15% SCHZ (ER .04)

    Emerging Markets ex. Korea - 5% SPEM (ER.12)

    REITs broad selection 5% - SCHH (ER.07)

- Here's another portfolio offered by <u>Kiplinger, taking advantage of super low Vanguard fees:</u>

    S&P 500 - VOO 35%

    Mid cap - VO 10%

    Small cap - VB 10%

    International (developed markets) - VEA 17%

    Emerging Markets - VWO 8%

Short Term Corporate Bonds - VCSH - 20% (1-5 yr. maturity, avg. duration 2.7 yrs. If yields rose 1%, principal impairment would be 2.7%)

For larger portfolios where you would like to review and make changes at least quarterly, consider all of the assets listed below, overweighting and underweighting as you see fit based upon all of the comments in this paper. I presently have my portfolio in 16 ETFs.

Because I cannot find an acceptable commodities ETF, I have none, but would like to find one. I have 5% in gold as an attempt to add diversity into anything not correlated highly to stocks. I am always searching for investments which do not correlate highly with common stock prices so as to reduce risk in a market pullback.

You will read lots of articles online predicting huge market crashes, or bear markets, or charts which predict serious trouble for stocks, or tipping points we're about to eclipse, and these all sound scary, since your life savings is at stake. I don't know why there are so many doomsayers, but there are. If you react by putting everything in a savings account or gov't bonds, you may end up outliving your savings. Take comfort that your ETFs spread risk, and that there will probably be a number of market pullbacks and then recoveries, before you retire.

VII. ETF CHOICES

There will always be secular changes taking place in any economy. The largest of these changes in the US were the shift from an agricultural economy, to an industrial one, to one dominated by energy, and to one dominated by technology. The process of diversifying investments and over and underweighting business sectors based upon your assessment of changes taking place in our economy, and its effect on business profitability, serves as your compass for choosing investments which are likely to do well going forward. You don't have to be clairvoyant. Just be mindful of what's happening around you and apply common sense.

First read the cash section of this paper and make a thoughtful determination of the amount of cash you believe is necessary to set aside from investments. Keep in mind that cash increases safety, but earns almost nothing, and the more you set aside the lower your returns will be. Then divide the balance into the ETFs listed below, going for as much diversification as possible. Overweight where you are confident, and vice versa. Your allocation to each asset can be any amount. Remember making changes to your allocations costs almost nothing - $5 to sell and $5 to buy a replacement. ETF symbols below are capitalized with 3 or 4 letters. Never hesitate to make a change because of transaction fees.

Listed below are the major ETF categories you should consider for your portfolio. This list is of the basic categories only - there are many others. Companies bringing to market new ETFs have reached further and further into lesser known securities, or new and creative ways to group them. I have limited the list to those which are fundamental to our market, understandable, not without undue risk, and suited to long term investors. If you want to explore some of the other options, go to ETF.com and search for whatever type of security you are interested in.

BONDS

As noted, bonds come in countless numbers of durations, purposes, means of repayment, seniority, country, business segment, etc. As Warren Buffet has said, over the long-term stocks will outperform bonds, so the greater proportion of bonds you hold, the lower your overall return will be. Here are just a few suggestions in the core segments.

<u>Short term</u> – This category of bonds reduces the risk of principal loss when interest rates rise, and therefore has a low coupon – low risk, low reward. The longer a bond is, the greater its inverse sensitivity to interest rates. This sector is very similar to near cash, which has a very low return, but is better than letting money sit totally idle. You may view this category as a place to park cash if you are willing to take a small degree of risk. For ETF choices see <u>Near Cash</u> below.

<u>Total Bonds</u> – These funds follow indices which include <u>all</u> investment grade bond types; gov't, public, taxable, asset backed, and corporate (no high yield). If you decide to have just one bond ETF, consider AGG or BND (Vanguard). They both have very low expense ratios, are very large, have similar yields, and have very similar performance histories. Bond ETF yields do not very widely. If you want to drill down a bit look at the following categories below. Over the last year (7/19) both ETFs have performed equally - both up 5%. They have YTD yields of 2.7%. They have performed well in 2019 due to falling interest rates, but most do not think rates can go much lower.

International Bonds – I do not own this sector, but it might be considered since it has performed much better than US investment grade bond funds. BNDX is a Vanguard, investment grade, dollar denominated, non-US global bond fund, with a low expense ratio (.11%). Made up of mostly European bonds, 75% is in gov't bonds. The yield is 2.9%, however its YTD return is 6.9% (7/19) due to falling interest rates.

High Yield bonds – As investment grade bond funds yields have declined, investors have piled into high yield funds, also known as junk bonds. These are non-investment grade (S&P rated BB and below classification) which carry a higher yield and higher risk of default. ETFs provide diversification of risk in an otherwise somewhat risky investment. Most popular are large ETFs HYG, JNK, and SJNK. All of these have expense ratios in the .4-.5% range and have yields in the 5.2-5.6% range. All of these have similar performance. So many investors have moved into this bond sector that yields are believed by many to now be too low for the degree of risk assumed. Sticking with a well-diversified ETF mitigates this somewhat. A subset of this category is leveraged bank loans which are made to subprime borrowers. I would avoid this category altogether (I worked in this business, too risky).

Corporate bonds – These are investment grade bonds issued by large US corporations. Risk is very low and so is return. A safe place for cash unless rates are rising. LQD dominates with an expense ratio of .15% and a yield of 3.4%. It has gained 12% YTD (7/19) due to the fall in interest rates.

Municipal bonds – These are best suited to high tax bracket investors. They are very low risk and therefore have a very low yield, however, the yield is even lower than other bond types because they are usually tax free (Fed and State usually), and so their after-tax yield is enhanced by the reciprocal of your tax bracket. VTEB, a tax free muni bond ETF, has a low cost, and a yield of 2.9%, and is up 5.7% YTD (7/19).

Long Term bonds – Not recommended for periods of rising interest rates. These would be OK in economic downturns or recessions. TLT tracks 20-year US gov't treasury bonds, yields 2.4% and has a low ER of .15%. For a super low return low risk investment, I'd much rather a bank CD, and pick a near term maturity like 18 months to two years. With a CD, you'll not bear any impairment of principal if interest rates rise. If yields ever return to 5% or more, these are perhaps worth considering.

Fixed Term Defined Maturity Corporate Bonds – New in 2011, these are bond portfolios purchased and held to mature as of a specific date. They're designed to act more like a bond than a bond fund. At maturity, investors receive a distribution equivalent to the fund's net asset value, and the fund is closed. Each maturity has a different symbol. Consider Guggenheim's Bulletshares corporate bond ETFs at Guggenheim Investments.com (click on ETF products). BSCP for example, is for corporate bonds maturing in 2025. iShares has a similar product, see IBDP for example, for their 2024 fund. These are actively managed but trade as an ETF. To read more see Schwab Target Maturity Bond ETFs.

Treasury Inflation Protected Bonds - Treasury inflation protected securities (TIPS) refer to a treasury security that is indexed to inflation in order to protect investors from the negative effects of inflation. They are very low risk, very low return bonds, lower than US Treasuries. Many recommend these ultra conservative securities, but I don't because their return is too small. The ETF TIP has a yield of 2.1% and a low expense ratio of .19%. Its YTD gain of 6.5% is deceivingly high due to the drop-in rates, not likely to reoccur. It protects against inflation but doesn't help against higher interest rates.

Other bonds – If you want to consider other types of bond funds I recommended you look at Vanguard's list here: Vanguard.com ETFs Here you will find long and intermediate term bonds, mortgage backed, inflation protected, corporate, and gov't. All will have yields between 2-3%. You won't find anything exciting here. Bonds will reduce your portfolio volatility, but that comes with a return which may be less than dollar inflation.

COMMODITIES

Commodities are sometimes counter cyclical and therefore are a diversification hedge. They react to increased demand in areas of the world which are growing and are also sensitive to the value of the dollar. China is currently the dominant factor in commodity demand.

In my view the commodity ETF choices currently available to the average investor all have too many negative issues. There are three ways to participate in commodities. ETFs of material company stocks such as VAW, XLB, or MXI (global) which are companies which principally produce, transport or supply commodities, like DuPont. They will go up and down in tandem with the rest of the stock market and therefore do not diversify your portfolio. ETFs which track the Bloomberg Commodity index – these unfortunately have very complex technical issues relating to owning futures contracts. Thirdly, ETFs attempting to duplicate the ownership of the actual commodities, also have technical problems, as they must continually buy and sell futures contracts.

Also large swings in oil prices whipsaw these ETFs - when oil prices decline it can wipe out your gain on everything else. Over the last year (7/19) GSG has done the "best" down 10% and down 50% over the last 5 years and has a high ER of .75%. I have devoted a considerable amount of time trying to find a suitable ETF for commodities to no avail. Until something better is introduced, I would settle for one of the company stock ETFs as described above.

COMMUNICATION SERVICES

Last year, Standard & Poor's and MSCI, two of the largest providers of indexes for use by issuers of exchange-traded funds, said that the telecommunications sector was being transformed. With telecom companies moving to the newly created communications services sector, this resulted in major changes to previous sector classifications.

Previously, the telecom sector – one of the smallest sector weights in the S&P 500 – and the related ETFs were dominated by Verizon Communications and AT&T. By pulling some stocks out of the consumer discretionary and technology sectors, the new communications services sector contains dissimilar businesses.

From the consumer discretionary sector, the media, entertainment, interactive media and services, and interactive home entertainment sub-industries have been added to the new communications services group.

In addition to AT&T and Verizon, the top 10 holdings in the new sector Index includes three of the four FANG stocks – Facebook, Netflix, and Google, as well as Disney. That means the Technology Select SPDR ETF (XLK) and other technology ETFs part ways with Alphabet and Facebook. Consumer discretionary ETFs tracking S&P and MSCI benchmarks, such as the Consumer Discretionary Sector SPDR ETF (XLY), lost exposure to Netflix and Disney.

Looking backward, the Communication Services sector index returned annualized performance of 14.2 percent over three years, 12.7 percent over five years and 9.9 percent over ten years. The back-test period ran from late 2007 through April 30, 2018.

I am not a fan of this new classification. The problem is that from an investor standpoint, the businesses in this group are significantly different, and I cannot see how grouping them together makes sense for an investor selecting business sectors. The category was created for companies, "that facilitate communication and offer related content and information through various media". This is so broadly worded, it's almost laughable to me. How Disney's entertainment empire, Google's internet dominance, and Facebook's social media business can be considered together is nonsense.

The two largest ETFs in this new sector are XLC and Vanguards VOX. I cannot recommend either, or any other ETF following this sector, as the businesses are so fundamentally different, they should not be invested in logically as one classification.

CONSUMER DISCRETIONARY

These are companies who sell non-essential goods and services to consumers. It includes durable goods, retail, autos, apparel, leisure, entertainment, travel, restaurants, and apparel. It encompasses 9 of the 11 S&P sectors. These are purchases people make when they have discretionary funds available, which do well in a strong economy, and vice versa. They are expenditures people reduce or postpone when their money's tight – the opposite of consumer staples. These group includes Amazon, Disney, McDonalds, and Home Depot.

The most popular ETFs here include XLY, VCR, FDIS, and IYC. All of these are very heavily concentrated. XLY holds Amazon over 20%, Home Depot at 10%, with the top 5 equaling 50%. All of these have benefited greatly because of Amazons incredible price rise in the last couple of years (up 100% over the last 2 years). FXD has a nice equal weighted index but a high ER (.64%). XRT is a retail ETF which is equal weighted and an ER of .35%. Also, if you want to avoid the Amazon monolith, the small RCD is an equal weighted choice (ER .40%).

For the 1 year ending 6/19, of all of the ETFs listed above IYC performed the best, followed by XLY. XRT was very poor, also poor was FXD and RCD.

If you look at past performance, any of these ETFs which is heavily Amazon weighted will have the best return. Amazon is an incredible company which should support continued growth. However professional Investors will rush to the exits on many of the companies in this sector as soon as the economy begins to slow down. Therefore, if you choose this group, you should be prepared to reduce your position if that happens. Also, an ETF having more than 20% in one company begins to defeat the diversification objective of passive investing. This group also includes luxury goods - not my favorite.

If you want to be invested in Amazon, consider buying it outside of an ETF. This contradicts the main thesis of this book, however, Amazon is a very unique company. The massive scale, strong management, obsessive focus on customer satisfaction and convenience, and wide divergence in their sources of income including web services, makes it hard to argue the company will not be successful for many years to come. I only own two stocks individually, Amazon is one of those (Becton Dickinson is the other).

CONSUMER STAPLES

This is considered a defensive sector, which survives recessions better as consumers need to keep buying even in bad times. Mostly food and beverage stocks, but it also includes grocery retailers, which are currently getting hurt by Amazon, which has dragged this group down in recent years. Growth is very slow, but dividends are quite high. It does worse than the market in favorable economic growth periods.

These stocks did terribly in 2018 because of an increase in the cost of commodities, and higher labor costs, while unable to pass on these higher costs with higher prices. Therefore, profit margins were getting squeezed. Large retailers like Walmart, Target, and Costco are forcing prices down. The group turned totally around in 2019 as investors became very cautious and piled into defensive stocks. Note that investors chasing yield from strong dividend payers sometimes sell this group and invest in bonds when bond yields get up to 3% or higher, eclipsing dividends paid by these companies.

I would choose this group only if a market downturn is likely. Consider RHS, XLP, and VDC. I ran a one-year comparison (7/19) and RHS had the best performance of these three, up 13%.

DIVIDENDS

This group is highly popular because dividends play a major role in long term stock performance. There are hundreds of different variations of dividend stock ETFs, mostly large companies. They slice and dice not only by size of dividend, but the number of consecutive years paid, amount of average increase, US or global, common or preferred stocks, REIT's, etc. The strength here is the annual return, the weakness is that when bond yields increase, some investors will sell these equities and buy bonds instead. I consider this an important group to own. With US growth slowing in 2019, and bond rates falling, many investors have moved more heavily into dividend stocks. Because of that, P/Es have risen to very high levels for this group and may now possibly be considered too expensive.

Consider VIG (180 stocks); also look at DVY and SDY. I just ran a comparison of these 3 and over the last year VIG clearly outperformed the other two, up 13% (7/19) and has a very low ER of .08%.

EMERGING MARKETS

EM investors got hammered in 2018, down 20%, including me, because of the trade wars started by Trump, which were not anticipated by the markets. The three biggest ETFs here are Vanguard's VWO ($64B), IEMG ($59B), and EEM ($31B). They all have a similar Chinese bias but VWO and IEMG have a much lower ER. Over the last 5 years, they have returned similar returns - VWO has done slightly better. These ETFs are highly concentrated in China, So. Korea, Taiwan, and India = 67%.

Note: these will all overlap quite a bit with China ETFs like FXI and GXC. A relatively new emerging market ETF, EMQQ, focuses on internet and e-commerce companies, and has done well in YTD 7/19 up 20%.

If you decide to look at other emerging market ETFs, make sure you understand where the holdings are concentrated, although most follow the same two indices (MSCI & FTSE). There is so much weighting in China (30%) for these EM ETFs, I believe many mistakenly believe them to be more diversified globally than they actually are. Because of the trump created trade war with China, at the present time you must be careful in selecting Emerging Market ETFs which are heavily concentrated in China. If you wish to sit out this trade war until it's over, you may have to invest in an EM ETF which excludes China, such as EMXC (only $30 Million, ER .49%), or pass on this group altogether. For the 12 months ending 6/19, EEM was down 2.4% and EMXC was up 2.2%.

ENERGY

As mentioned above in the energy section, I stay away from this category because it is dominated by big oil, and I don't like being whipsawed up and down by the volatile price of oil. In early 2018 as oil prices rose (due to OPEC reducing supply) pundits were saying they were overweighting this sector. When oil prices declined in the 3rd quarter of 2018, taking energy stocks with it, these "experts" took significant losses.

The US is producing greater and greater amounts of oil. The 100 million barrels per day threshold is expected to happen in 2019. The US became the largest producer in the world in 2018. Is worldwide demand going to increase as fast? I am personally averse to fossil fuels as an investment in the long run, simply because of its nature as a pollutant, even though gains may be available in the short run.

People who want a broad ETF to invest in this sector often pick XLE or VDE, but they might not be aware that both are almost totally oil based - all ten of the top ten holdings. There are also ETFs for the subgroups like refining and oil field services if you are interested.

Natural gas is a clean and cheap fuel which is slowly replacing oil. Demand is expected to increase 40% over the next ten years, however it is in such abundant supply, prices for the commodity and for ETFs have been falling since 2008. Wind and solar continue to struggle. ICLN, a clean energy ETF has not grown much, with only $170M in assets under management, it has declined 20% in the last 5 years. Today's reality is energy and oil are pretty much synonymous, investment wise. A personal preference, I leave this group for others.

FINANCIALS

This is a large segment of the S&P (15%) and includes commercial and investment banks, insurance companies, credit card companies, mortgage finance, consumer finance, specialized finance, stock brokers, asset management and custody, corporate lending, financial investment, real estate investment trusts (REITs), as well as companies engaged in real estate management & development.

This is a highly varied sector, and although you can invest in a very broad-brush ETF such as XLF, the most popular, I do not recommend that. I would recommend looking at the individual businesses within the sector and considering investments there, because these businesses have highly divergent characteristics, and therefore respond and act much differently.

Banks are popular currently because of rising interest rates, a growing economy which spurs loan growth, strong balance sheets, and relatively low P/E's. IYG is good broad choice for financial services, concentrating in the mega banks (56%), credit card, and payment processors (MA & V), as people reduce their use of currency. KBE is a good choice for banking, being equal weighted, so the concentration in the huge banks is avoided. KRE is popular regional banks only.

Large banks are also popular for their preferred stock which has strong yields and almost zero default risk. The preferred stock ETF PFF which I like (mostly, but not all banks) has a current yield of 5.6%, however, because of falling rates in 2019, the YTD return is 12.4% (8/19)

An overlooked sector is small cap financials, where you might consider PSCF, but it has been weak in 2019, up only 11.5%.

I do not think it imperative that you participate in this sector specifically. If you own any large cap index ETF, you will have ownership in the major banks, credit card companies, and payment processors through it. Favor this sector when interest rates are rising.

GOLD

For ETFs which hold gold as a commodity I recommend BAR, IAU, or GLD, which all perform exactly the same however BAR has the lowest ER at only .17%. These are trusts which actually hold gold bullion in vaults and follow the spot price for gold daily. I would limit my purchase to 5-8% of your portfolio. Do not buy stock in gold miners, which are too volatile, moving as a multiple of the price of gold, and have done very poorly.

The biggest negative is that there is no way to value gold, so price movement is impossible to understand or predict, unless you can somehow measure fear and future inflation. Also owning and selling gold is considered a "collectable" and any capital gain is taxed by the Fed at 28% presently. Owning GLD, IAU or BAR is considered owning gold. (No tax if in an IRA).

HEALTHCARE

This sector has benefitted as more investors see it as both a growth business and a defensive investment. Also, if and when the economy begins to contract, this segment will decline less.

Some investors are worried that left leaning Democratic candidates will push for a universal healthcare system, which most consider highly doubtful. Also, pressure from all politicians to reduce the cost of prescription drugs, is negatively affecting pharmaceutical companies. Healthcare is my largest holding. ETFs breakdown into 6 sub-categories:

1. Pharmaceutical companies – I don't recommend for a number of reasons - See "Healthcare". ETFs in this

category have performed poorly in 2018, again, although trending slightly upward in the second half of '18.

2. Healthcare Providers—hospitals, nursing homes etc. I don't recommend these either - See "Healthcare". Too difficult for them to operate profitably.

3. Healthcare insurers - (Aetna, Cigna) etc. I don't recommend them either - See "Healthcare". I can't understand if their future is bright, or not.

4. Healthcare Equipment and Supplies – This sector has been unstoppable. I highly recommend IHI for larger companies (up 144% over the last 5 years) and also equal weighted XHE. I would make these a major portfolio segment. There is just no way our healthcare requirements are going to go down in future years, as our population ages, and people expect a higher standard of care.

5. Biotechnical companies - Consider <u>ETFs only</u> as company level risk is too great. I prefer XBI. XBI is equal weighted and up 18% for the first 8 months of 2018 vs, the S&P 500 which is up 9.7%. Volatility is well above average, XBI has a beta of 1.94, almost two times the volatility of the whole market, so expect large swings. Avoid IBB the largest biotech ETF which has had weak performance, a high ER, and has concentrations.

6. Broad, all-inclusive ETFs containing all of the above categories such as XLV, VHT, and IYH. These three ETFs are up between 13% and 16% in 2018, slightly better than the S&P 500 (up 10%). All three perform about the same, and all three are held back by a 9-10% concentration in Johnson and Johnson, a very large, weak performer. JNJ is a bit of an enigma, very diversified, pays a good dividend, and grows sales about 8%/year, and is huge - sales of $21B/quarter. It is presently being hurt by potential gov't price pressure, and litigation losses (talcum powder).

I would pass on these broad ETFs, because they contain too much of a concentration of categories 1-3 above, and categories 4 and 5 do so much better. Of these three, VHT has performed the best and has an ER of only .1%.

INTERNATIONAL

<u>All World</u> – consider VEA - Europe and the Far East excluding US (so no overlap), developed countries, 3700 stocks of all sized companies, very diversified, super low ER of .07. A first choice to get exposure outside the US, and a good pick if you only have one international ETF. It is up 13% in the first half of 2019.

<u>Europe</u> – look at VGK - a balanced developed market European index including Britain. A good start internationally as long as their economy is growing. The European central bank is still pushing growth which has slowed this year. The Trump trade war is definitely hurting the economies there, as their economic growth is very tied up with the US. VGK is up 15% in the first half of 2019.

<u>Eurozone</u> – consider EZU – This index only includes countries that use the Euro, so excludes Britain (uses Sterling). Because of the very negative consequences of Britain exiting the Eurozone, the British stock market has done very poorly recently (worst of 90 countries in 1st qtr. 2018) therefore this index may do better than VGK until the Brexit issue is resolved. Absolutely no one knows how Brexit will affect UK commerce. EZU is up 16% in the first half of 2019.

<u>China</u> – The fastest growing large country deserves some exposure in my view. Consider FXI – China's 50 largest companies (no Alibaba??) with .74 ER; GXC, the total Chinese market, more diversified, .59 ER, with a heavier tech element (Alibaba and Tencent); and ASWR, which follows the Shanghai CSI 300 index. FXI is older more stable companies and is less volatile. GXC is more volatile but has higher returns over the last year. ASWR has gyrated because of the ups and downs of Trump's trade war, however this ETF is <u>up 28%</u> in the first half of 2019 as investors are expecting an

eventual settlement. (positive technical changes are also helping ASWR)

Risk is somewhat elevated here, in part because the accounting and reporting practices in China are considerably below US standards. On the other hand, the Chinese government is engaging in a large number of simulative measures to boost the economy. If you want Chinese exposure but not exclusively, look at emerging market ETFs like EEM or VWO, which are highly concentrated in China.

Pacific – VPL – Developed markets including Japan, Australia, South Korea, Hong Kong, and Singapore. No China exposure because it is considered an emerging market (a dubious classification). Highly diversified but mostly Japan and So. Korea, low ER. Also, EPP – Another Pacific developed country ETF except it excludes Japan. For decades Japan's economy hardly grew at all because of an aging and declining population. Investors wanted to exclude it (including me) hence this ETF. The central bank finally got the economy growing again in 2016 with below zero interest rates, punishing savers. EWJ, the largest Japan ETF was down slightly in 2018, and is up 8% for the first half of 2019.

Individual Country ETFs – These are ETFs which own stocks domiciled in a particular non-US country, like Brazil, or India. Other than China, I would not recommend any of these, unless you have an above average familiarity with the economic and political conditions in a particular country. For example, you spend considerable time living there, have relatives living there, or some other connection. These ETFs carry greater risk than a regional choice, and it is more cautious to include geographical groups containing more than one country. The narrower scope results in greater risk and greater volatility. For example, rather than Korea chose the Far East, perhaps VPL.

LARGE CAP

The S&P 500 index has a number of ETF choices, however there is absolutely no reason not to pick the lowest expense ratio, since they all follow the same index. At present that is Vanguard's VOO (.04% - almost zero) or SPY (.09%). It's hard to beat this ETF, as Warren Buffett has demonstrated, it should be a core holding, and your largest holding.

Another approach, which I also recommend, is buying an equal weight S&P 500 such as RSP. Each S&P 500 company is weighted equally in the index, reducing the effect of the mega companies (like FAANG), reducing volatility and reducing risk. The ER is slightly higher at .2%. For the first half of 2019 RSP and VOO performed equally, however over the last 2 years VOO did best (up 22%).

You may notice that your own portfolio will not go up, or down, as much as the S&P 500, even if VOO or SPY is all that you own. That's probably because the cash component of your portfolio earns next to nothing, and the S&P 500 has no cash component. Professional asset managers have the same problem. They need to hold cash for redemptions, and to make future purchases when market dips occur.

LARGE CAP GROWTH

For capturing fast growing large companies you hear about on TV every day, like Apple, Oracle, Amazon, etc., Look at Vanguards VUG, and slightly different VGT. Also consider XLK. The QQQ is also popular based on the NASDAQ 100, which includes NASDAQ stocks which are heavily skewed toward technology.

To choose, look up the symbol on Yahoo and click holdings, where you can see what the ETF owns in its top ten. FAANG stocks will dominate all of these ETFs, and because they are cap weighted, they are highly concentrated. If you are not careful you may end up with too much FAANG in your portfolio, as many did in Sept. and Oct. '18 when these stocks started to fade, some significantly.

Its human to want to invest in areas that have been doing well recently (and vice versa), however jumping into something which has risen dramatically as the FAANG stocks did in '17 and '18 leaves you open to an increased risk that the momentum traders may be about to jump out. It's wise to remain diversified, which means you don't want to own only what's going up right now.

As an example, the leading sectors in 2019 through May are Real Estate and Utilities, two left for dead categories when interest rates were rising, and high-tech stocks were leading all groups. The significant and unexpected downturn in interest rates in 2019 is causing these sectors to outperform.

Large cap growth is a broad category and you may wish to focus on a smaller segment of it. I like IGV for software stocks, a seemingly unstoppable sector. I also like XSD, an equal weighted semi-conductor category, which is less volatile than the popular SMH.

LARGE CAP VALUE

This is a defensive category, and one you might pick to reduce risk if you believe the risk of a downturn is at hand. Stable, slower growth companies often have low P/Es, such as financials, where you trade off rapid stock price appreciation for more stability and if a market downturn does occur, these stocks will decline less. Value stocks have underperformed growth stocks for the last ten years, leading many to decide to give up on this sector.

However, value stocks have become more popular in May 2109 as some believe the ten-year recovery we have experienced may be in its final stages. Will value stocks get their day in the sun if the US growth rate declines even more through the remainder of 2019? If you are pessimistic about our 10-year recovery you may wish to overweight this sector. Be aware however that you will be overweighting banks and other large Dow underperformers.

If you are interested, look at Vanguard's VTV or MGV, and look at its holdings. It will center in large and somewhat mature companies which often grow slowly and are household names which people often choose because they are looking for safety. If you broaden out to include some not quite as large companies, look at VOOV, which as of 2019 has outperformed the two ETFs listed above.

An alternative is to broaden out into smaller value companies. Mid-cap value, VOE, small-cap value, VBR, and the Russell 1000 value VONV, had underperformed the large cap ETFs noted above for several years, however this has reversed in 2019, with these three outperforming the larger company choices. This possibly indicates investors are looking for value, without concentrating in financials, as interest rates have remained very low in 2019 (unfavorable to banks).

LOW VOLATILITY STOCKS

ETFs for this group were designed to give investors greater stability in their portfolios by selecting large company stocks which move up and down less than the overall market - low betas. In return for less volatility, your return will normally be somewhat lower. Investors plowed a great deal of money into these ETFs in 2019, because aversion to risk has been a common theme among ETF investors in 2019, who are worried about slowing global economic growth, ongoing tariff wars, Brexit, and the uncertain outlook for interest rates.

Strictly speaking, risk and volatility are not the same thing, however volatility is one aspect of risk.

There are 27 low vol ETFs in the market today, but when it comes to U.S. large cap equities, the low vol battle centers on two popular funds: the iShares Edge MSCI Min Vol U.S.A. ETF (USMV), and the Invesco S&P 500 Low Volatility ETF (SPLV).

SPLV and USMV (both have betas of .68), use different methodology but similar returns. USMV has a very low ER of .15%, and a slightly better return over the last year. The collection of companies varies widely, mostly large cap, well-known names as found in the Dow. In the present environment of caution, low volatility ETFs have done well.

USMV and SPLV are actually outperforming the S&P 500, as measured by the SPDR S&P 500 ETF Trust (SPY) (6/19).

MATERIALS

Materials ETFs provide investors broad exposure to companies primarily engaged in extracting and processing raw materials, including metals, minerals, chemicals and forest products (not oil). Options include ETFs focused on American materials companies broadly, on large-cap American materials companies, or on global materials companies. This as opposed to owning the materials themselves (commodities). They are a way to capture economic growth, especially when most major countries are growing, as they were in 2017-2018. They are essential to growth, as manufacturers must have these materials to operate. I recommend VAW or XLB for US companies (same index, low ERs), and MXI for global materials. This is a very difficult sector to predict. Owning some of this group may help diversification somewhat, but if markets are down, this group will probably be down also.

MID CAP

A clear winner is IVOO, Vanguard's S&P based ETF of the next largest 400 companies after the S&P 500 (ER .15%). Vanguard's other midcap, VO, is OK but it overlaps the S&P 500. There are a couple of different indexes being used here depending on how best to divide the market by size, however over time IVOO has been the best choice.

MID CAP AND SMALL CAP GROWTH

In moving toward growth, you may do better with lesser known companies not in the large cap bracket, because the large growth mega companies become overbought, as people tend to buy what they know or recognize, and not buy unknown names. For mid-cap growth look at VOT. In their top ten holdings you will recognize 2 or 3 names. In small cap growth, consider VIOG and VBK, you may recognize only one of the top ten names, however the diversification is very great – each holding is less than 1%, which gives you protection if one or two of these companies fail to survive. Of these three, VIOG has performed the best over the last 12 months - it is up only 12% in 2019s first half while the S&P 500 is up close to 18%.

MID CAP AND SMALL CAP VALUE

As above, I believe value investors tend to crowd into large caps, and you may do better with small and mid-cap value. This category has not done particularly well since the current recovery started in 2009, which has been dominated by growth stocks, however many believe value will outperform growth as we approach the end of the current bull market, whenever that is. There are many choices here with varying results – no clear winner. Consider SLYV, RFV, RZV, PXSV, and SMDV. When comparing performance, chart them together on Yahoo Finance - chose one, click chart, click comparison and add the others, then choose different time periods and compare which has done the best. The lowest ER of this group is SLYV and RFV at .15%.

NEAR CASH

There are a large number of choices here because when the Fed reduced short term interest rates to 0-.25%, investors began to search for investments which paid a little more than zero, but had a very low risk element. This could be the place you park your cash held for safety, cash held to reduce losses in a market pullback, or cash held back as dry powder for buying opportunities which evolve over time.

The choices here cross several asset categories including short or ultra short term bonds, money market funds, bank CD's, and short term treasuries. Remember that any bond fund, including gov'ts will lose principal value if interest rates rise, however, if the bonds are short term, the decline will be very small. If you want zero risk and unlimited access to your money you have to stay with a bank savings vehicle.

Managed money market accounts have close to zero risk and are not FDIC insured, however no provider has broken the

$1/share promise since 2008 and Gov't rules have tightened the rules (floating NAV rule). Most providers have dozens of choices which as of 6/19 yield about 1.1%.

I used to invest in some of the near cash ETF alternatives, however Fidelity will put your "core cash" in any money market you chose, and their default core holding, FDRXX, is hard to beat. It invests in low risk government bonds and has a 7-day yield of 2.08%, and a 1 year return of 1.95% (7/19).

Bank CDs are a choice with close to zero risk, however you give up having liquidity over the term of the instrument. Yields depend on the length of the term and the financial strength of the issuer. One-year bank CDs vary significantly as of 6/19, ranging from as little as .5% for major banks, up to 2.5% for riskier financial institutions. The average per Bankrate.com is 1%. With money market funds over 2%, I cannot see why anyone would accept a 1% yield while tying up the funds for one year.

Also, there are money market ETFs with low ERs which yield around 2.5% (9/19) such as the JPMorgan Ultra short Income JPST, and Invesco Bulletshares Corp. bond BSCJ which holds a collection of US and corporate short-term bonds (2.3% 6/19).

If you are willing to take a very small amount of risk there are lots of choices, most of which use various forms of very short-term gov't, corporate, or municipal bonds. They all have similar yields (2.5% to 2.8%) with the higher yielding choices having more corporate and less gov't and bank holdings. I ran a one year (6/19), comparison of 8 ETFs and 3 stood out from the rest. Best performing, was NEAR, followed by MINT, and FTSM. They all have ERs between .20 and .35%, all are actively managed (needed in this sector) and all have yields of 2.5-2.8%.

My current favorite for parking cash with a very small amount of risk is IGSB, iShares investment grade short term corporate bond ETF with a yield of 3.08% and an expense ratio of .06% as of 10/19.

The shorter the bond, the less interest rate increases will affect performance, so for least risk in a rising rate environment choose under 3-year maturities, or better, under one-year maturities.

There is a new service offered by Max at MaxMyInterest.com which will automatically select the highest yielding FDIC insured on-line bank's insured savings accounts and move your funds there monthly for a quarterly fee of .002%. There is no lock up period. If you want zero risk, you may want to investigate it further.

> ***Takeaway***: As of 6/19, if you want close to zero risk, go with a money market like Fidelity's FDRXX currently 2.1%. If you want a slightly higher yield with some risk I would go with NEAR at 2.6%, and if you don't mind locking the funds up for a period, search bank or broker provided CD rates and pick the maturity you want and an institution you are familiar with. Leaving the money in your brokers core account is the simplest option and its yield is not very different from the other choices - .1% or one tenth of one percent times $1000 is only $1, so it might not be worth the time to try to find something with a .1 or .2 percent higher yield.
>
> Be sure to check which fund your broker's default cash holding fund is for proceeds from any sales you make. Clicking on that fund will lead you to its current yield. Also note that most brokers including Fidelity will give you a choice of which of their funds you want your cash to be held in.

PREFERRED STOCK

Preferred stock has some stock characteristics but acts more like a bond with a fixed dividend, which is similar to a bond's coupon rate. The price moves inversely to interest rates, like bonds. Each company's issuance has its own set of conditions and features, and they vary quite a lot from company to company. An ETF spreads your risk out, reducing risk considerably. Preferred ETFs have been stable in price since 2009.

They have higher yields than comparable bonds and provide a steady quarterly income. Bonds have a higher preference in a liquidation, but this feature is not relevant unless the issuer is, or near, filing bankruptcy. Add the diversification protection of owning an ETF, and I would classify this risk as almost totally irrelevant - bankruptcies among major corporations just don't happen often.

The two popular ETFs of preferreds, PFF and PGX are highly diversified, and contain primarily large bank preferreds, and represent a relatively low risk for a 5.8% yield. Both have appreciated considerably in 2019 because of falling interest rates (PGX by 13.4% through 7/19). Expense ratios are somewhat higher at about .5%. Another choice is the international IPFF.

REITs

For most small investors you will probably want no more 6-8% of your portfolio in REITs and so you probably have room for only one ETF. Most widely held is the extremely broad, low cost, VNQ by Vanguard. It has a yield today (6/19) of 4.0% however it has risen 19% in the first half of 2019 as more investors buy REITs in a falling rate environment.

<u>REITs are very sensitive to interest rates and should be underweighted when rates are rising</u> (and vice versa). Over the last 14 years, VNQ has increased only 4.6% per year, so it hasn't been very exciting, so you cannot expect the outsized returns as has been seen in some real estate sectors. If you

want to focus on a property type, the very high price of home ownership is helping residential apartment REITs (EQR, AVB) and conversely, Amazon is wiping out mall REITs, where vacancy recently hit 9%.

SEMICONDUCTORS

Many had written off this industry when desktop PC's started to fall continually, however as we now know we need chips in practically everything we buy. Automobiles are becoming rolling computers, automated machinery, mobile devices, household devices, everything connected to the internet, games, artificial intelligence, the cloud, (everything?). These companies are in many ways the future, and entry into the industry is difficult due to high fixed costs. This group has been blowing the doors off over the last 3 years, up 250%, however did go down in 2018. The pullback is understandable because of the huge gains they had made.

It's hard to envision a future without these chips. The negative is that chips become a commodity item quite quickly in their life cycle, so relentless innovation is required. Companies which have gained the lead in gaming have led the industry. Gaming is a fast growing but also a fast changing industry. The risk factor is therefore somewhat higher. (What happens if kids decide gaming isn't fun anymore?)

Consider SOXX, SMH, and PSI, however because this group has been extremely volatile in recent years (beta 1.5), I now prefer the equal weighted XSD. Also, size weighted ETFs will have close to 30% concentrated in only 3 companies. In the first half of 2019, XSD has outperformed the highly popular SMH by 4.5%.

SILVER

The largest ETF for silver is SLV with gains also taxed at 28% (except in an IRA). I don't see any reason to buy silver. It has been $15-17/oz. give or take, for the last 5 years, hit a recent low of $14 in 9/18, and if you are seeking a commodity investment which usually moves opposite to equities, choose gold.

People sometimes balk at the high price of gold however with an ETF you can invest any amount you chose. The demand for silver for industrial purposes is broader than gold, however demand is less driven by fear than gold, which means it doesn't respond as much to geopolitical risks. Precious metals seem to respond more to inflation and the dollar than other factors and trying to anticipate price movements is fruitless. The price of silver has been going down since 2011. As gold has increased in price in 2019, so has silver, in response to fear over the trade war and that it might lead us into a recession. Because ETFs allow you to make any size purchase (no dollar minimums), gold is a better choice for your precious metals allocation.

SMALL CAP

For the next largest 600 companies after the mid-caps, I like Vanguard's VIOO (ER .15%) which has less overlap than their other small cap, VB. You can expand this to the next 2000 by picking a Russell 2000 index like the Vanguard VTWO (ER.15%). (There are also Micro cap ETFs, which I don't think are needed.)

Small cap stocks outperformed in early 2018 because Trump's trade war doesn't affect them significantly, selling mainly in the US. Also, the corporate tax cuts approved in 2018 (corporate rate reduced from 35% to 21%) have an outsized effect on smaller companies which tend to have higher income tax rates. Small companies do not have dozens of tax lawyers finding ways to avoid or reduce taxes, and do not have international operations to funnel profits through.

However, the fear of an economic slowdown hit the small caps in August '18 and have performed poorly since then. If the economy slows down, some small companies may experience problems meeting debt obligations, and their profit margins may decline, if they cannot pass through higher costs created by the tariff war. Small stocks are believed to be somewhat more risky than large corporations, as a number of these small companies may have little or no profit, and VIOO has a somewhat elevated beta, 1.25. ETFs, however, diversify this risk.

Some portion of your portfolio should have exposure to the small caps. For small cap value look at VIOV or VTWV - I would favor the former.

SOFTWARE

It may be redundant to separate software from technology, as the categories of companies classified as "tech" is becoming blurred. It's hard for any company to not be involved in technology in some fashion, and software is a critical component of almost every company today. Amazon, classified as communication services, is a heavy user of technology in all phases of its business, including the internet purchase interface, warehousing, and delivery.

Many believe software is the common link for strong corporate future growth, and therefore ETFs such as IGV, PSJ, and XSW capture this segment. All of these are up around 30% for the first half of '19, with PSJ slightly outperforming the other two, consistently over the last 5 years, despite a high ER (.63%).

Most of the top ten holdings in the space have been moving up dramatically in the last couple of years. Note these companies have very high P/Es (are they overpriced?) but perhaps should be looked at over the longer term. Also note ETFs in this segment will overlap considerably with tech ETFs. XSW is equal weight and therefore no concentrations, and a .35% ER.

TECHNOLOGY

Also called information technology, the fastest growing and most popular investment sector recently, this group represents 21% of the entire S&P 500, in large part because of the FAANG stocks. Many believe that these are the companies of tomorrow, with strong growth justifying very high P/E's. It's very hard to generalize about this group, for the same reason it is very hard to decide which companies belong here.

Many of these companies are so called "disruptors", tipping upside down traditional businesses as Netflix has done to entertainment, and Amazon has done to retail. Some older companies are declining, such as IBM, which haven't diversified into faster growing businesses, whereas Intel has succeeded in developing chips for uses other than PC's, which is a shrinking sector. About all these companies have in common is a heavy reliance on digitized data, use of the internet, and accumulation, transfer, and storage of data – otherwise their businesses vary widely.

You will want a considerable portion of your long term portfolio in this segment. Portfolio managers, especially value investors, who avoided this sector due to high P/E's are falling behind. I suggest you give up trying to understand what is or is not technology and focus on ETF selection.

Because of strong investor interest in this group the number of ETFs available is huge. There are many ways to slice and dice this segment. When choosing, start with a business category you want to invest in and then click "holdings" on the ETF summary page and look at the top ten holdings to understand what companies are included, and how concentrated it is.

I suggest you own more than one ETF here, and note there will be some overlap, which is OK. (Note: see also mid cap growth and small cap growth which include less well-known companies.)

Be aware that if the economy slows down these companies may be affected to a greater degree, because their betas are higher than the S&P 500, meaning greater than 1. However, if you are a long-term investor you will likely achieve better growth on the other side of the slowdown, when things pick up again. Just be aware that higher beta companies will have above average volatility in both directions.

Consider XLK, concentrated in FAANG (Facebook, Apple, Amazon, Netflix, Google) .13% ER up 30% over YTD 6/19. Also, VGT, concentrated in FAANG .1% ER, up 30% through 6/19. QQQ, the most popular, also concentrated in FAANG, .2% ER up 24% through 6/19.

If you want to reduce the concentration in FAANG, buy RYT which is <u>equal weighted</u>, .4% ER, up 29% through 6/19.

The most popular semiconductor group is SMH, however it is highly concentrated. I much prefer XSD which is equal weighted and has the same .35% ER as SMH.

Consider Vanguards growth ETFs VUG (large) VOT (midcap) and VIOG (small-cap) which are all good. VUG has the same FAANG concentration as the other large cap ETFs listed.

You can invest in a collection of internet-based companies which includes many fast growers, and consider a small position in XWEB, as I have, which is up 19% through 6/19.

I ran a 1-year comparison of all of these large growth ETFs (XLK, VGT, RYT, QQQ, VUG) as of 6/2019, VGT was best, XLT second (QQQ was last). Don't just buy big companies. Small cap VIOG outperformed all these ETFs.

Instead of one large position in tech, make a smaller contribution to perhaps 3 or 4 of these ETFs. As with any higher beta sectors, it's best to diversify to a greater extent, which includes paying a slightly higher ER for an equal weighted alternative.

A final caveat, social media companies are coming under fire for invading the privacy of the subscribers, monopolistic behaviors, not policing fraudulent users, acting as an unwitting source of foreign users attempting to influence our elections, and not filtering racial and divisive content. Facebook and Google (Alphabet) have borne the brunt of this, and both are down in price over the last year (6/19). In choosing ETFs you may want to be mindful of your concentrations in these two companies. I personally disfavor Facebook, which seems to ignore public concerns, while I am OK with Alphabet, whose issues appear less offensive.

TOTAL US MARKET

There used to be over 5000 total stocks on the NYSE but because of mergers (not replaced by IPOs) there are only 3640 left. You can get them all with Vanguard's total US market ETF VTI, if you do not wish to overweight and underweight different sectors. A simplified portfolio where you are not interested in reviewing it often, sometimes referred to as the lazy man's or woman's portfolio, might consist of VTI in the US, VEA (all world excluding US), and AGG (US aggregate bond), in proportions of 50/20/30 for example.

TOTAL WORLD

Vanguard has what they call a total world ETF, VT, which would seem like a simplistic way of investing money in stocks, however it has a drawback. The FTSE index which it follows states that it includes 7,781 stocks of companies located in 41 countries, including both developed and emerging markets, is a bit misleading. Because it is capitalization (size) weighted, all ten of the top ten holdings are large US companies including FAANG and large Dow members. These ten comprise 9.8% of the total holdings and will dominate the total return. I would skip VT, and if looking for utter simplicity, choose VTI for US, and VEA for International, and chose the percentage breakdown between the two, perhaps 70% VTI, and 30% VEA.

TRANSPORTATIONS

I have never favored this group, which consists primarily of railroad, trucking and airline companies. They have high capital equipment needs which lead to high debt and replacing capital goods requires heavy cash needs. They perform a necessary and never-ending need, but competition is fierce, keeping pressure on profit margins. They are seen as a bellwether for the economy, with increased revenues signaling a growing economy, and this seems to be the primary reason they are discussed so often.

The trucking group has received new strength from the consumer switch to e-commerce, and its positive effect on shipping, however they are being impacted negatively by driver shortages, with unemployment currently so low. A headwind for this entire group is oil prices - price increases hurt trucking, but really impact the airlines significantly, which consume huge quantities of fuel. Airlines are a group I do not favor for a number of reasons (see Sectors I avoid). There are not many good choices for ETFs here. You'll notice relatively small AUMs, and relatively high ERs. IYT and XTN were the only acceptable choices I found, and IYT performed the best over the short and long term. (I would pass on TPOR, FTXR, XKST, and JETS). I do not invest in this group.

UTILITIES

I used to ignore this defensive group, only 3% of the S&P 500 - as slow growing and unexciting - but steady revenue and strong dividends are a plus to add some stability to your holdings, especially when the market is looking weak going forward. It has been popular in 2019 with investors who are fearing a stock market pullback.

Utilities tend to move inversely to the stock market and therefore add diversification. The caveat is, like bonds, they do poorly in periods of rising interest rates (and vice versa), because they have heavy interest expense, and their revenue is very slow to increase. In 2019, this group has risen sharply, benefiting from increased investor caution.

I would add this group when the economy is starting to slow, and you expect economic weakness (and lower interest rates) ahead. They can be a substitute for buying bonds, with some upside appreciation possible (up 46% over the last 5 years). I have owned VPU, mainly for diversification, which is as good as any other ETF. It has a 2.9% yield and is up 16% through 6/19.

Utilities are often thought of as having zero risk. PGE, the largest utility in California is now bankrupt, due to fires and deaths resulting from their negligence in clearing trees from their power lines. (You might also remember Enron). "Zero risk" is similar to "free lunch" - a non-existent phenomenon.

VIII. FINAL THOUGHTS (June 2019)

By almost every measure that exists, the US economy had been doing extremely well through the end of 2018: GDP growth, GDP per capita, personal income growth, job growth, purchasing managers' report, labor participation, jobless claims at a 48 year low, unemployment lowest since 1959 (3.7%), retail sales growing, consumer sentiment high, CEO sentiment high, corporate earnings, industrial spending, ISM manufacturing survey, reduced consumer loan delinquency, record average consumer FICO score (704), record low home mortgage defaults and foreclosures, consumer savings up, consumer debt ratios lower, inflation moderate (2.5%) for CPI and PPI, car sales somewhat slower but still high, increased house prices, the dollar is strong, and the US can now export oil. These factors presented a very favorable basis for US stock prices over the last several years.

Late 2018 and the first half of 2019 ushered in a sea change in economic performance. Several economic reports and indicators are slowing down, causing the Fed to switch toward lowering and not raising interest rates. We have fears of a consumer spending slowdown due to trade tariffs raising prices, home prices far exceeding personal income growth (and about to go up even more because of tariffs on building materials), and a slowing in auto sales.

Autos and houses represent the backbone of the consumers 70% share of GDP, so slowing in both sectors does not bode well. Perhaps most concerning is a worldwide slowdown affecting emerging markets, Europe, and most importantly China. The slowdown in China is reducing aggregate world demand, however their growth rate is still quite astounding at about 6.0% (if data is believable) eclipsing all developed countries. By comparison, the Fed is forecasting the US growth rate at about 2%.

Stocks fell over 10% in Oct. '18, more than wiping out the entire YTD gain, and the S&P 500 declined by 6% for the full year. The cause, or causes, of this decline are not known but among the reasons suggested - the long term of the present expansion (are we in the 9th inning?), unresolved trade tariff wars, peaking corporate profits, and a sentiment shift toward increased caution. Also, since more than half of all share trades are promulgated by computers responding to predetermined algorithms, when prices declined, the algos increased selling to preserve capital.

Stocks recovered dramatically in 2019, responding to a very oversold condition in 2018, announcements from the Fed chairman that they would begin to lower interest rates if the economy slowed further, and a cessation of trade hostilities between the US and Mexico. This happened despite a significant slowdown in corporate profits in the first quarter of 2019.

So the fears of investors in late 2018 turned out to be not only wrong, but financially costly for those who sold everything or became defensive. Those who held on to their stock holdings did the best, again. It is another example of staying invested when the doomsayers are forecasting another Armageddon.

With the forward S&P 500 P/E at 17, and the three main market averages hitting record highs in early July 2019, (Dow, S&P 500, NASDAQ) stocks are considered "fully valued", meaning future growth in prices is liable to be much slower going forward.

It's sad that those of us simply trying to put money away for the future have to endure this volatility, but computers have put us here, and they're not going away. These large price swings damage the market because many investors will decide that stocks are too risky for them, and will resort to bond yields which are barely, if at all, above the rate of inflation.

It's been true many times before, and I believe it will be true again - markets will always respond to the strength of the economy in the long term, and it's remarkably strong at present, so we'll have to be patient, again, (not my long suit).

OF GREATER CONCERN

There are, however, two longer term US trends of deep concern, for which we seem to have no answer. Firstly, politicians have learned that spending money which benefits their constituents gets them more votes, whereas increases in taxes or reduced spending on benefits, gives voters reason to vote them out of office. For many years the Republican Party was a voice for spending restraint, but this has now disappeared. Regardless of the party in power, Washington keeps increasing spending or decreasing taxes, and increasing the national debt at an alarming rate.

Our political leaders prophesize that the spending and/or reduced taxes will produce enough economic growth to pay for the increased deficit, but that never happens. All that happens is a larger deficit. The garnering of votes surpasses their desire to keep spending in line with GDP growth. We continue to push an increasing debt load onto our children.

We all cringe at the prospect of inadequate tax revenues to support Medicare and Social Security, but politicians don't even *address* the issue for fear of scaring people and losing votes. As if not talking about it makes it go away. Our last 8 years of unsurpassed low interest rates has enabled the treasury to manage the debt, however super low interest rates cannot last forever.

The consequences of too much debt are catastrophic: a possible downgrade of US debt to lower than triple A, a failure, or severe cutbacks in Medicare and Social Security, a loss of confidence in our ability to repay our debt ala Greece and Italy, a reduced dollar value, and the need for significant tax increases, which will slow the economy immeasurably. If you think I'm exaggerating, do some reading on the subject of the increasing US deficit, especially after the corporate tax cuts of 2018 were passed. When you start adding up the current and projected national debt, and the projected resources to repay it, (even if you don't include the unfunded pension liability), you'll be reaching for something around 90 proof - hold the water.

How can you reign in excessive spending when politicians are rewarded for doing so, and removed from office for reducing spending or increasing taxes? I have no answer for that unless all political positions are reduced to one term. No one in office runs again. Politicians will not have to raise funds for their next election, will not have to pander to special interest lobbying groups, and will have no reason not to govern for the good of our country. I don't think politicians are going to go for that idea, but it's the only solution I can think of.

The second intractable problem is more worrisome, and systemic to the US economy. The inequality of income in the US increases every year, and at an increasing rate. It has been worsening particularly since the 1970's. The 2018 tax cut adding to the relentless upward movement in the share of the nation's income being received by higher income households, and vice versa. That the rich are getting richer and the poor are getting a smaller and smaller piece of the pie is borne out by the data every year without exception. The overwhelming majority of Americans do not want a communist or socialist state, but how long can this problem continue to worsen?

Can we have 40 million people on food stamps while others buy $5000 ladies' handbags, $5000 watches, or a garage full of unused Ferraris? Billionaire investor Ray Dalio recently said (1/19) that capitalism wasn't working. A small percentage of our population receives a larger and larger percentage of our total national income every year. There has been no "trickle down", the flawed concept proposed by Ronald Reagan economic advisor Arthur Laffer. By some estimates 80% of the US population lives from paycheck to paycheck. How has the last 50 years benefited them?

I have no answer for this one either, however based on what has happened in other countries it doesn't end well. When the fabric of society is torn enough, rebellion occurs. We have seen innumerable governments fall because the people at the top took way more than their share, and the rest of the population struggled. I hope the guillotine is outlawed before we get there.

I'm sorry to end on such a grim thought, but we need more people addressing these longer term issues. If we wait until a crisis is already at hand, the remedies will be that much more difficult, but sadly that is what is most likely to happen.

Thank you for reading. I hope you enjoy a comfortable retirement.

— Gary Palmer

ACKNOWLEDGEMENTS

To *Investopedia.com*, which I referred to in defining some investment terms, and *Fidelity.com* and *Yahoo.com*, which I referred to in citing performance of ETFs and market movements and statistics.

To my son, *Jeff Palmer,* who convinced me to go forward with this project and who generously donated his time, design and editorial skills in helping me get this book to publication.

ADDENDUM

SOME BASICS ON CORPORATE FINANCIALS

Very basic stuff here but bear with me...it's short.

The two principal documents of a corporation of interest to investors are the balance sheet and the income statement, which most companies release quarterly. The balance sheet of a company provides information on what the company owns (its assets), what it owes (its liabilities) and the value of the business to its stockholders (the shareholders' equity) as of a specific date. It's called a balance sheet because the two sides balance out. This makes sense: a company has to pay for all the things it has (assets) by either borrowing money (liabilities) or getting it from shareholders (shareholders' equity).

Total Assets - Total Liabilities = Shareholders Equity

- **Assets** are economic resources that are expected to produce economic benefits for their owners.

- **Liabilities** or debt are obligations the company has to outside parties. Liabilities represent others' rights to the company's money or services. Examples include bank loans, debts to suppliers and debts to employees.

- **Shareholders' equity** or net worth is the value of a business to its owners after all of its obligations have been met. This net worth belongs to the owners. Shareholders' equity generally reflects the amount of capital the owners have invested, plus any profits generated that were subsequently reinvested in the company.

Example Company
Balance Sheet
December 31, 2017

ASSETS		LIABILITIES	
Current assets		Current liabilities	
Cash	$ 2,100	Notes payable	$ 5,000
Petty cash	100	Accounts payable	35,900
Temporary investments	10,000	Wages payable	8,500
Accounts receivable - net	40,500	Interest payable	2,900
Inventory	31,000	Taxes payable	6,100
Supplies	3,800	Warranty liability	1,100
Prepaid insurance	1,500	Unearned revenues	1,500
Total current assets	89,000	Total current liabilities	61,000
Investments	36,000	Long-term liabilities	
		Notes payable	20,000
Property, plant & equipment		Bonds payable	400,000
Land	5,500	Total long-term liabilities	420,000
Land improvements	6,500		
Buildings	180,000		
Equipment	201,000	Total liabilities	481,000
Less: accum depreciation	(56,000)		
Prop, plant & equip - net	337,000		
Intangible assets		STOCKHOLDERS' EQUITY	
Goodwill	105,000	Common stock	110,000
Trade names	200,000	Retained earnings	220,000
Total intangible assets	305,000	Accum other comprehensive income	9,000
		Less: Treasury stock	(50,000)
Other assets	3,000	Total stockholders' equity	289,000
Total assets	$ 770,000	Total liabilities & stockholders' equity	$ 770,000

The notes to the sample balance sheet have been omitted.

Shares of stock are referred to as equities. A single share of stock represents a fractional ownership of the corporation in proportion to the total number of shares. Control of the company is held by whomever holds or controls a majority of the shares. Minority shareholders, like us, buy the shares to receive dividends and potentially capital appreciation in the price of the shares going forward. The price, or value, of the shares will go up if the companies' earnings go up, and vice versa.

Company liabilities may include long term debt issued in the form of corporate bonds. When we invest by buying a small portion of those bonds, we are in effect loaning money to the company, and do so in order to receive interest, and at maturity, our principal repaid.

Bonds issued by the US government are called Treasuries, and when we buy those, we are in effect lending to the Federal government.

The income statement of a company, or the profit and loss statement or P&L, shows the total revenues for the stated period, followed by deductions for the cost of sales (resulting in the gross profit) sales, general, and administrative expenses, (resulting in operating income) followed by other income and expense, resulting in pretax income. After taxes are deducted the result is net profit (after taxes). Net after tax profit is divided by the number of outstanding shares to report the income or earnings per share, also known as the EPS.

When companies report their results for the quarter, investors focus primarily on the total revenues, as an indication of the growth of the company's business, and the EPS, as an indication of how profitable the company is. Investors focus on how those revenues and EPS compared with the estimates which have previously been released by investment firms. Company's hope to "beat" those estimates and drive the share price higher, increasing the value of the company, and increasing the shareholders' value.

When most companies report earnings, they issue "guidance", which is the company's estimate of future revenues and earnings. The stock price moves primarily, but not always, in response to whether this guidance is seen as resulting in strong future earnings growth, or vice versa, going forward. Investors are interested in how the company did in the previous quarter and year but are _more_ interested in the future prospects for revenue and profits, because that will determine whether the shares are likely to increase, or decrease, in price.

A third financial statement of importance to investors, which most companies provide, is the cash flow statement. It ignores all non-cash accounting measures such as depreciation expense, asset write-downs, and changes to reserves, all of which do not affect the company's cash flow for the period. If a company has negative cash flow (even if under accounting rules it is showing a net profit), at some point it will need to borrow, (increasing interest expense), sell assets to raise cash, or issue additional stock. A new stock issuance will dilute the value of existing shares, causing their price to decrease. Many investors consider the cash flow statement to be the most important of the company's financial reports. Having a net profit is important but having a positive cash flow is critical.

Many investors believe that free cash flow is the most critical way to measure a company's economic health. It measures how operations are actually affecting the company's cash balance, which is critical to meeting expenses, and making debt payments as they come due. It eliminates accounting treatments such as depreciation and reserves, which have no effect on a company's cash balance.

Free cash flow is Net Income plus non-cash expenses such as Depreciation and Amortization less Capital Expenses (Capex) and less increases in working capital (some add decreases in working capital). Free cash flow is the amount of cash the company generated during the period which is available for discretionary items, such as R&D, stock dividends, and future purchases. The presence of free cash flow indicates that a company has cash to expand, develop new products, buy back stock, pay dividends, or reduce its debt. High or rising free cash flow is often a sign of a healthy company that is thriving in its current environment. It gives you a picture of how much cash the company is putting in the hands of management.

Companies who file for bankruptcy do so because of cash losses or insufficient cash flow to service future debt payments, or both. Annual increases to the company's cash flow are a strong indicator that the company's business plan is working properly and will positively affect the share price accordingly.

Analyzing and making sense of corporate financial statements isn't easy. The company will always seek to show itself in the best possible light, while staying within accounting guidelines. Also, there is always a lot going on within a company which never appears in the statements. Are their products becoming outdated? Are competitors selling a superior product? Are their costs for labor and materials rising? Are a handful of lawsuits coming in the future due to product liability cases? Have a number of key executives left the company? Is the board of directors and senior management in disagreement over the direction of the company? Are key product patents about to expire? The list is endless.

This is one of the reasons to avoid owning individual company stocks and owning ETFs for diversification. When a company has a serious problem, like Boeing has with their 737 Max plane, which lead to numerous deaths, a large drop in their stock price will not cause a significant drop in your retirement savings if you own it in an ETF.

APPENDIX 1

LIST OF ALL URLs

you are eligible to receive half of your ex-spouse's full benefit	https://www.ssa.gov/planners/retire/divspouse.html
maximizemysocialsecurity.com	https://maximizemysocialsecurity.com/
report	https://weforum.ent.box.com/s/w6cth9cdasx1k7g1vjnsqxttkv34t2su
IRA vs. Roth Calculator	https://www.bankrate.com/calculators/retirement/roth-traditional-ira-calculator.aspx
iShares 7-10 Year Treasury Bond ETF (IEF)	https://www.etf.com/ief
Technical indicators	https://www.investopedia.com/terms/t/technicalindicator.asp
fundamental	https://www.investopedia.com/terms/f/fundamentals.asp
gross domestic product	https://www.investopedia.com/terms/g/gdp.asp
low-cost investing	https://www.rebalance360.com/cri/u-s-dept-of-labor-video-featuring-scott-puritz/?utm_source=marketwatch&utm_medium=column&utm_campaign=oleary-save-ten-2018-03-26&utm_content=mt
The Shift from Active to Passive Investing: Potential Risks to Financial Stability?	https://papers.ssrn.com/sol3/papers.cfm?abstract_id=3321604
P/E ratio	https://en.wikipedia.org/wiki/P/E_ratio
consumer staples	https://www.investopedia.com/terms/c/consumerstaples.asp
business cycle	https://www.investopedia.com/terms/b/businesscycle.asp
recession	https://www.investopedia.com/terms/r/recession.asp
durables	https://www.investopedia.com/terms/d/durables.asp
Barclays U.S. Aggregate Bond Index	https://www.thebalance.com/the-barclays-capital-aggregate-bond-index-2466398
hedge funds	https://www.thebalance.com/what-is-a-hedge-fund-357524
Shorting stock	https://www.thebalance.com/short-selling-definition-short-a-stock-357792
hedge	https://www.investopedia.com/terms/h/hedge.asp
downside risk	https://www.investopedia.com/terms/d/downsiderisk.asp
buy-and-hold	https://www.investopedia.com/terms/b/buyandhold.asp
day traders	https://www.investopedia.com/terms/d/daytrader.asp

swing traders	https://www.investopedia.com/terms/s/swingtrading.asp
mutual funds	https://www.investopedia.com/terms/m/mutualfund.asp
margin account.	https://www.investopedia.com/terms/m/marginaccount.asp
Breakwave Dry Bulk Shipping	https://www.etf.com/bdry
buy limit order	https://www.investopedia.com/terms/b/buy-limit-order.asp
portfolio	https://www.investopedia.com/terms/p/portfolio.asp
level of asset allocation	https://www.investopedia.com/articles/04/031704.asp
asset allocation	https://www.investopedia.com/terms/a/assetallocation.asp
individual retirement account	https://www.investopedia.com/terms/i/ira.asp
capital	https://www.thebalance.com/what-is-financial-capital-3305825
Expansion	https://www.thebalance.com/economic-boom-4067682
cause serious price inflation	https://www.thebalance.com/causes-of-inflation-3-real-reasons-for-rising-prices-3306094
asset bubble	https://www.thebalance.com/asset-bubble-causes-examples-and-how-to-protect-yourself-3305908
supply	https://www.thebalance.com/aggregate-supply-what-it-is-how-it-works-3306216
outperform the market	https://www.thebalance.com/outperform-the-market-3305874
derivatives	https://www.thebalance.com/what-are-derivatives-3305833
Contraction	https://www.thebalance.com/economic-contraction-4067683
a recession	https://www.thebalance.com/causes-of-economic-recession-3306010
increase in interest rates	https://www.thebalance.com/when-will-interest-rates-go-up-3306125
confidence	https://www.thebalance.com/consumer-confidence-index-news-impact-3305743
stocks	https://www.thebalance.com/what-are-stocks-3306181
utilities	https://www.investopedia.com/terms/u/utility.asp
HYG	https://finance.yahoo.com/quote/HYG?p=HYG&.tsrc=fin-srch
overbought	https://www.investopedia.com/terms/o/overbought.asp
oversold	https://www.investopedia.com/terms/o/oversold.asp
pullback	https://www.investopedia.com/terms/p/pullback.asp

Inverted Yield Curve	http://www.investopedia.com/articles/basics/06/invertedyieldcurve.asp
store money long-term	https://www.cnbc.com/2018/07/25/self-made-millionaire-grant-cardone-i-dont-save-money-heres-why.html
that's what experts recommend	https://www.cnbc.com/2018/06/19/warren-buffett-and-tony-robbins-agree-invest-in-index-funds.html
https://www.msci.com/market-classification	https://www.msci.com/market-classification
United Nations	https://humbledollar.us11.list-manage.com/track/click?u=96956b2db43346c5a7e6c6246&id=3a2bc7ace1&e=6bb3b8afbe
article	https://humbledollar.us11.list-manage.com/track/click?u=96956b2db43346c5a7e6c6246&id=2bb794292c&e=6bb3b8afbe
Standard and Poor's	https://www.investopedia.com/terms/s/sp.asp
junk	https://www.investopedia.com/terms/j/junkbond.asp
convertible bonds	http://etfdb.com/2009/convertible-bond-etfs-best-of-both-worlds/
uncorrelated to their equity holdings	http://etfdb.com/2010/five-etfs-to-give-your-portfolio-much-needed-diversification/
a Merrill Lynch study	http://www.investopedia.com/articles/01/052301.asp
par value	https://www.investopedia.com/terms/p/parvalue.asp
Consumer Price Index	https://www.investopedia.com/terms/c/consumerpriceindex.asp
Bond vs. Bond Funds	https://www.fidelity.com/learning-center/investment-products/mutual-funds/bond-vs-bond-funds
Guggenhem Investments	https://www.guggenheiminvestments.com/etf/bulletshares
Vanguard Total Stock Market ETF (VTI)	https://www.etf.com/vti
Vanguard Mid-Cap ETF (VO)	https://www.etf.com/vo
Vanguard Risk Assessment Tools	https://personal.vanguard.com/us/FundsInvQuestionnaire
Guggenheim Investments.com	https://www.guggenheiminvestments.com/etf/bulletshares
Schwab Target Maturity Bond ETFs	https://www.schwab.com/active-trader/insights/content/target-maturity-bond-etfs-diversified-baskets-single-year-maturity
Vanguard.com ETFs	https://investor.vanguard.com/etf/list
indexes	https://www.investopedia.com/terms/i/index.asp
exchange-traded funds	https://www.investopedia.com/terms/e/etf.asp

telecommunications	https://www.investopedia.com/terms/t/technology-media-and-communications-tmc-sector.asp
consumer discretionary	https://www.investopedia.com/terms/c/consumer-discretionary.asp
technology	https://www.investopedia.com/terms/t/technology_sector.asp
consumer discretionary	https://www.investopedia.com/terms/c/consumer-discretionary.asp
FANG	https://www.investopedia.com/terms/f/fang-stocks-fb-amzn.asp
XLK	https://www.investopedia.com/markets/etfs/xlk/
XLY	https://www.investopedia.com/markets/etfs/xly/
exposure	https://www.investopedia.com/terms/m/marketexposure.asp
annualized performance	https://www.investopedia.com/terms/a/annualized-rate.asp
back-test	https://www.investopedia.com/terms/b/backtesting.asp
27 low vol ETFs	https://www.etf.com/channels/low-volatility-etfs
iShares Edge MSCI Min Vol U.S.A. ETF (USMV)	https://www.etf.com/USMV
Invesco S&P 500 Low Volatility ETF (SPLV)	https://www.etf.com/SPLV
SPDR S&P 500 ETF Trust (SPY)	https://www.etf.com/SPY
balance sheet	https://www.investopedia.com/terms/b/balancesheet.asp
liabilities	https://www.investopedia.com/terms/l/liability.asp
shareholders' equity	https://www.investopedia.com/terms/s/shareholdersequity.asp
share	https://en.wikipedia.org/wiki/Share_(finance)
cash	https://investinganswers.com/node/5011
stock	https://investinganswers.com/node/5150
debt	https://investinganswers.com/node/5752

www.ingramcontent.com/pod-product-compliance
Lightning Source LLC
Chambersburg PA
CBHW070616220526
45466CB00001B/22